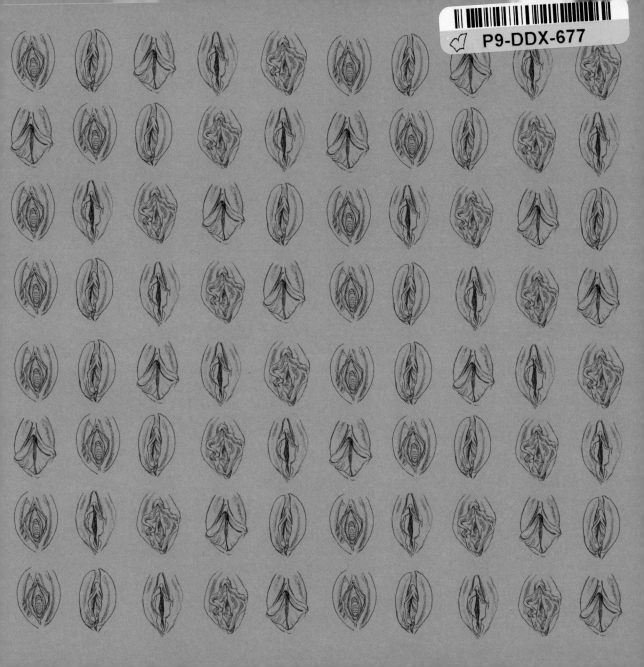

Katja Klengel

Girlsplaining™

A (Sorta) Memoir

Published by
ARCHAIA™

Katja Klengel

Girlsplaining ™

A *(Sorta)* Memoir

Colored by
Adrian vom Baur and Katja Klengel

Translated by
Nika Knight

Lettered by
AndWorld Design

ARCHAIA ™
Los Angeles, California

Cover by
Katja Klengel

ENGLISH EDITION

Designer
Scott Newman

Assistant Editor
Allyson Gronowitz

Editor
Sierra Hahn

Ross Richie CEO & Founder
Joy Huffman CFO
Matt Gagnon Editor-in-Chief
Filip Sablik President, Publishing & Marketing
Stephen Christy President, Development
Lance Kreiter Vice President, Licensing & Merchandising
Arune Singh Vice President, Marketing
Bryce Carlson Vice President, Editorial & Creative Strategy
Kate Henning Director, Operations
Spencer Simpson Director, Sales
Scott Newman Manager, Production Design
Elyse Strandberg Manager, Finance
Sierra Hahn Executive Editor
Jeanine Schaefer Executive Editor
Dafna Pleban Senior Editor
Shannon Watters Senior Editor
Eric Harburn Senior Editor
Sophie Philips-Roberts Associate Editor
Amanda LaFranco Associate Editor
Jonathan Manning Associate Editor
Gavin Gronenthal Assistant Editor
Gwen Waller Assistant Editor

Allyson Gronowitz Assistant Editor
Ramiro Portnoy Assistant Editor
Kenzie Rzonca Assistant Editor
Shelby Netschke Editorial Assistant
Michelle Ankley Design Coordinator
Marie Krupina Production Designer
Grace Park Production Designer
Chelsea Roberts Production Designer
Samantha Knapp Production Design Assistant
José Meza Live Events Lead
Stephanie Hocutt Digital Marketing Lead
Esther Kim Marketing Coordinator
Breanna Sarpy Live Events Coordinator
Amanda Lawson Marketing Assistant
Holly Aitchison Digital Sales Coordinator
Morgan Perry Retail Sales Coordinator
Megan Christopher Operations Coordinator
Rodrigo Hernandez Operations Coordinator
Zipporah Smith Operations Assistant
Jason Lee Senior Accountant
Sabrina Lesin Accounting Assistant

GIRLSPLAINING, March 2021. Published by Archaia, a division of Boom Entertainment, Inc. © Katja Klengel, 2018 © Reprodukt for the original German edition, 2018 All Rights Reserved. Translation made in arrangement with Am-Book (www.am-book.com). Archaia™ and the Archaia logo are trademarks of Boom Entertainment, Inc., registered in various countries and categories. All characters, events, and institutions depicted herein are fictional. Any similarity between any of the names, characters, persons, events, and/or institutions in this publication to actual names, characters, and persons, whether living or dead, events, and/or institutions is unintended and purely coincidental.

Originally published in German by Reprodukt.

The translation of this work was supported by a grant from the Goethe-Institut.

BOOM! Studios, 5670 Wilshire Boulevard, Suite 400, Los Angeles, CA 90036-5679. Printed in China. First Printing.

ISBN: 978-1-68415-662-7 , eISBN: 978-1-64668-147-1

Contents

Sex and the City

They don't know me. I don't know them, either. But that will soon change...

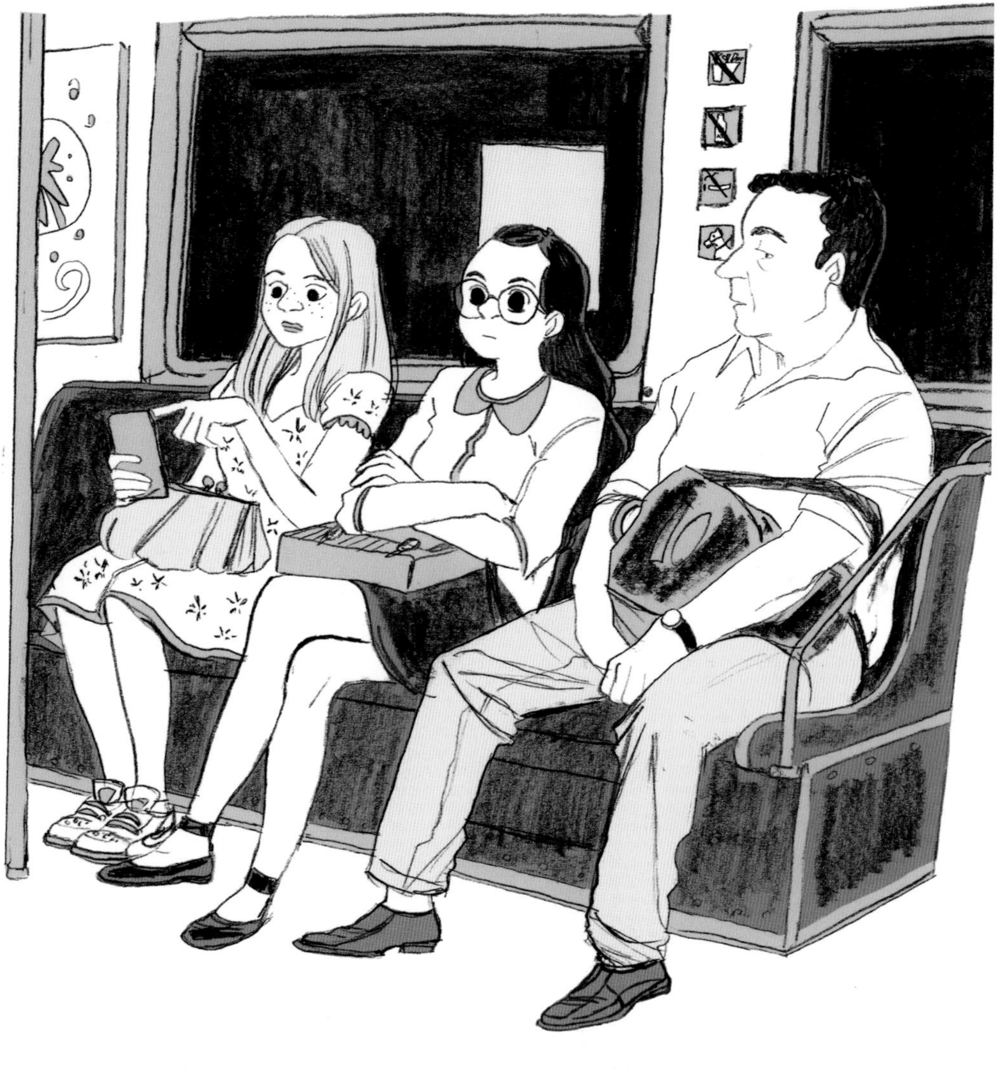

My name is Katja Klengel. I'm 29 years old, I live in Berlin, and guess what--

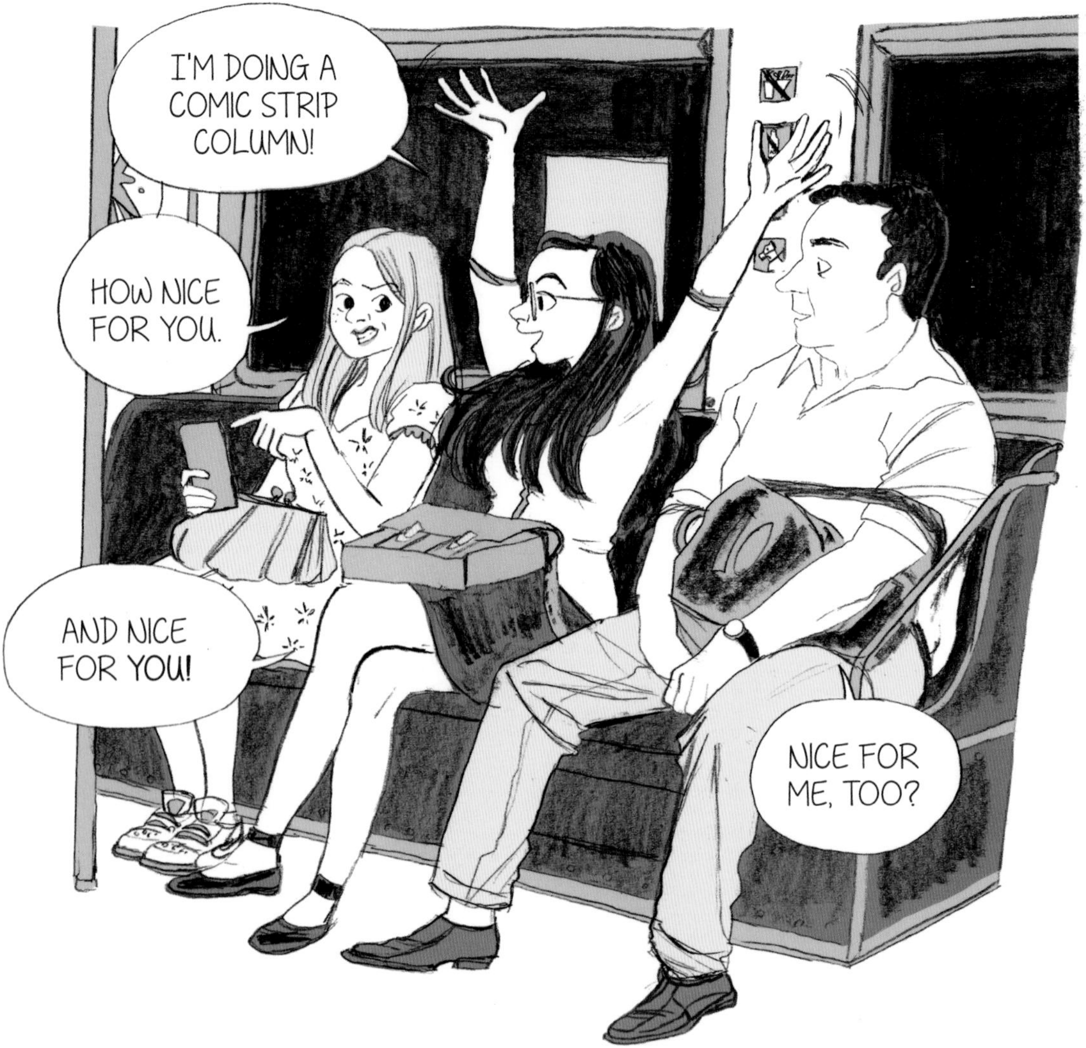
I'M DOING A COMIC STRIP COLUMN!
HOW NICE FOR YOU.
AND NICE FOR YOU!
NICE FOR ME, TOO?

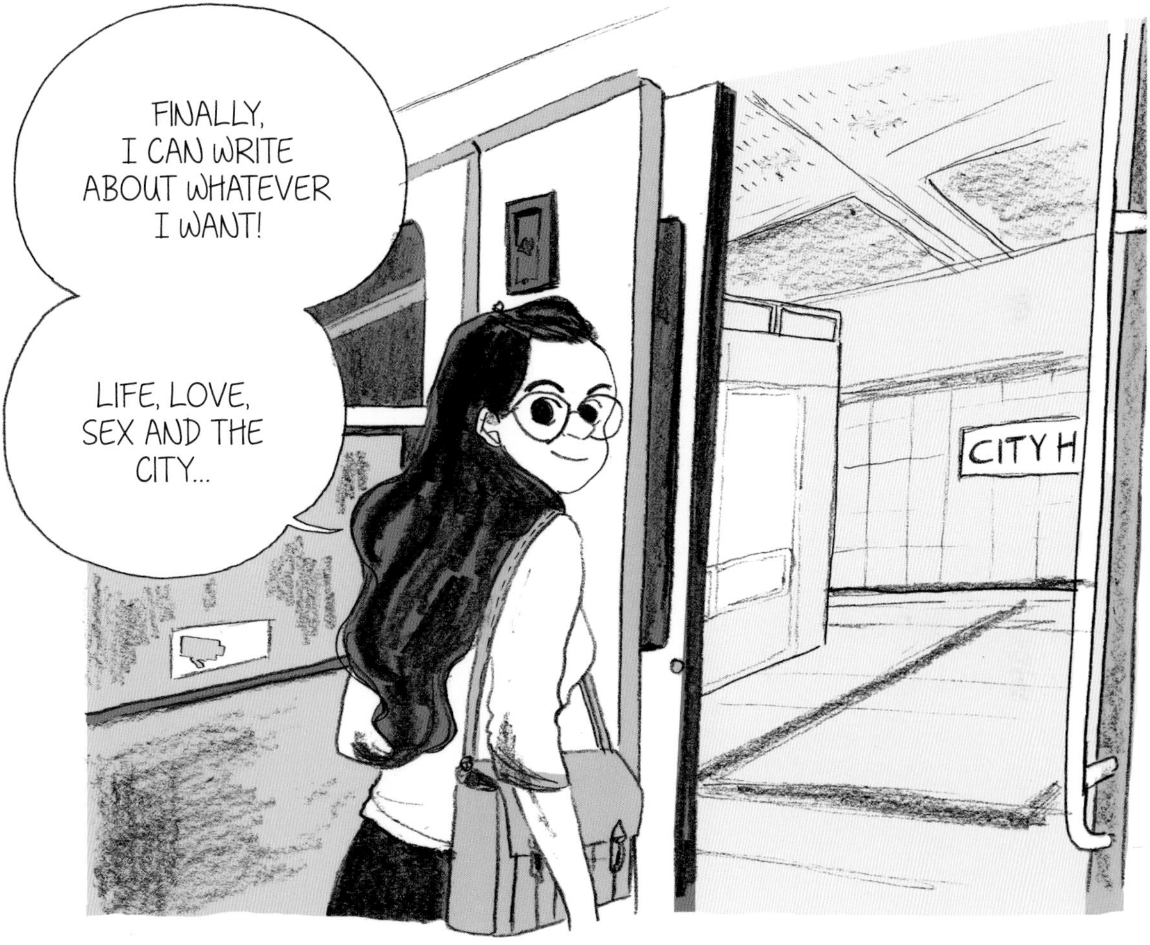
FINALLY, I CAN WRITE ABOUT WHATEVER I WANT!
LIFE, LOVE, SEX AND THE CITY...
CITY H

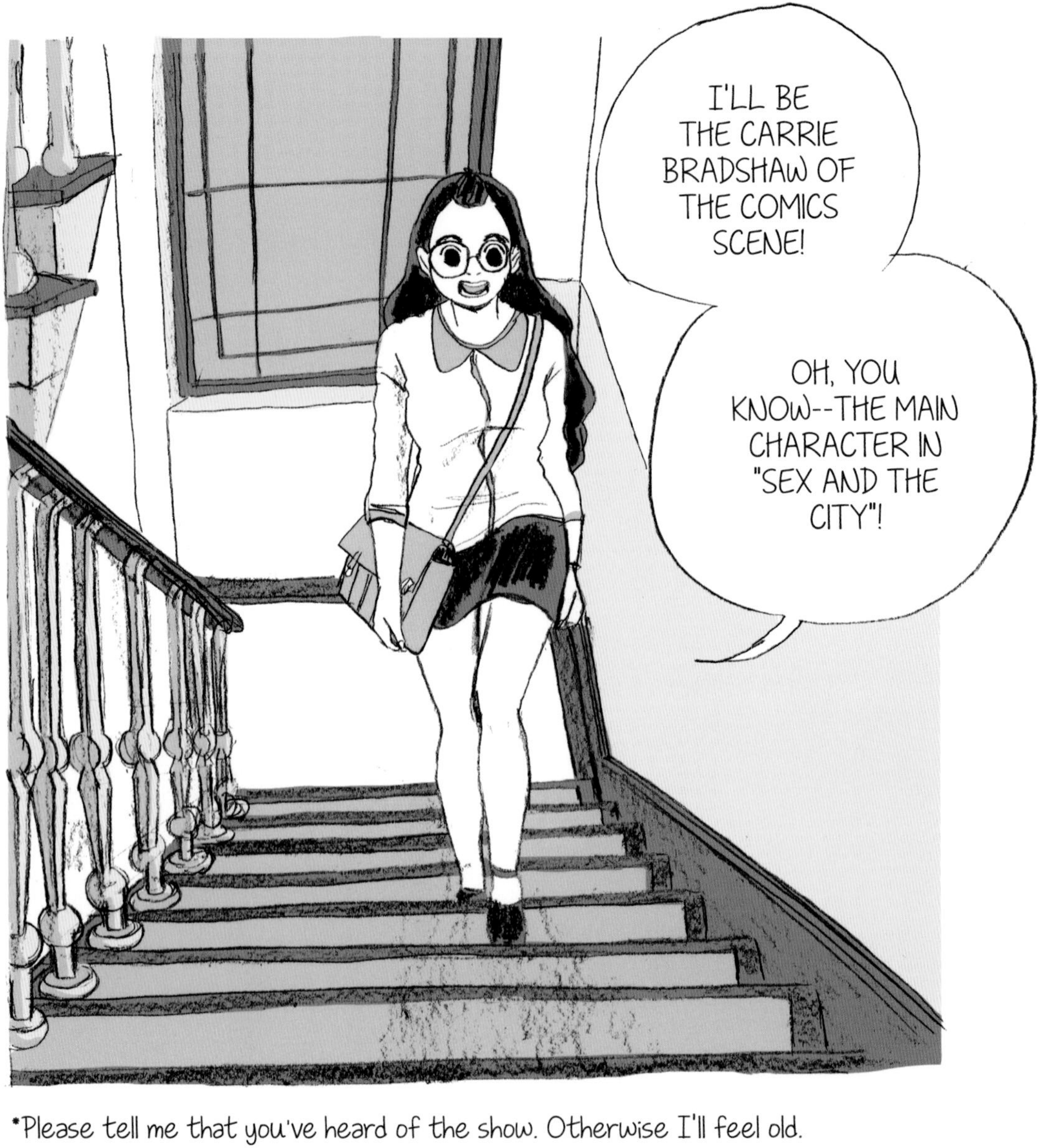
I'LL BE THE CARRIE BRADSHAW OF THE COMICS SCENE!
OH, YOU KNOW--THE MAIN CHARACTER IN "SEX AND THE CITY"!

*Please tell me that you've heard of the show. Otherwise I'll feel old.

Maybe I should take a page from Carrie's book and do what she does. The "success principle," you might call it.

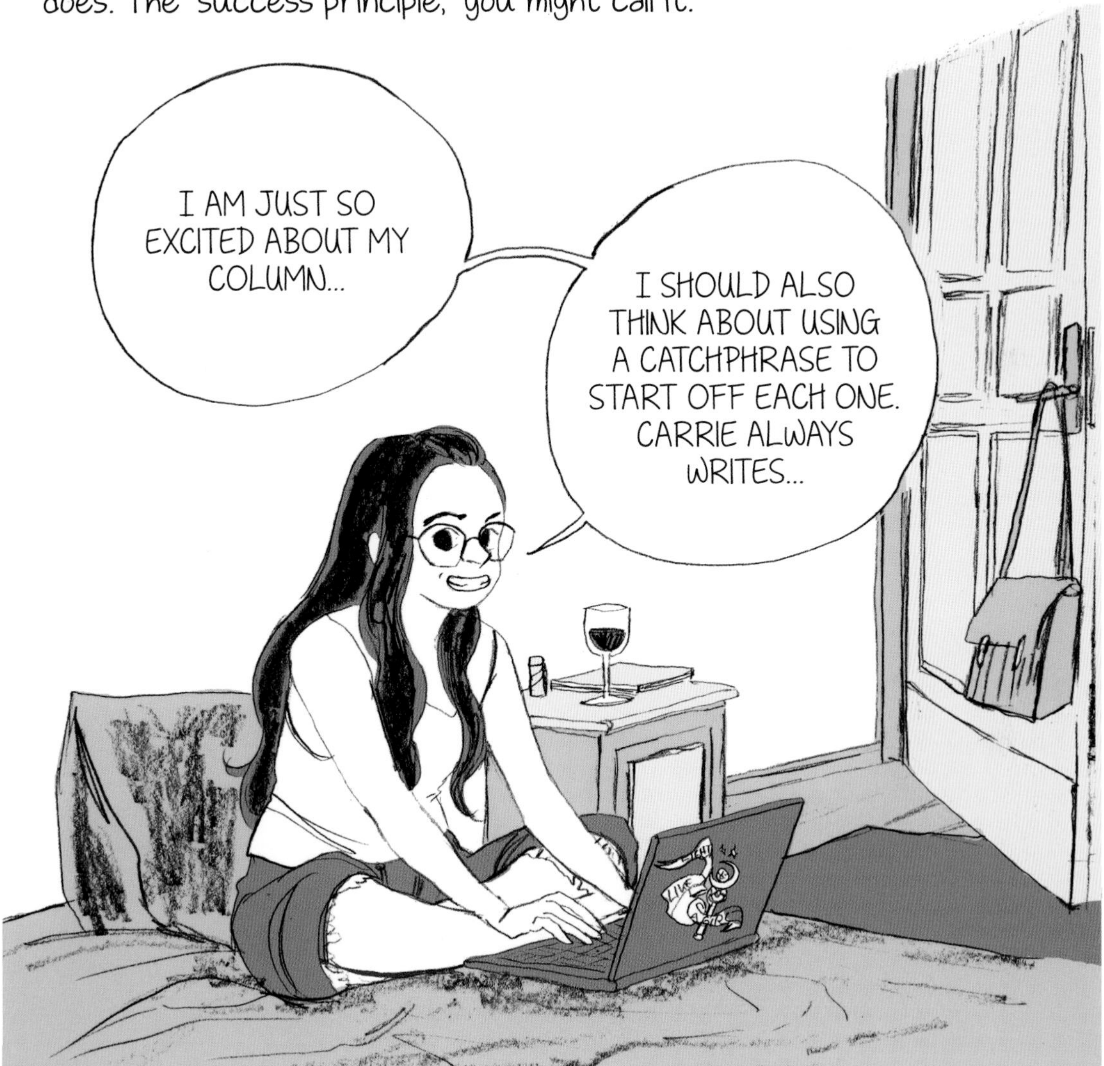
I AM JUST SO EXCITED ABOUT MY COLUMN...
I SHOULD ALSO THINK ABOUT USING A CATCHPHRASE TO START OFF EACH ONE. CARRIE ALWAYS WRITES...

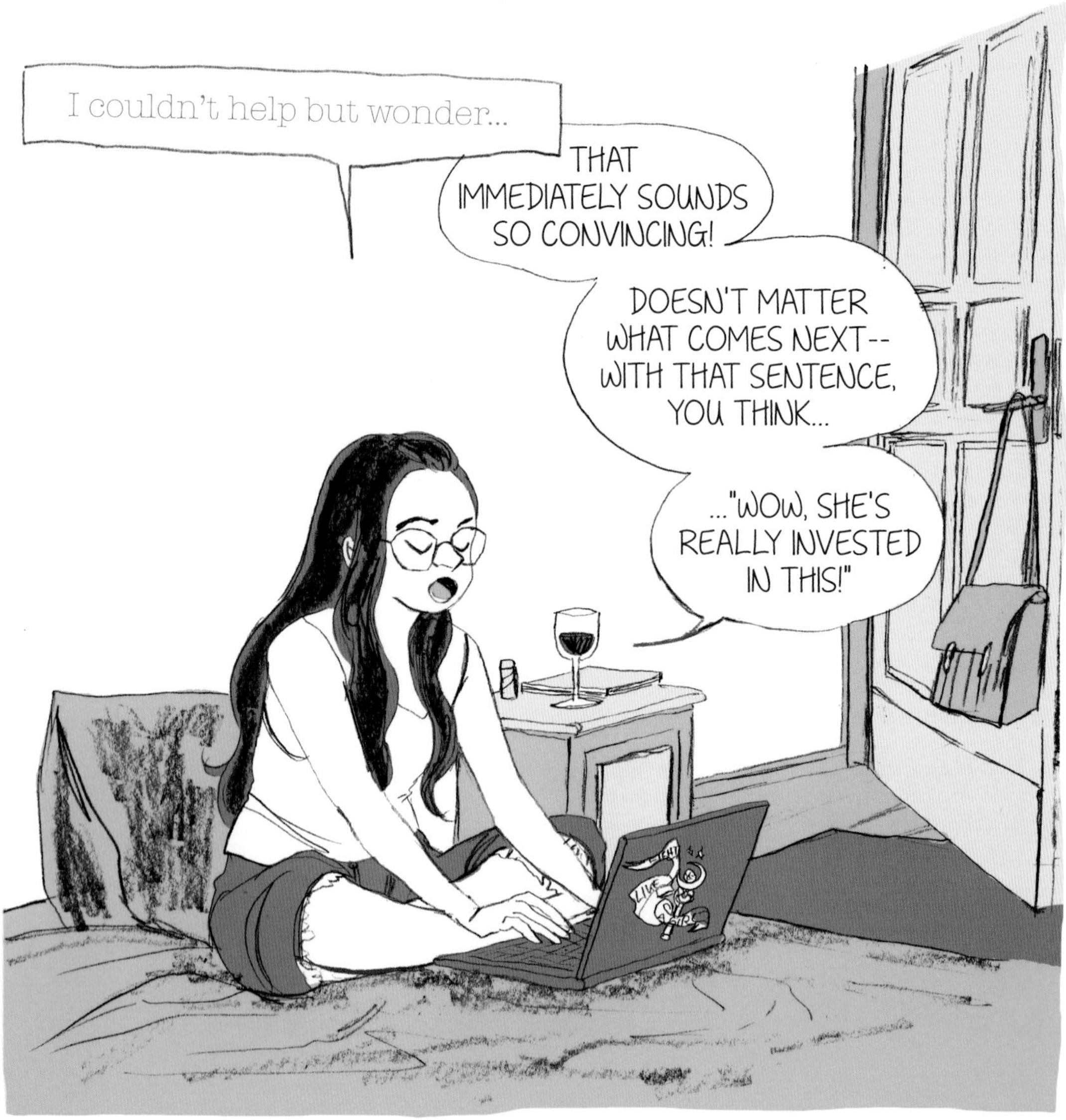
I couldn't help but wonder...
THAT IMMEDIATELY SOUNDS SO CONVINCING!
DOESN'T MATTER WHAT COMES NEXT-- WITH THAT SENTENCE, YOU THINK...
..."WOW, SHE'S REALLY INVESTED IN THIS!"

I would, of course, walk around the city in the chicest designer clothes and find inspiration for my next column, just like Carrie.

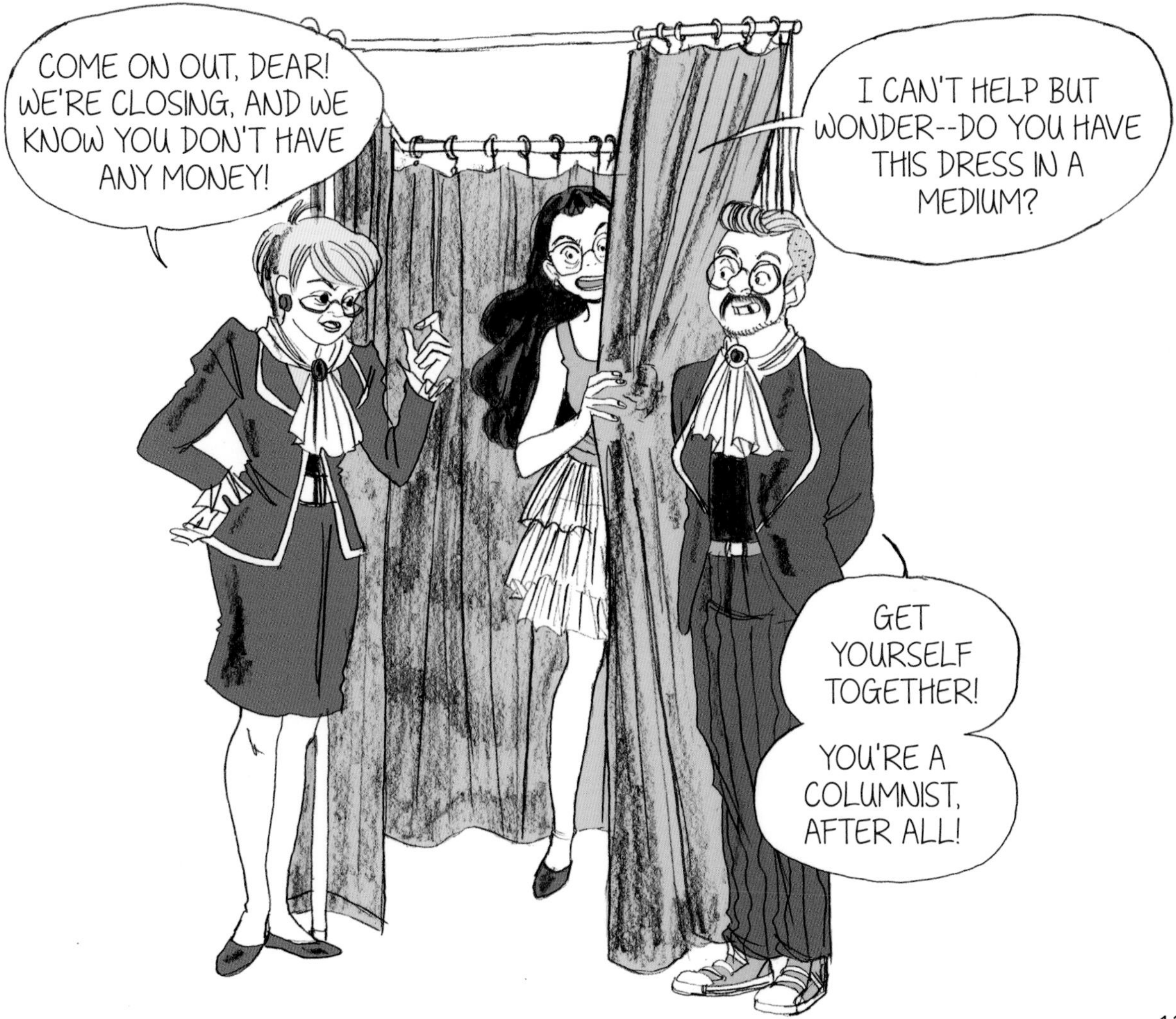
COME ON OUT, DEAR! WE'RE CLOSING, AND WE KNOW YOU DON'T HAVE ANY MONEY!
I CAN'T HELP BUT WONDER--DO YOU HAVE THIS DRESS IN A MEDIUM?
GET YOURSELF TOGETHER!
YOU'RE A COLUMNIST, AFTER ALL!

I would, of course, ~~walk around the city~~ stay at home in ~~the chicest designer~~ my completely normal clothes and find inspiration for my next column, ~~just like Carrie~~.

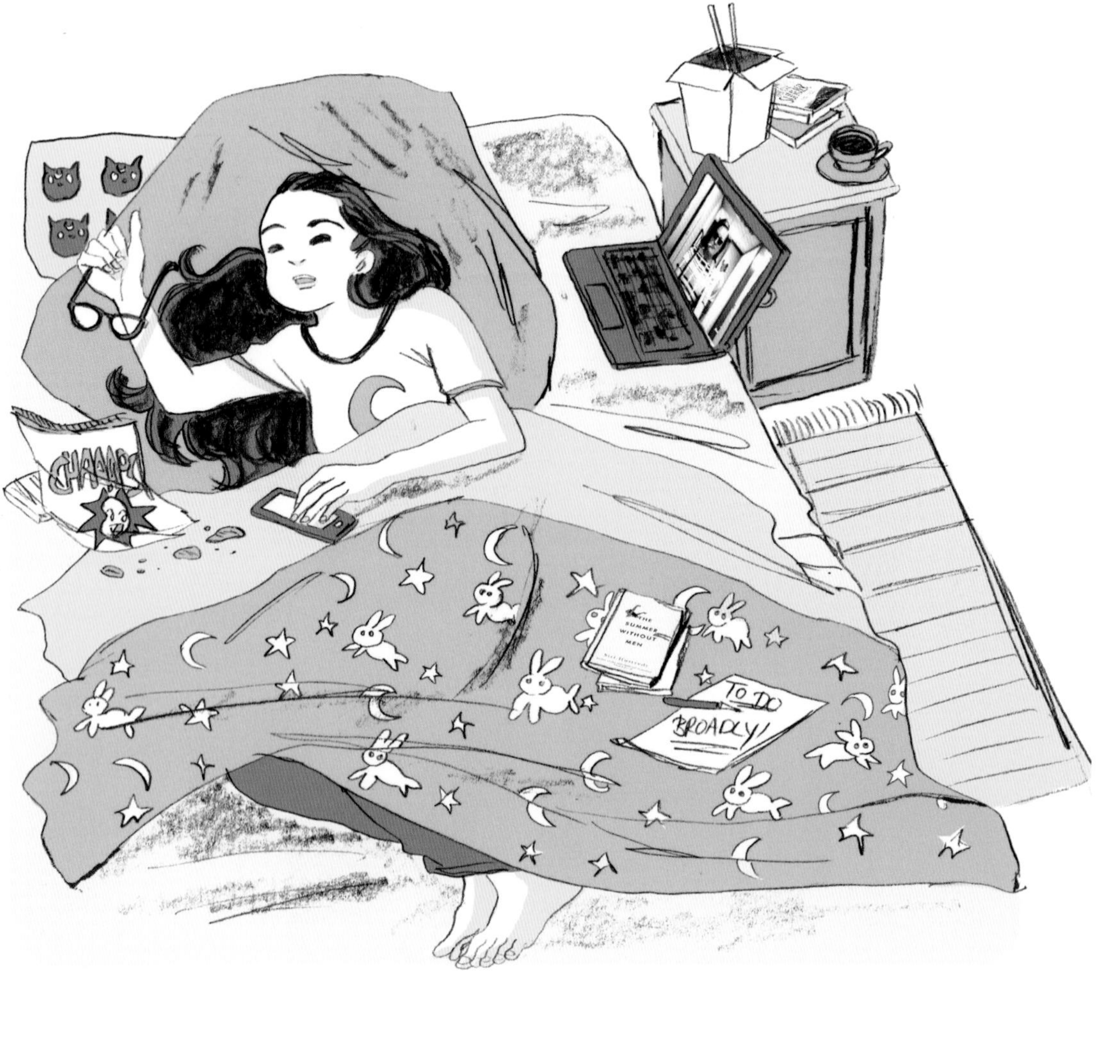
THE SUMMER WITHOUT MEN
TO DO
BROADLY!

Or I'll just meet my three girlfriends for lunch, like always, and get them to tell me whatever's new in their lives, and then very subtly put that in my column.

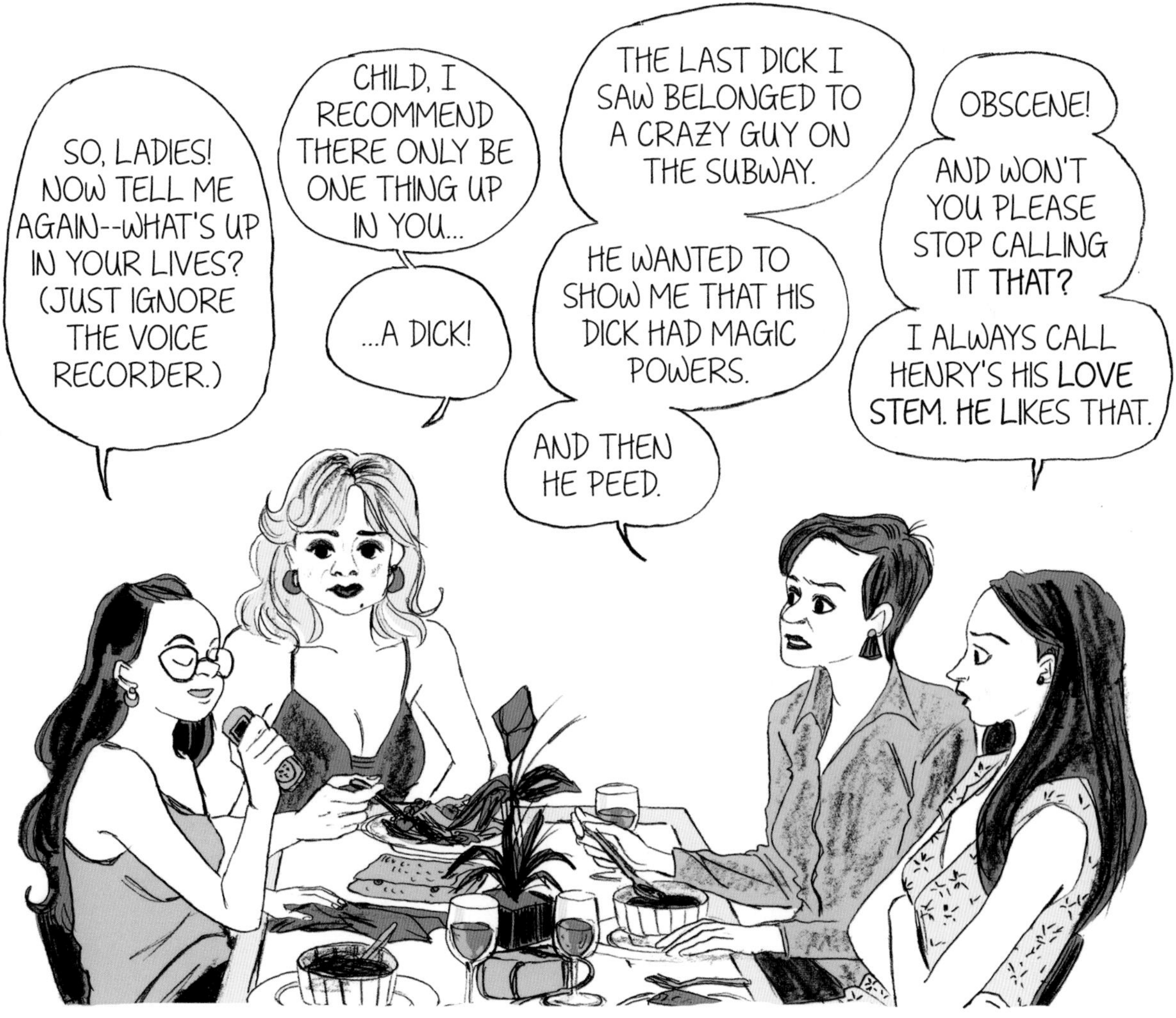
SO, LADIES! NOW TELL ME AGAIN--WHAT'S UP IN YOUR LIVES? (JUST IGNORE THE VOICE RECORDER.)
CHILD, I RECOMMEND THERE ONLY BE ONE THING UP IN YOU...
...A DICK!
THE LAST DICK I SAW BELONGED TO A CRAZY GUY ON THE SUBWAY.
HE WANTED TO SHOW ME THAT HIS DICK HAD MAGIC POWERS.
AND THEN HE PEED.
OBSCENE!
AND WON'T YOU PLEASE STOP CALLING IT **THAT?**
I ALWAYS CALL HENRY'S HIS **LOVE STEM. HE** LIKES THAT.

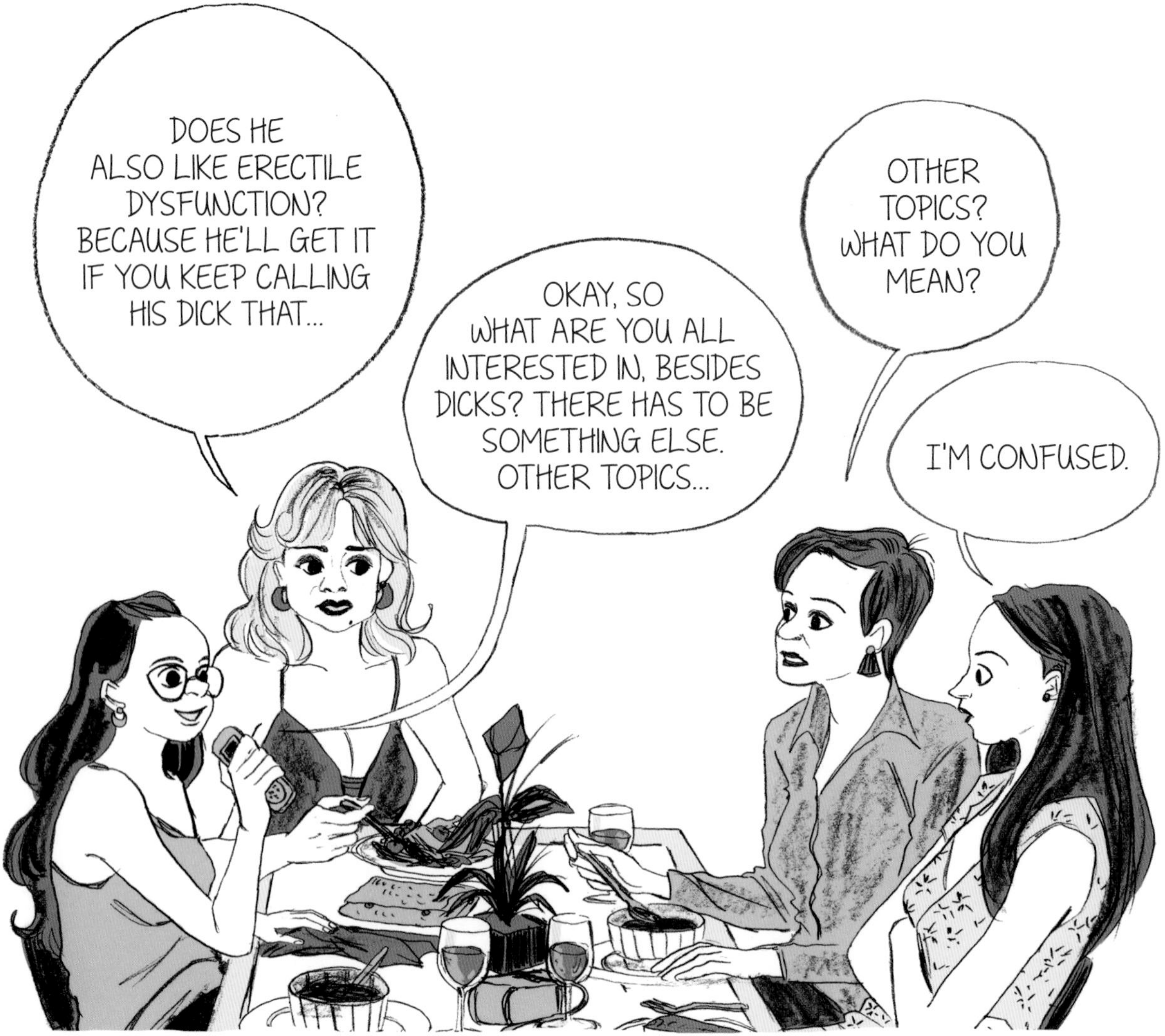
DOES HE ALSO LIKE ERECTILE DYSFUNCTION? BECAUSE HE'LL GET IT IF YOU KEEP CALLING HIS DICK THAT...
OKAY, SO WHAT ARE YOU ALL INTERESTED IN, BESIDES DICKS? THERE HAS TO BE SOMETHING ELSE. OTHER TOPICS...
OTHER TOPICS? WHAT DO YOU MEAN?
I'M CONFUSED.

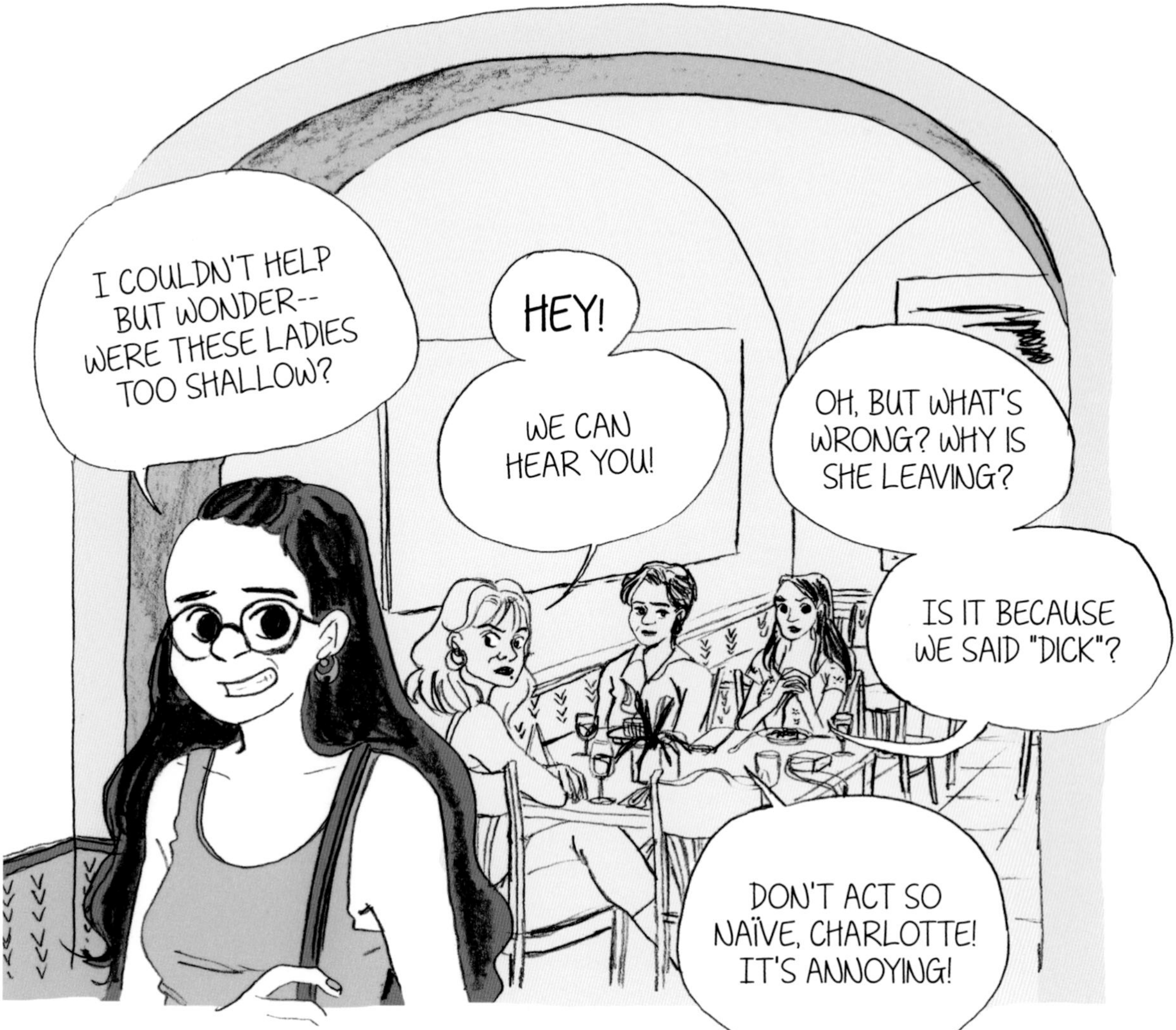
I COULDN'T HELP BUT WONDER-- WERE THESE LADIES TOO SHALLOW?
HEY!
WE CAN HEAR YOU!
OH, BUT WHAT'S WRONG? WHY IS SHE LEAVING?
IS IT BECAUSE WE SAID "DICK"?
DON'T ACT SO NAÏVE, CHARLOTTE! IT'S ANNOYING!

Or I'll just ~~meet my three girlfriends for lunch~~ hang out with my roommates on the couch, like always, and get them to tell me whatever's new in their lives, and then ~~very subtly~~ put that in my column.

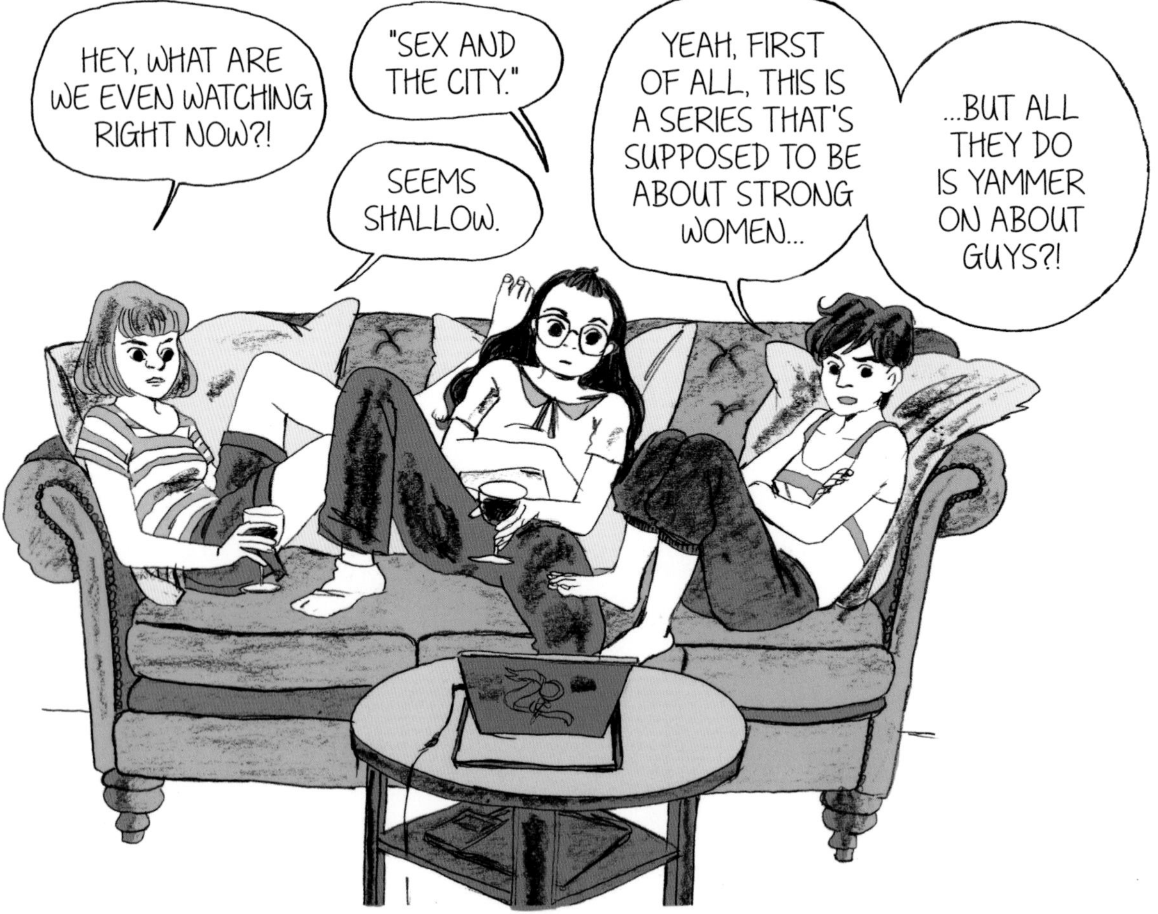
HEY, WHAT ARE WE EVEN WATCHING RIGHT NOW?!
"SEX AND THE CITY."
SEEMS SHALLOW.
YEAH, FIRST OF ALL, THIS IS A SERIES THAT'S SUPPOSED TO BE ABOUT STRONG WOMEN...
...BUT ALL THEY DO IS YAMMER ON ABOUT GUYS?!

I could also have an affair, like Carrie with Mr. Big. He would be the fulfillment of all my desires made flesh, the painful driving force of my column.

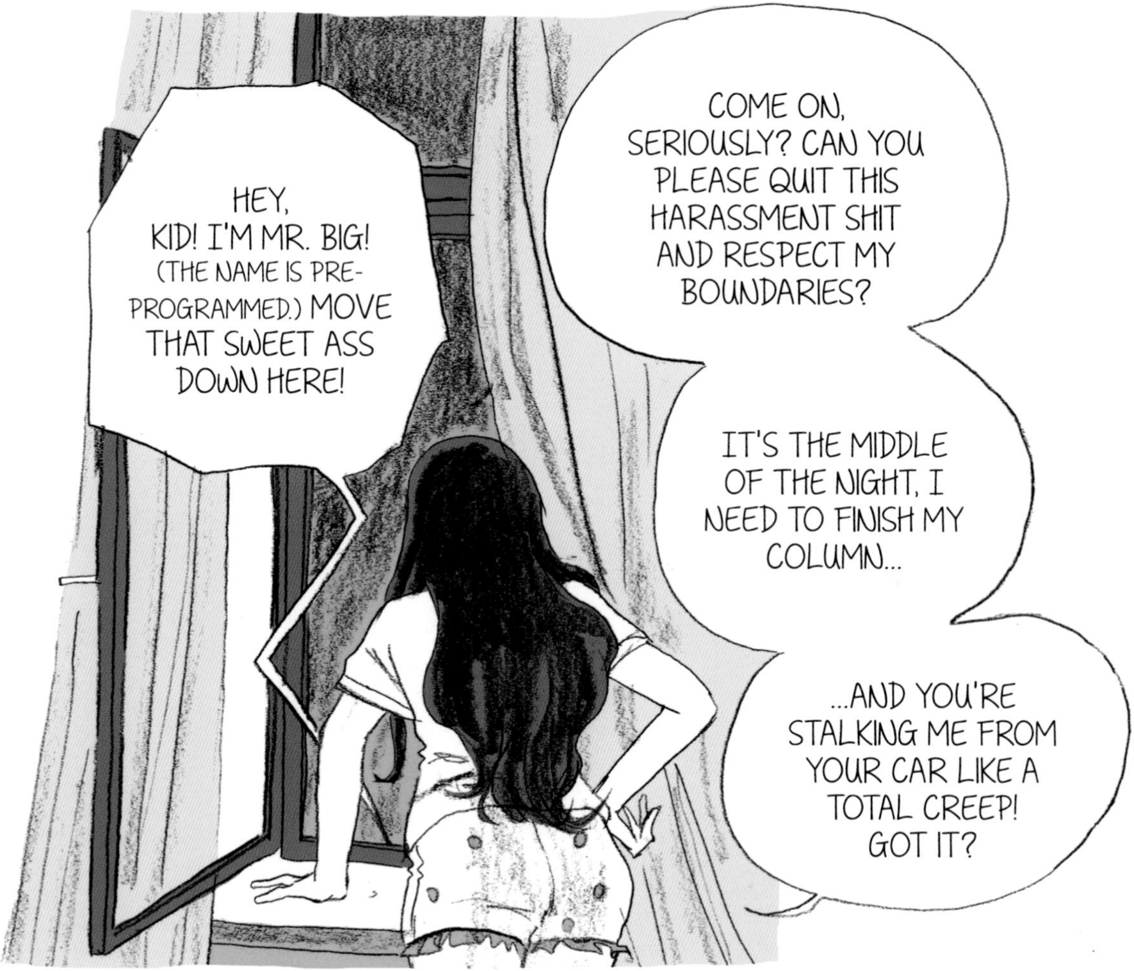
HEY, KID! I'M MR. BIG! (THE NAME IS PRE-PROGRAMMED.) MOVE THAT SWEET ASS DOWN HERE!
COME ON, SERIOUSLY? CAN YOU PLEASE QUIT THIS HARASSMENT SHIT AND RESPECT MY BOUNDARIES?
IT'S THE MIDDLE OF THE NIGHT, I NEED TO FINISH MY COLUMN...
...AND YOU'RE STALKING ME FROM YOUR CAR LIKE A TOTAL CREEP! GOT IT?

I could also ~~have an affair, like Carrie had with Mr. Big~~ realize that the fulfillment of all my desires is illusory and my column doesn't need a painful driving force, but rather something that does me good.

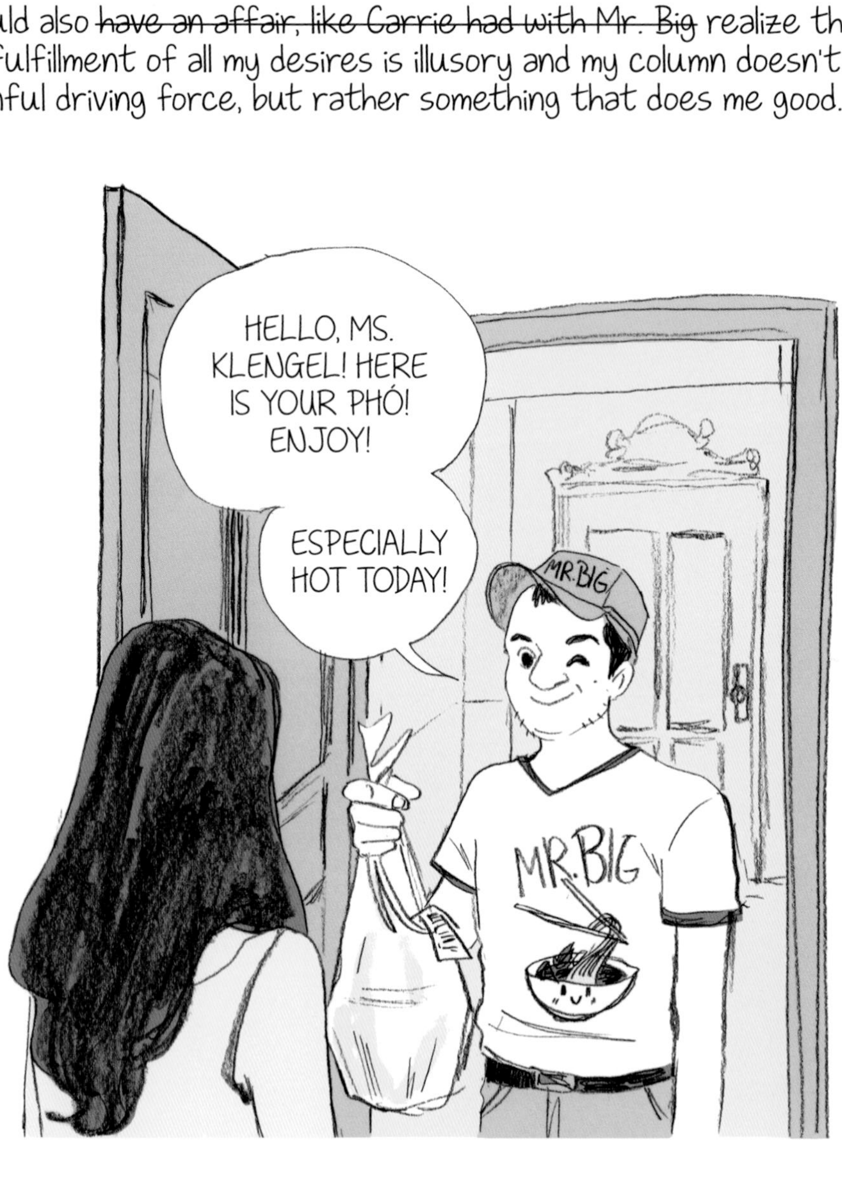
HELLO, MS. KLENGEL! HERE IS YOUR PHÓ! ENJOY!
ESPECIALLY HOT TODAY!
MR.BIG
MR.BIG

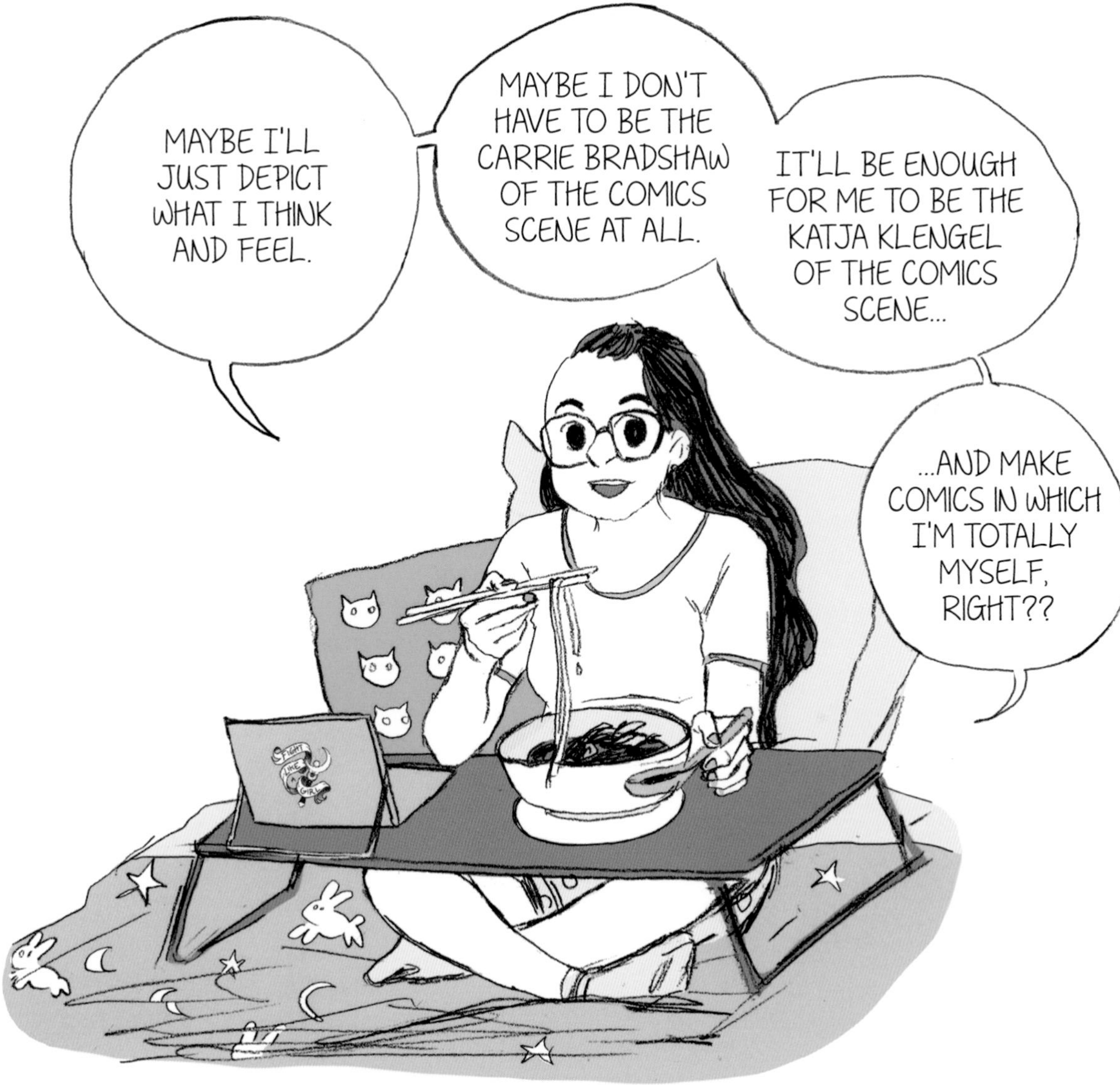
MAYBE I'LL JUST DEPICT WHAT I THINK AND FEEL.
MAYBE I DON'T HAVE TO BE THE CARRIE BRADSHAW OF THE COMICS SCENE AT ALL.
IT'LL BE ENOUGH FOR ME TO BE THE KATJA KLENGEL OF THE COMICS SCENE...
...AND MAKE COMICS IN WHICH I'M TOTALLY MYSELF, RIGHT??
FIGHT LIKE A GIRL

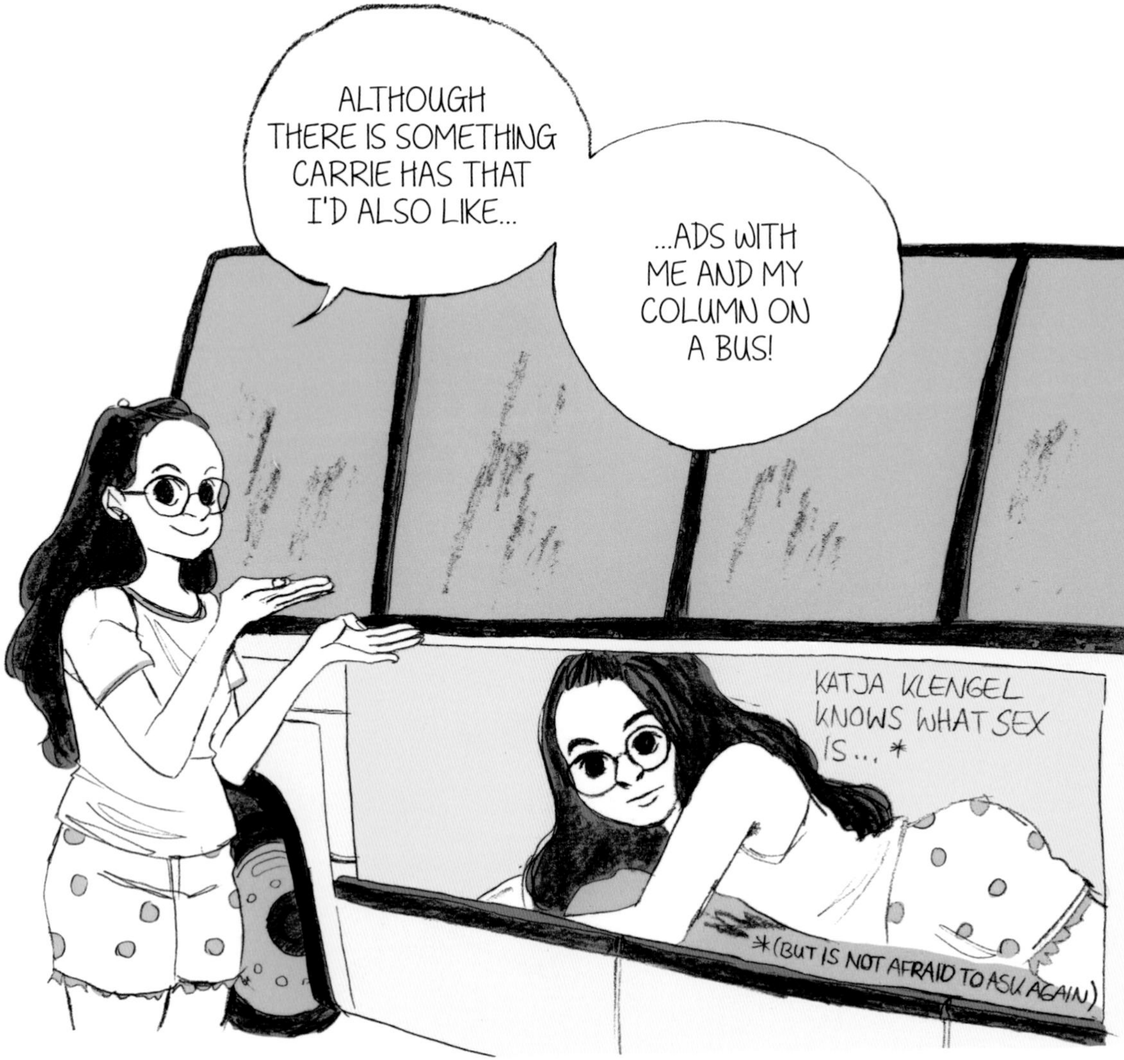
ALTHOUGH THERE IS SOMETHING CARRIE HAS THAT I'D ALSO LIKE...
...ADS WITH ME AND MY COLUMN ON A BUS!
KATJA KLENGEL KNOWS WHAT SEX IS..., *
*(BUT IS NOT AFRAID TO ASK AGAIN)

The Ghost of the
Rusty Razor Blades

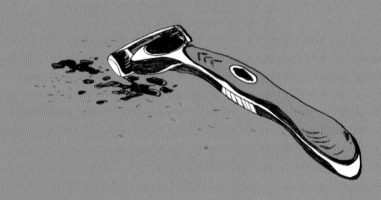

By the fourth grade, I already had pubic hair. I didn't think much of it until I was on a class trip one day. I never enjoyed class trips, and especially not this one. None of the other girls in my class had a single hair growing down there, so on the first night I had to pull down my underwear in front of all of them.

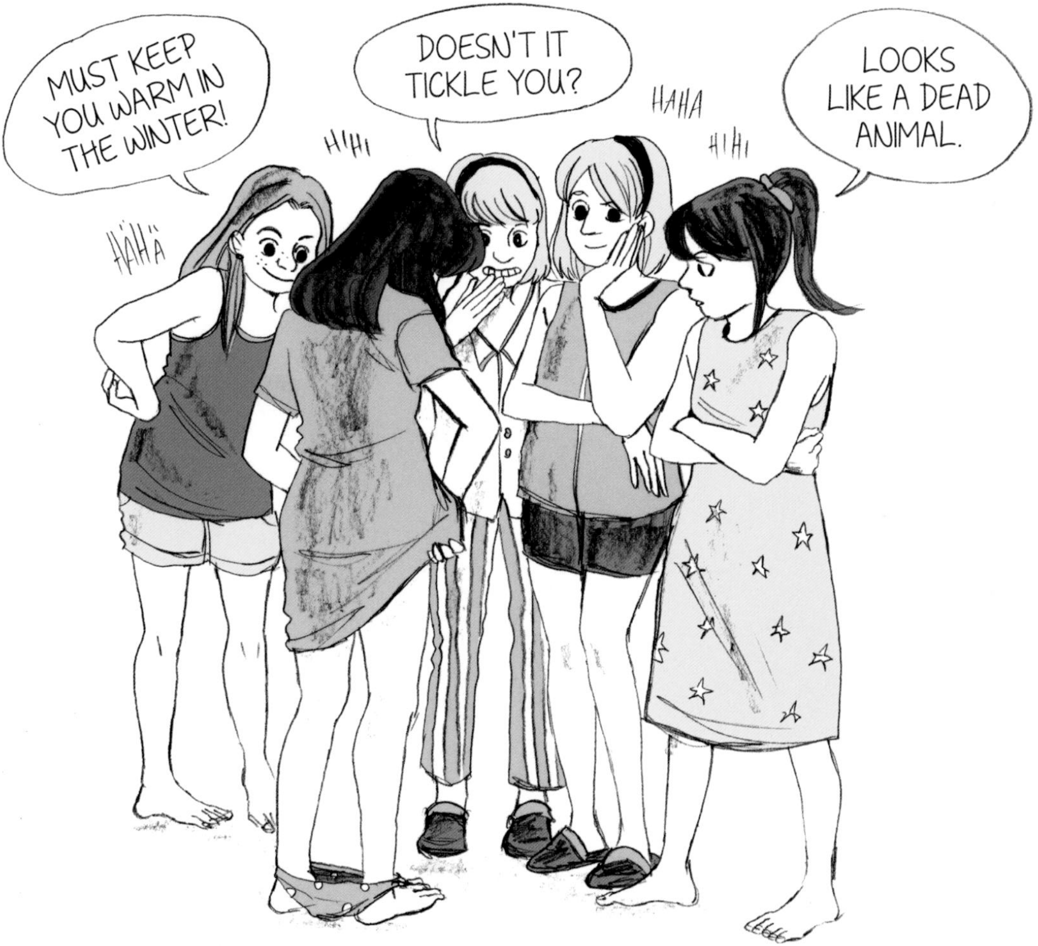
MUST KEEP YOU WARM IN THE WINTER!
DOESN'T IT TICKLE YOU?
HAHA
LOOKS LIKE A DEAD ANIMAL.
HIHI
HIHI
HÄHÄ

And one year later, it was an especially hot summer's day, my brother made the following remark--

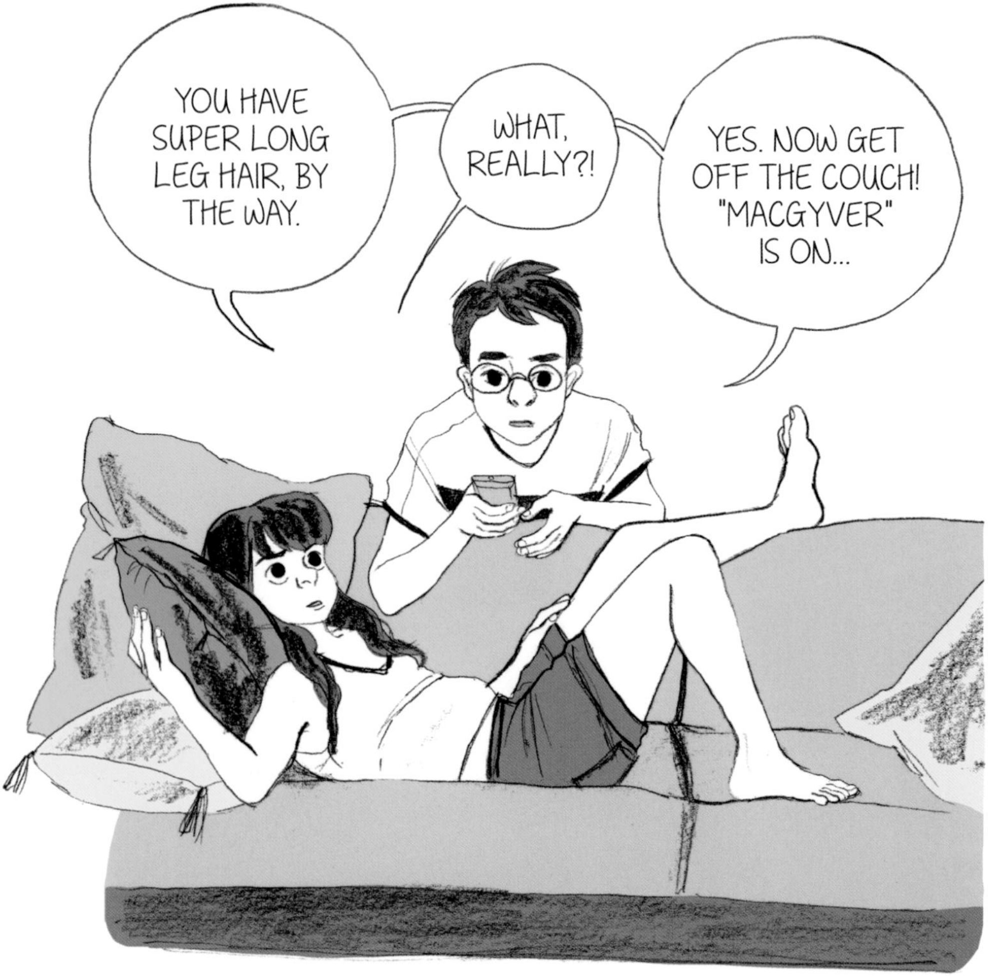
YOU HAVE SUPER LONG LEG HAIR, BY THE WAY.
WHAT, REALLY?!
YES. NOW GET OFF THE COUCH! "MACGYVER" IS ON...

Soon after, I bought my first razor. I'll never forget the cashier's expression.

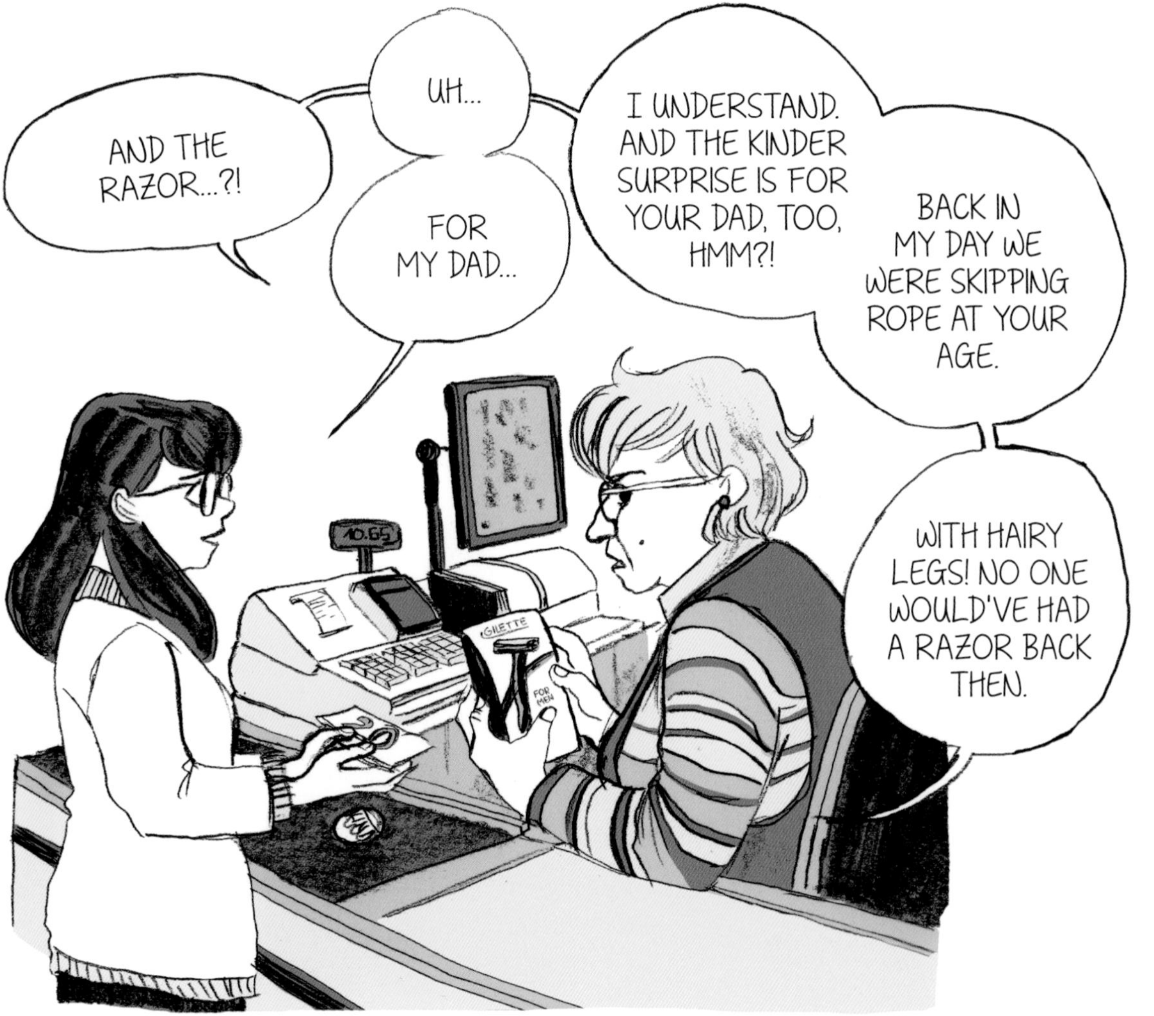
AND THE RAZOR...?!
UH...
FOR MY DAD...
I UNDERSTAND. AND THE KINDER SURPRISE IS FOR YOUR DAD, TOO, HMM?!
BACK IN MY DAY WE WERE SKIPPING ROPE AT YOUR AGE.
WITH HAIRY LEGS! NO ONE WOULD'VE HAD A RAZOR BACK THEN.
10.65
GILETTE
FOR MEN

At some point, my peers began to bully me, too. Even the boy with the desk next to mine, whom I had befriended. (And whom I secretly liked.)

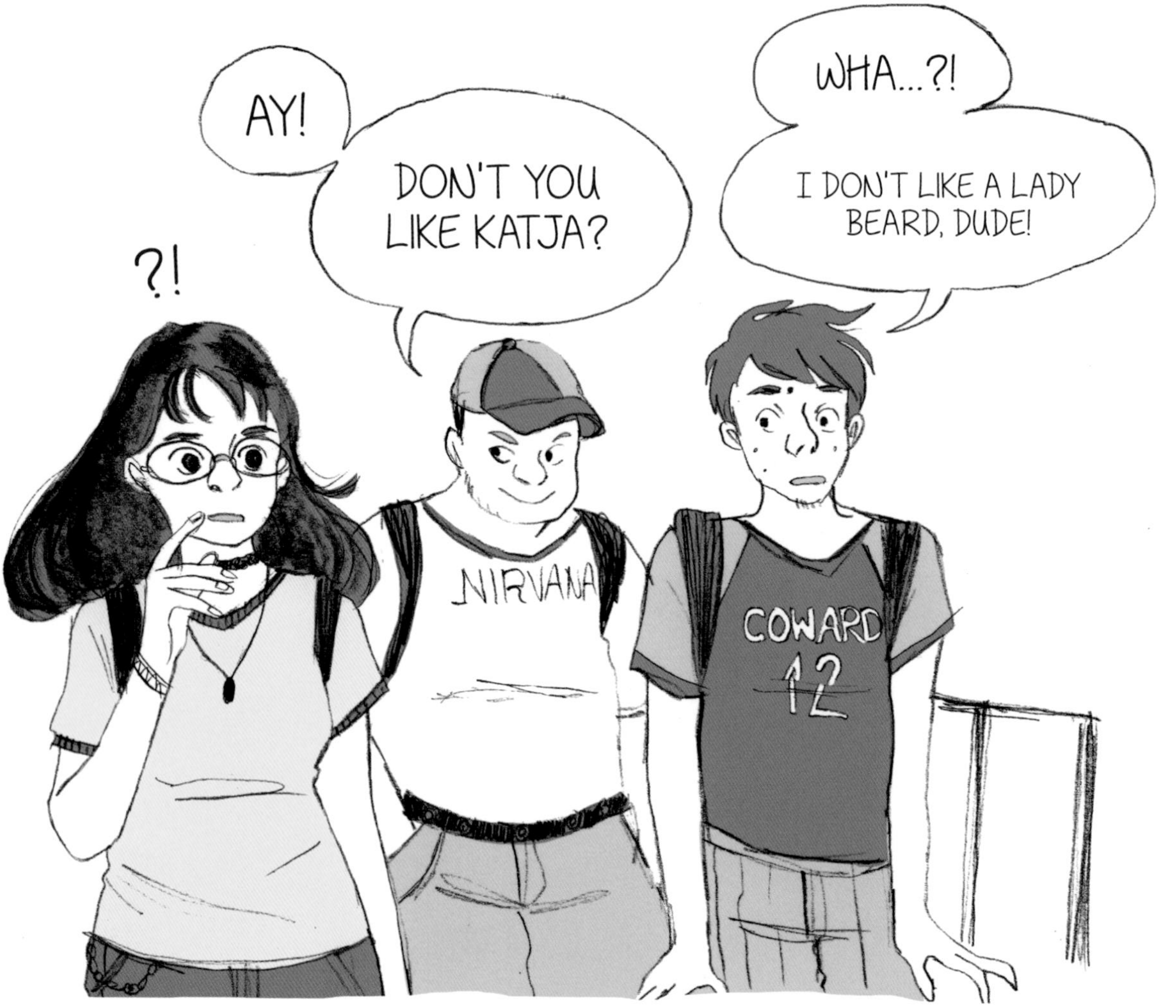
?!
AY!
DON'T YOU LIKE KATJA?
WHA...?!
I DON'T LIKE A LADY BEARD, DUDE!
NIRVANA
COWARD
12

Somehow, everything and everyone around me made me feel like a total freak...

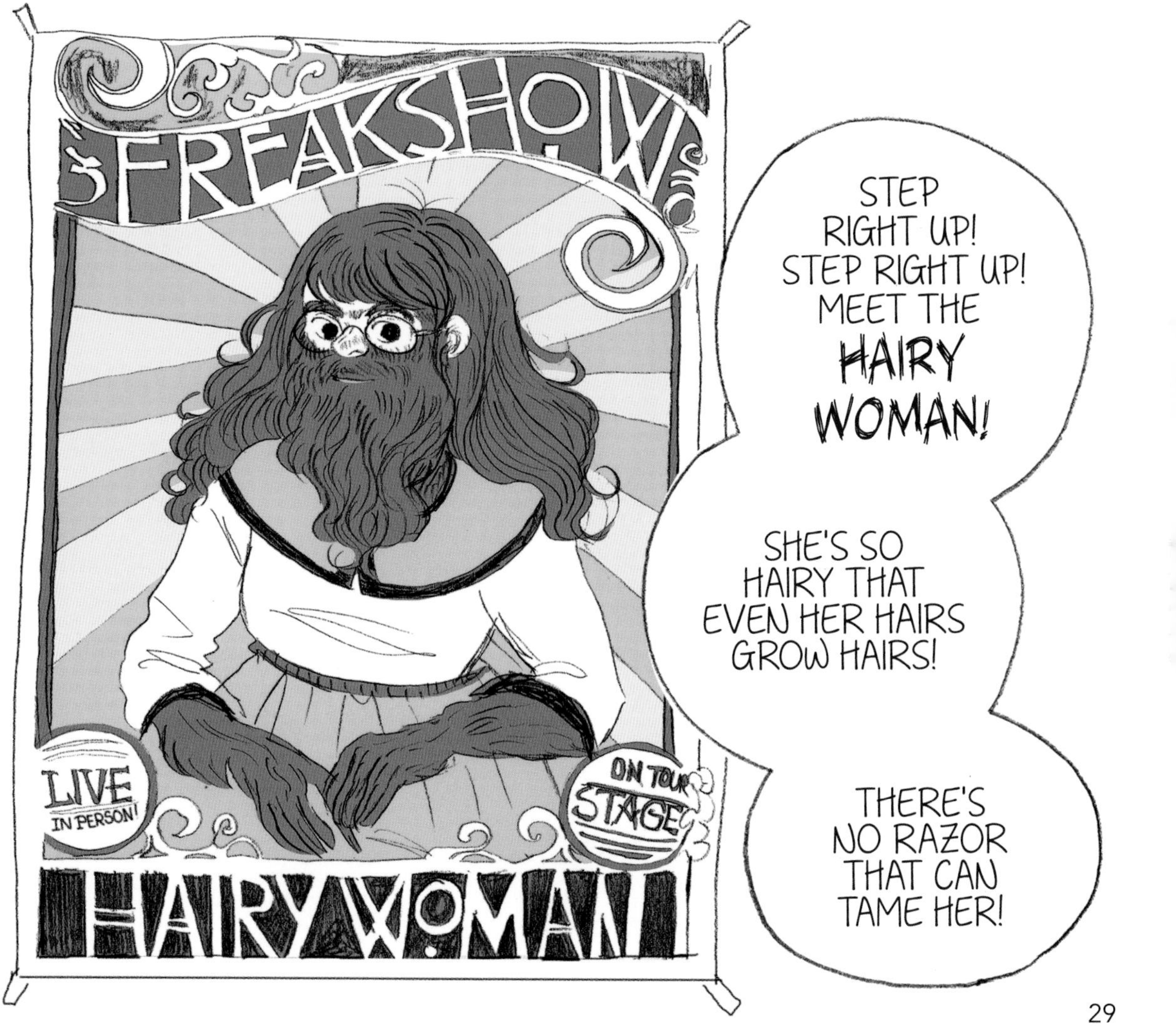
FREAKSHOW
STEP RIGHT UP! STEP RIGHT UP! MEET THE HAIRY WOMAN!
SHE'S SO HAIRY THAT EVEN HER HAIRS GROW HAIRS!
THERE'S NO RAZOR THAT CAN TAME HER!
LIVE IN PERSON!
ON TOUR STAGE
HAIRY WOMAN

To stop the teasing, I needed a lot of time with epilators, razors, and wax.

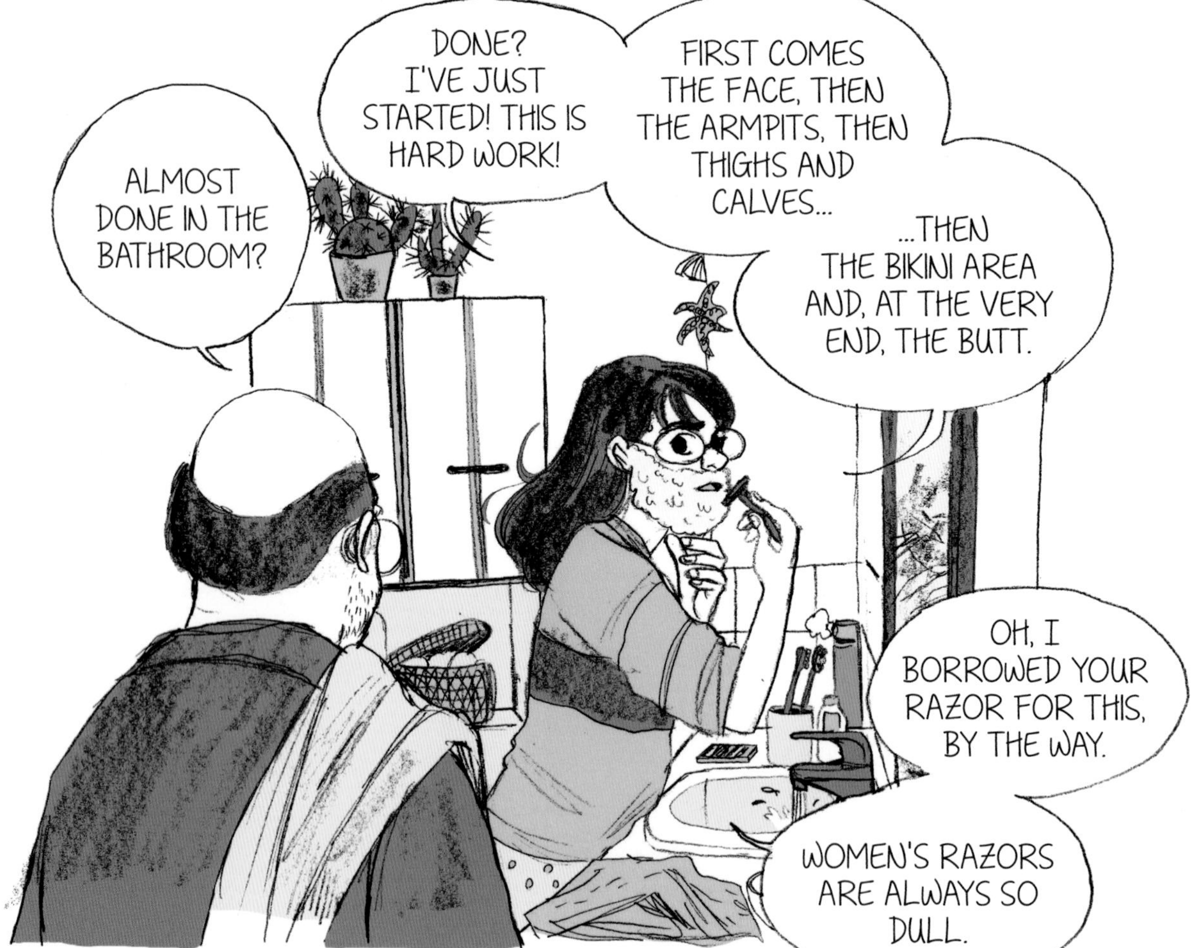
ALMOST DONE IN THE BATHROOM?
DONE? I'VE JUST STARTED! THIS IS HARD WORK!
FIRST COMES THE FACE, THEN THE ARMPITS, THEN THIGHS AND CALVES...
...THEN THE BIKINI AREA AND, AT THE VERY END, THE BUTT.
OH, I BORROWED YOUR RAZOR FOR THIS, BY THE WAY.
WOMEN'S RAZORS ARE ALWAYS SO DULL.

And then I needed more time for crying for whenever I cut myself or had ingrown hairs that turned into little pimples. Or I just sobbed because the stubble had grown back in again on the same day. I was tired of shaving myself every single day. And so I began to hide my body.

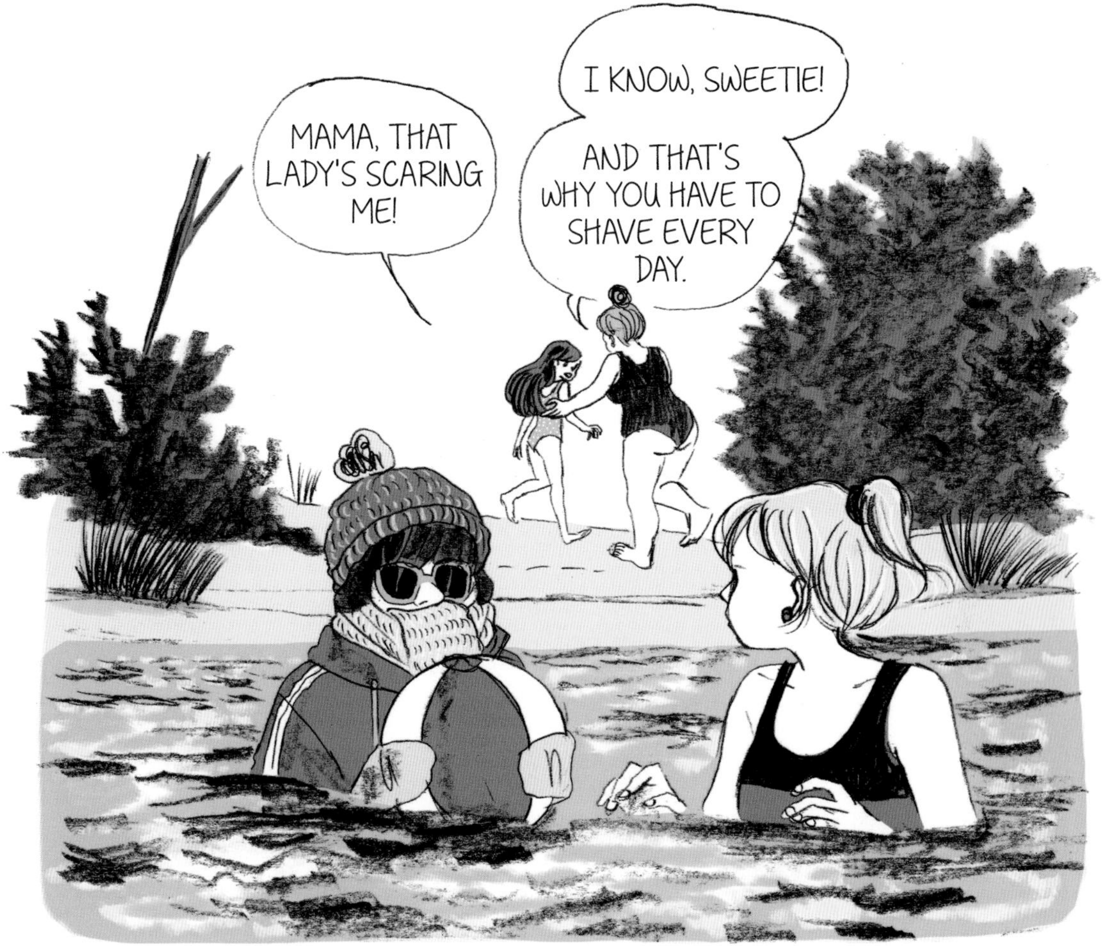
MAMA, THAT LADY'S SCARING ME!
I KNOW, SWEETIE!
AND THAT'S WHY YOU HAVE TO SHAVE EVERY DAY.

All the insults succeeded in reaching their goal: I was ashamed of myself, ashamed of my hair and of my body. And when I ended up in the hospital with a torn ligament, everyone saw what I had tried so desperately to hide.

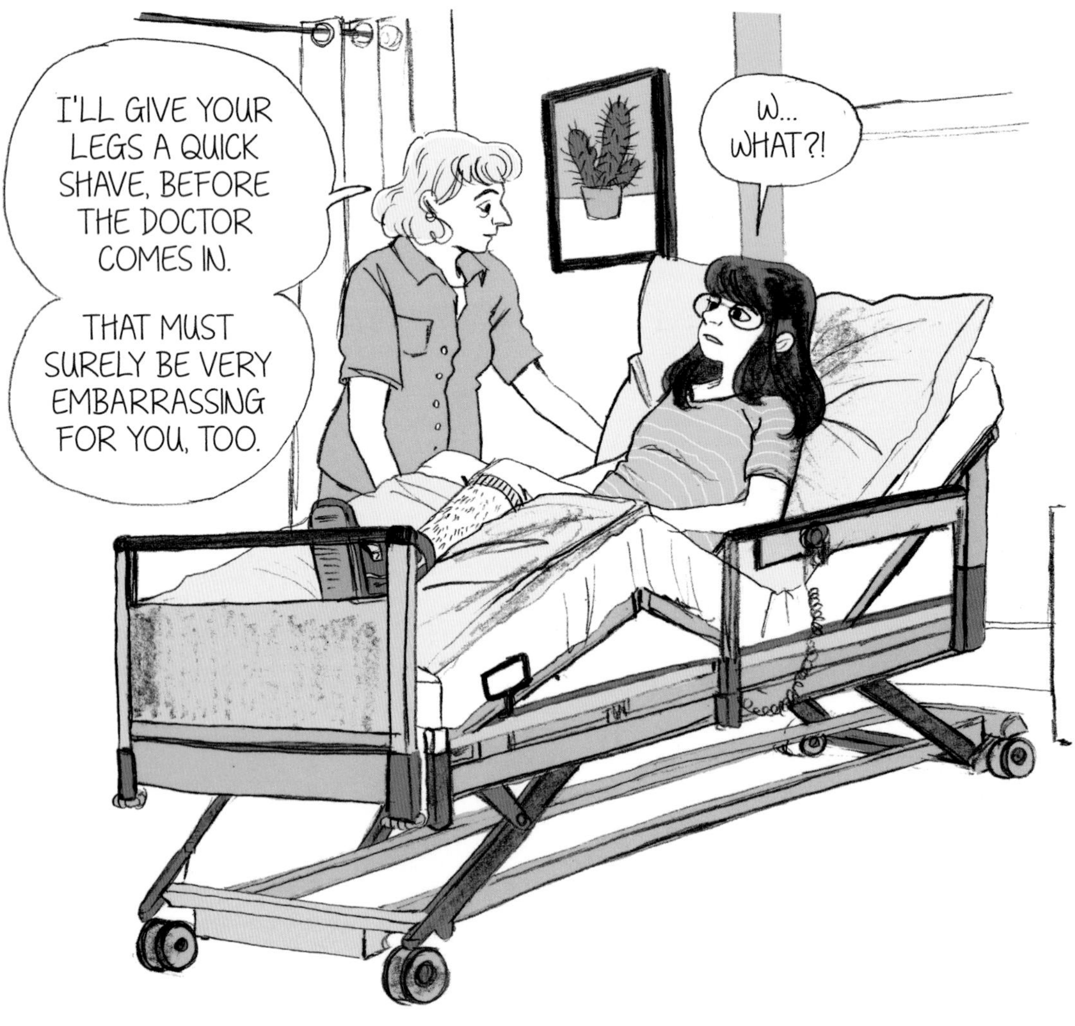
I'LL GIVE YOUR LEGS A QUICK SHAVE, BEFORE THE DOCTOR COMES IN.
THAT MUST SURELY BE VERY EMBARRASSING FOR YOU, TOO.
W... WHAT?!

Sometimes I imagined what would happen if I were in a car accident. The worst part wouldn't be my death. Much more terrifying was the thought that I'd be found at the accident site with unshaved legs.

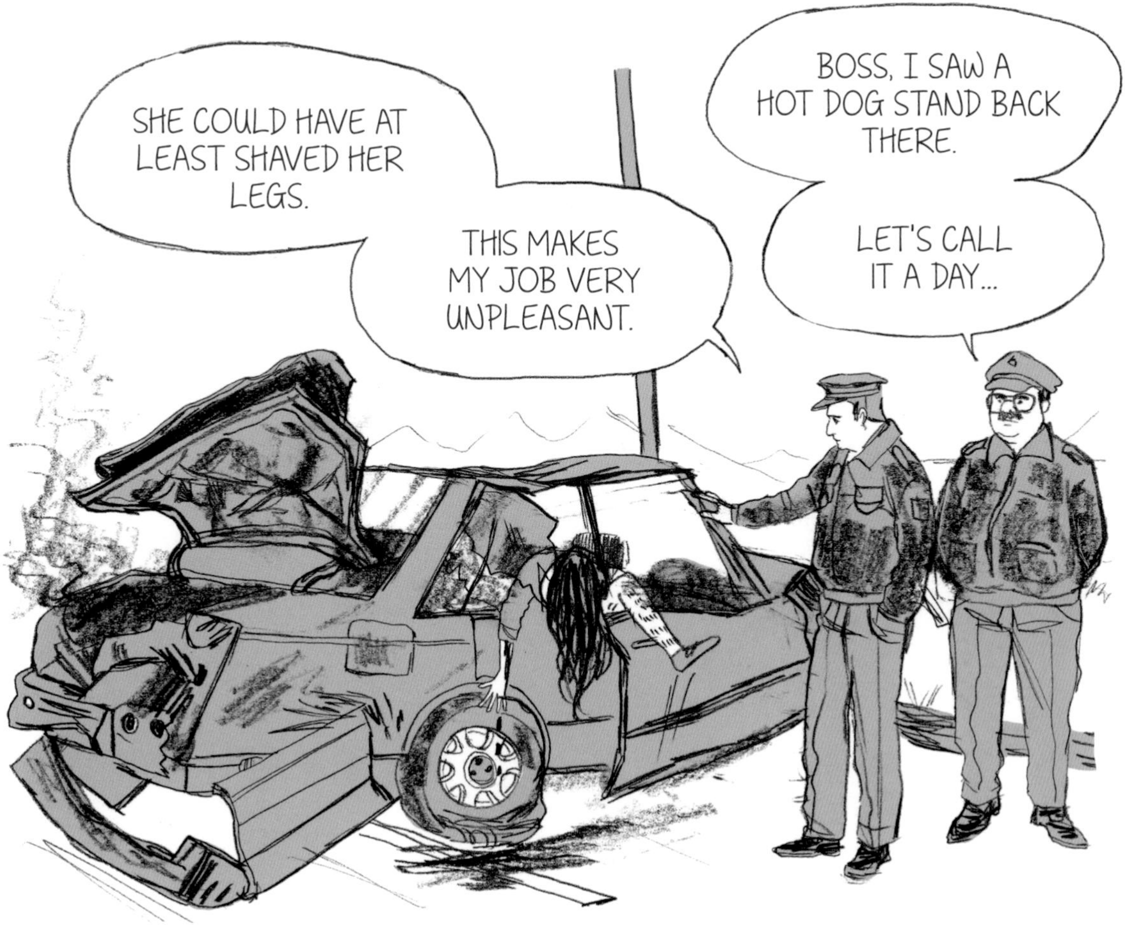
BOSS, I SAW A HOT DOG STAND BACK THERE.
SHE COULD HAVE AT LEAST SHAVED HER LEGS.
THIS MAKES MY JOB VERY UNPLEASANT.
LET'S CALL IT A DAY...

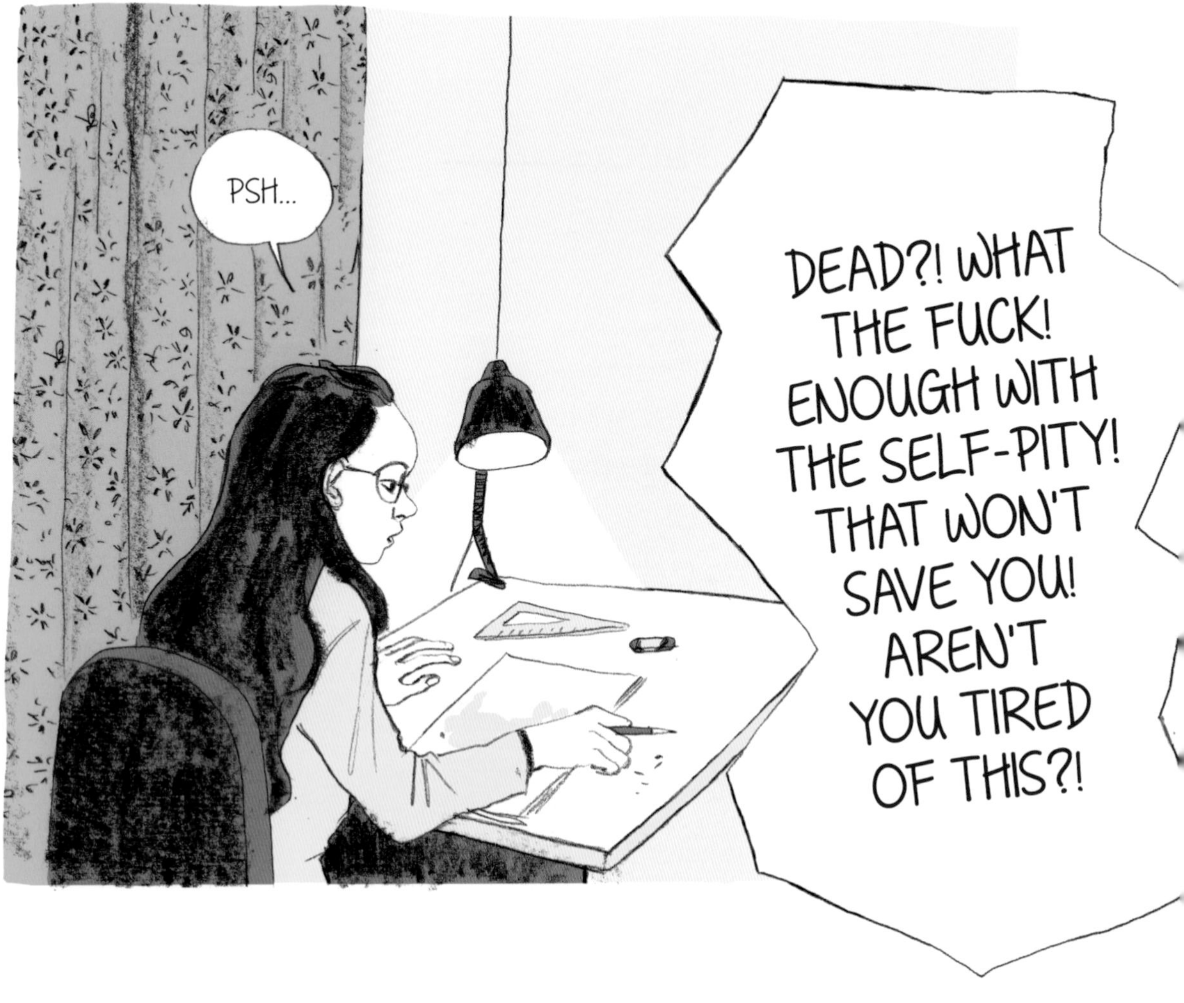
PSH...
DEAD?! WHAT THE FUCK! ENOUGH WITH THE SELF-PITY! THAT WON'T SAVE YOU! AREN'T YOU TIRED OF THIS?!

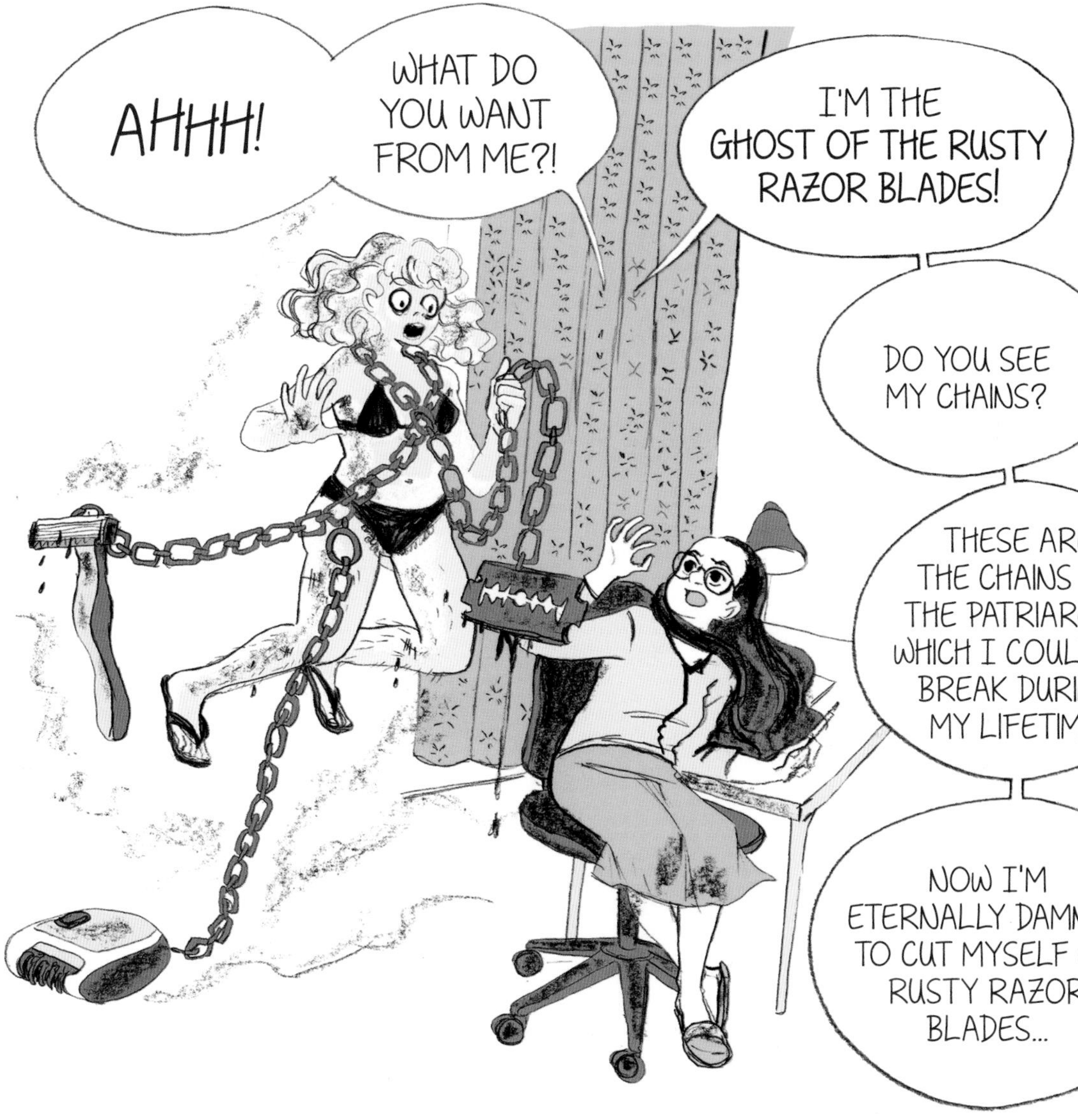
AHHH!
WHAT DO YOU WANT FROM ME?!
I'M THE GHOST OF THE RUSTY RAZOR BLADES!
DO YOU SEE MY CHAINS?
THESE ARE THE CHAINS OF THE PATRIARCHY, WHICH I COULDN'T BREAK DURING MY LIFETIME!
NOW I'M ETERNALLY DAMNED TO CUT MYSELF ON RUSTY RAZOR BLADES...

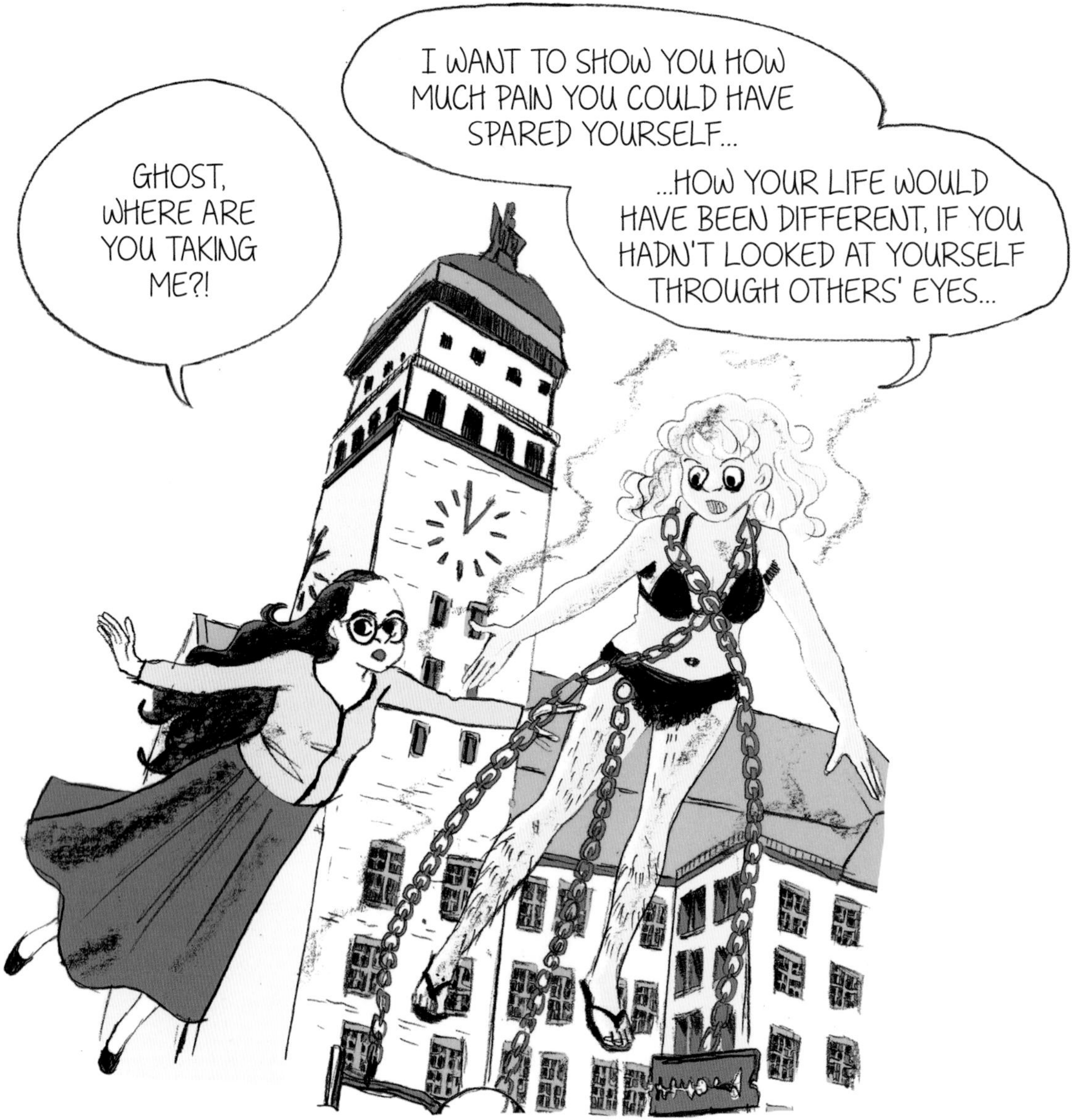
GHOST, WHERE ARE YOU TAKING ME?!
I WANT TO SHOW YOU HOW MUCH PAIN YOU COULD HAVE SPARED YOURSELF...
...HOW YOUR LIFE WOULD HAVE BEEN DIFFERENT, IF YOU HADN'T LOOKED AT YOURSELF THROUGH OTHERS' EYES...

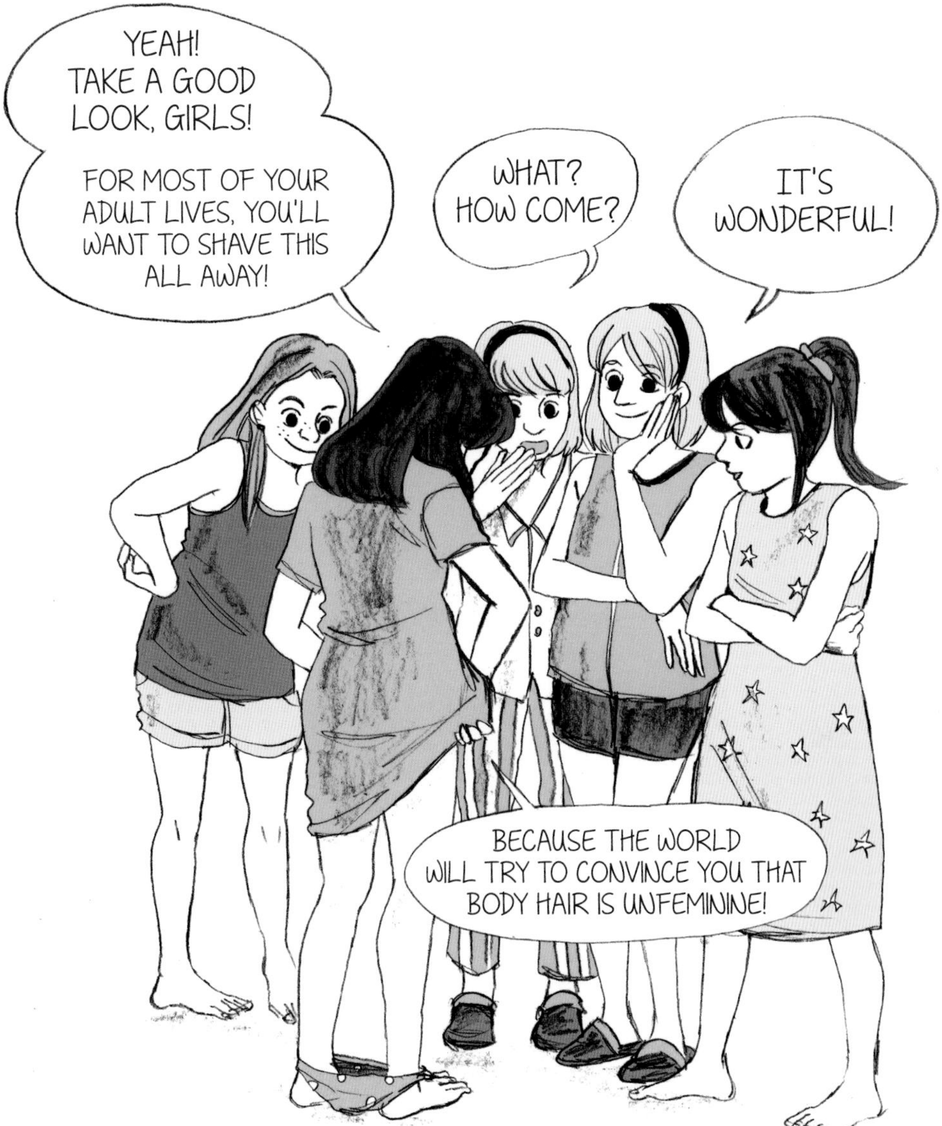
YEAH! TAKE A GOOD LOOK, GIRLS!
FOR MOST OF YOUR ADULT LIVES, YOU'LL WANT TO SHAVE THIS ALL AWAY!
WHAT? HOW COME?
IT'S WONDERFUL!
BECAUSE THE WORLD WILL TRY TO CONVINCE YOU THAT BODY HAIR IS UNFEMININE!

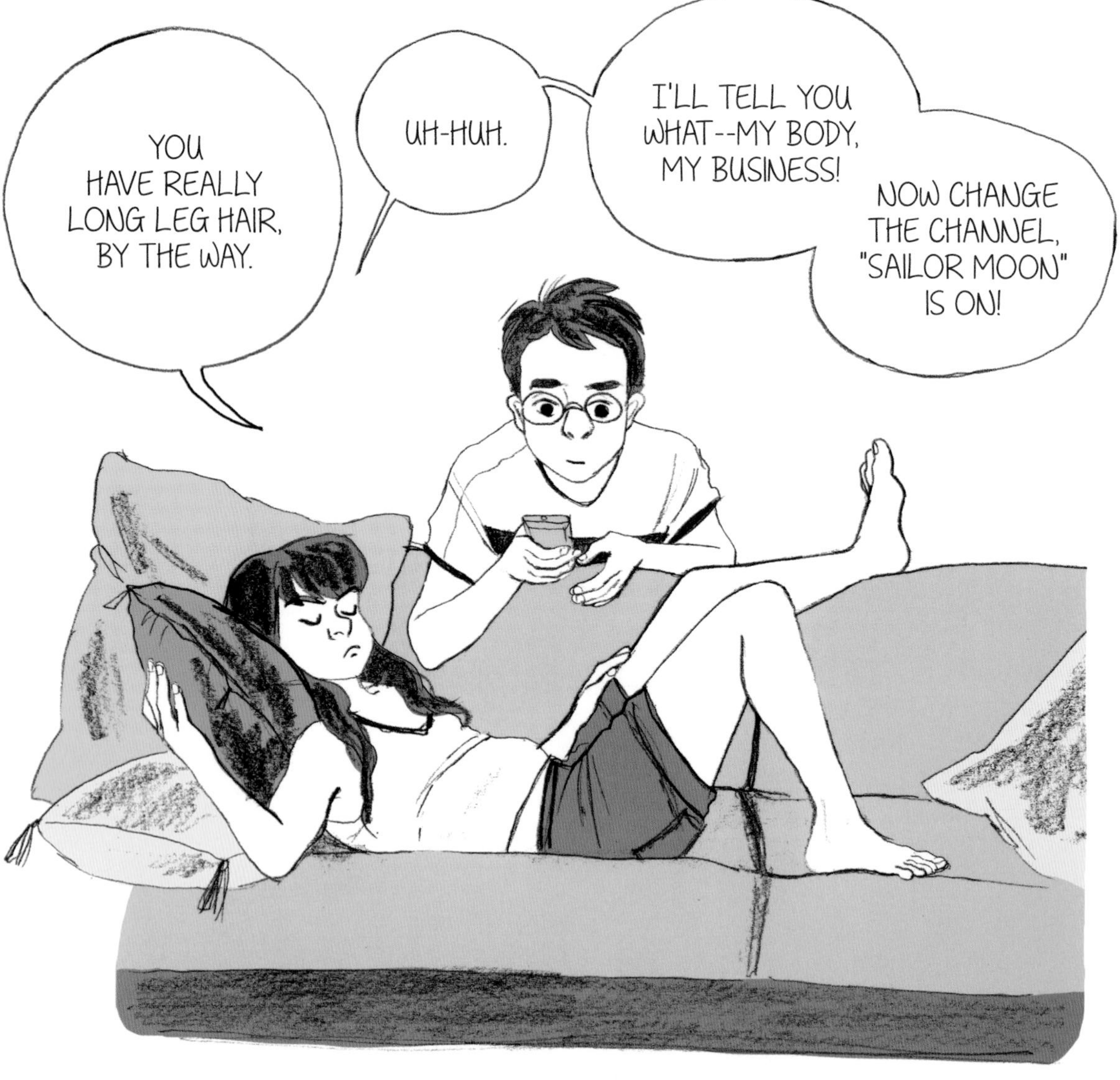
YOU HAVE REALLY LONG LEG HAIR, BY THE WAY.
UH-HUH.
I'LL TELL YOU WHAT--MY BODY, MY BUSINESS!
NOW CHANGE THE CHANNEL, "SAILOR MOON" IS ON!

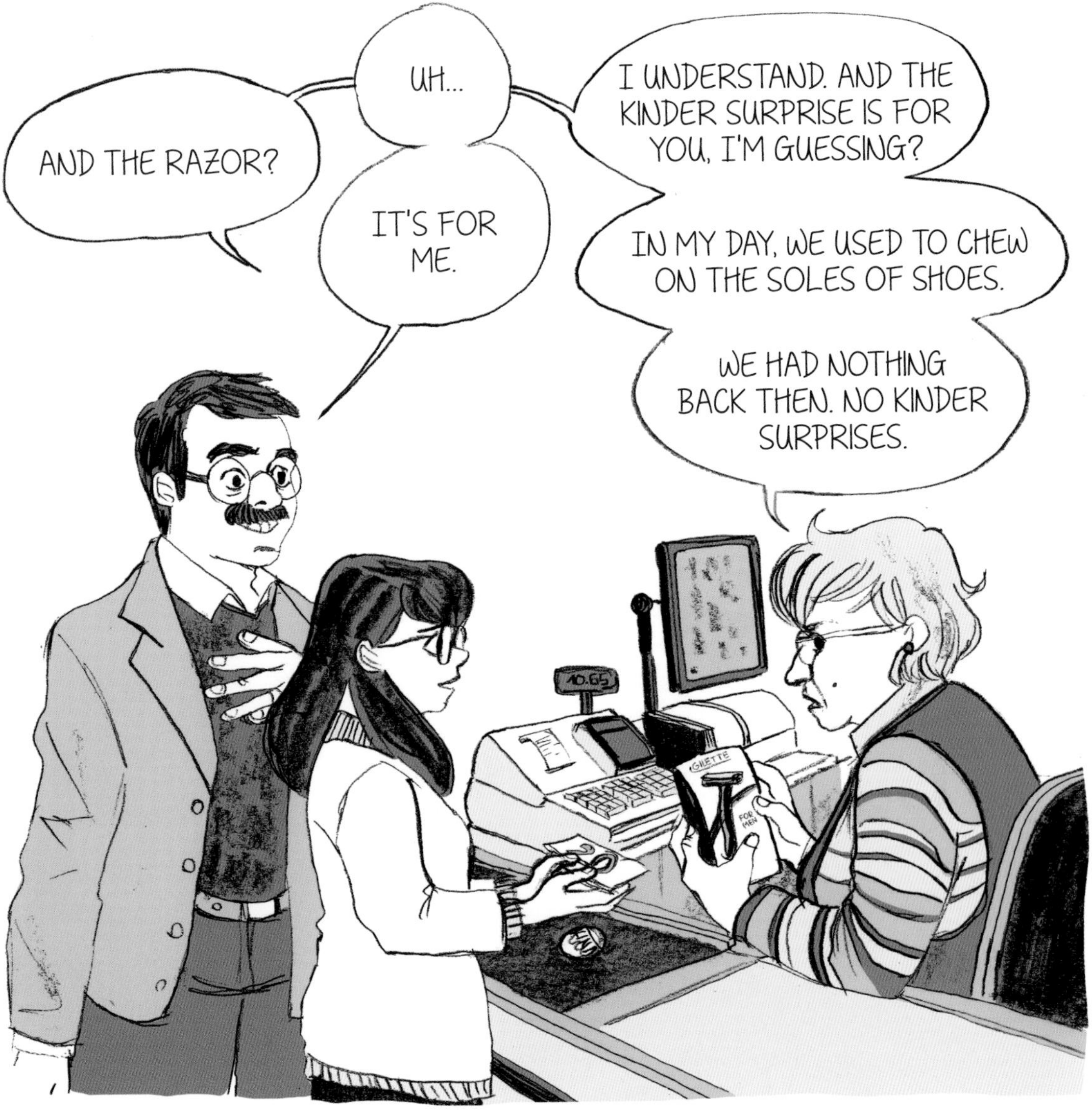
AND THE RAZOR?
UH...
IT'S FOR ME.
I UNDERSTAND. AND THE KINDER SURPRISE IS FOR YOU, I'M GUESSING?
IN MY DAY, WE USED TO CHEW ON THE SOLES OF SHOES.
WE HAD NOTHING BACK THEN. NO KINDER SURPRISES.
10.65
GILETTE
FOR MEN

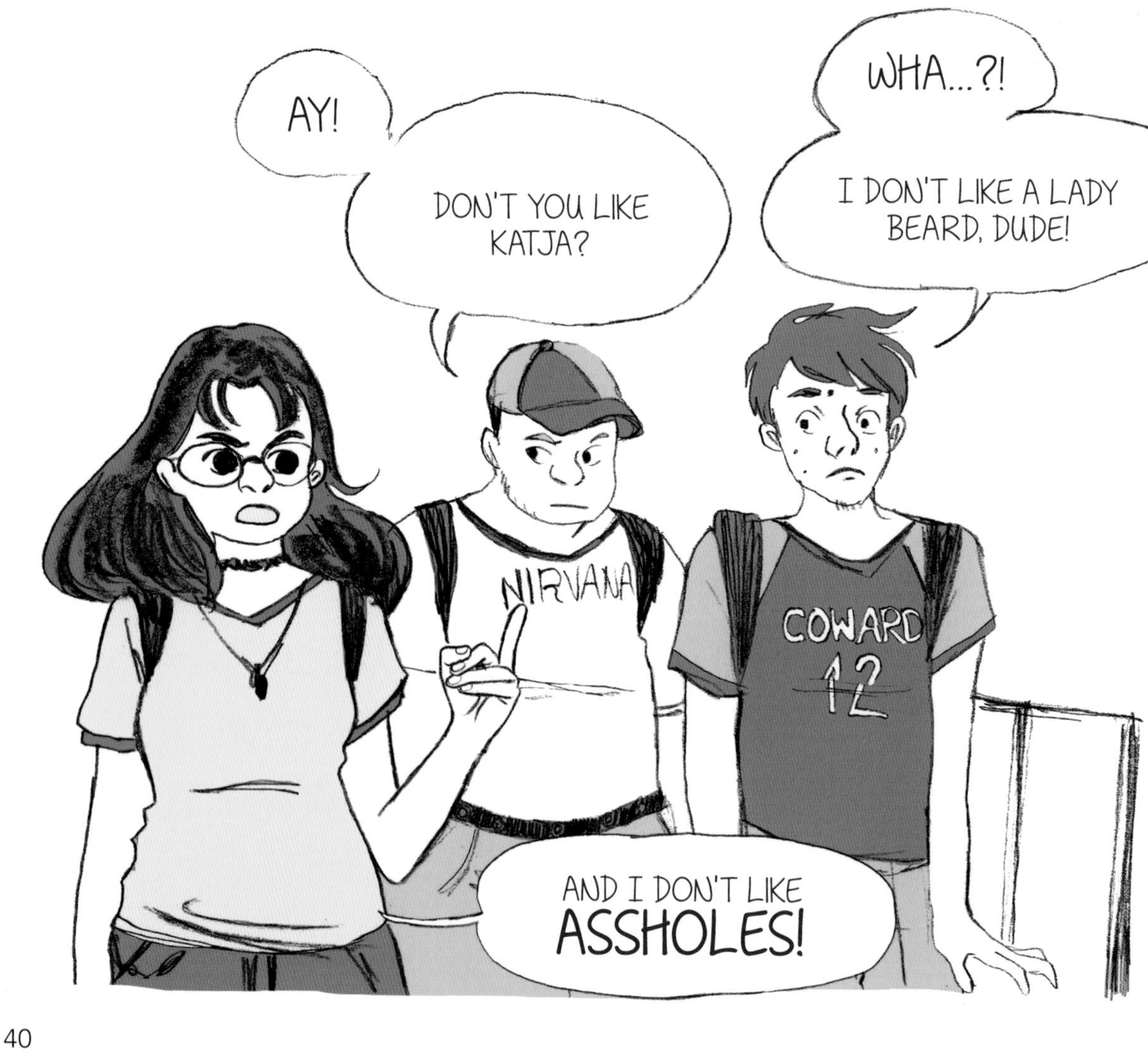
AY!
DON'T YOU LIKE KATJA?
WHA...?!
I DON'T LIKE A LADY BEARD, DUDE!
NIRVANA
COWARD
12
AND I DON'T LIKE ASSHOLES!

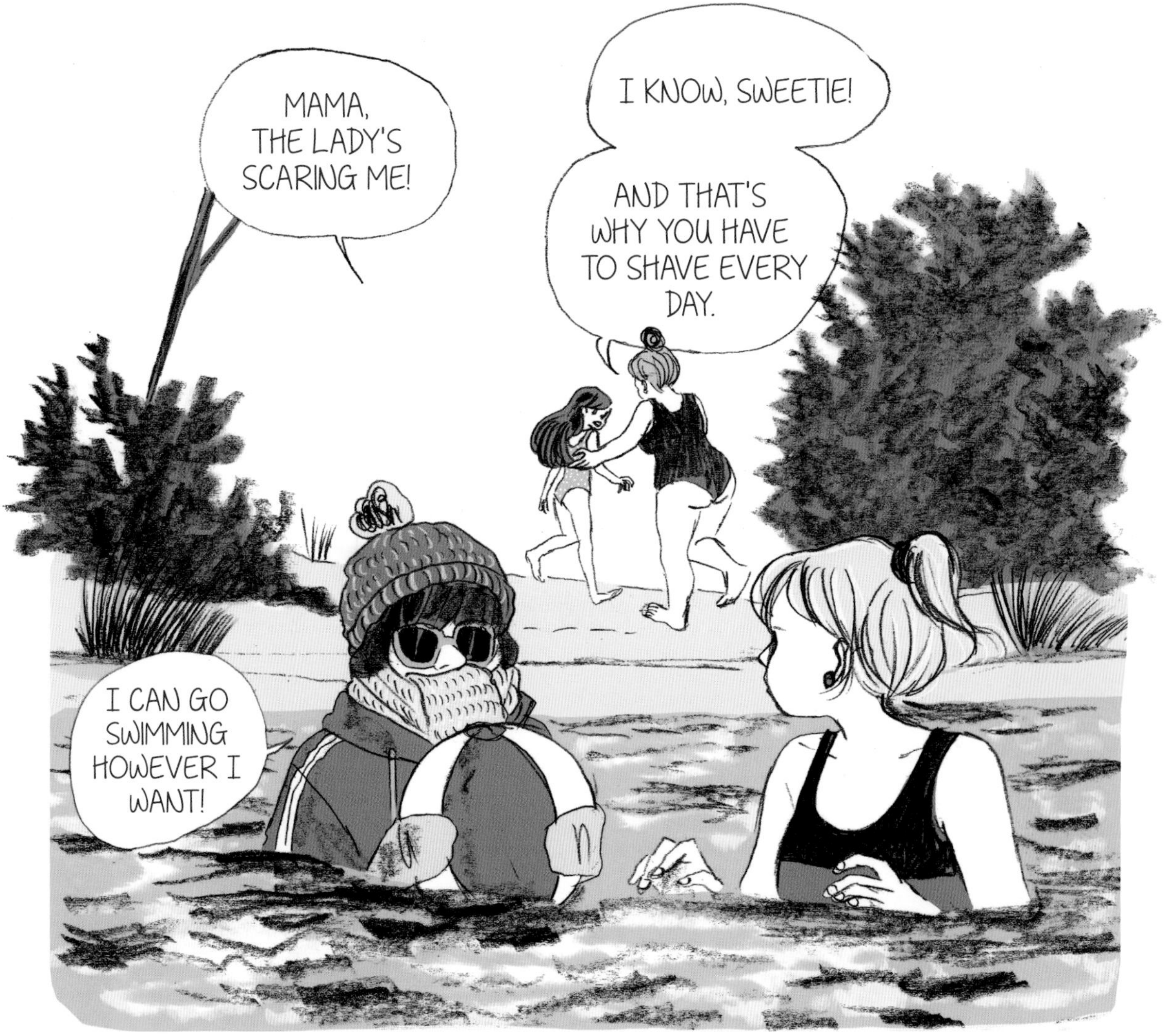
MAMA, THE LADY'S SCARING ME!
I KNOW, SWEETIE!
AND THAT'S WHY YOU HAVE TO SHAVE EVERY DAY.
I CAN GO SWIMMING HOWEVER I WANT!

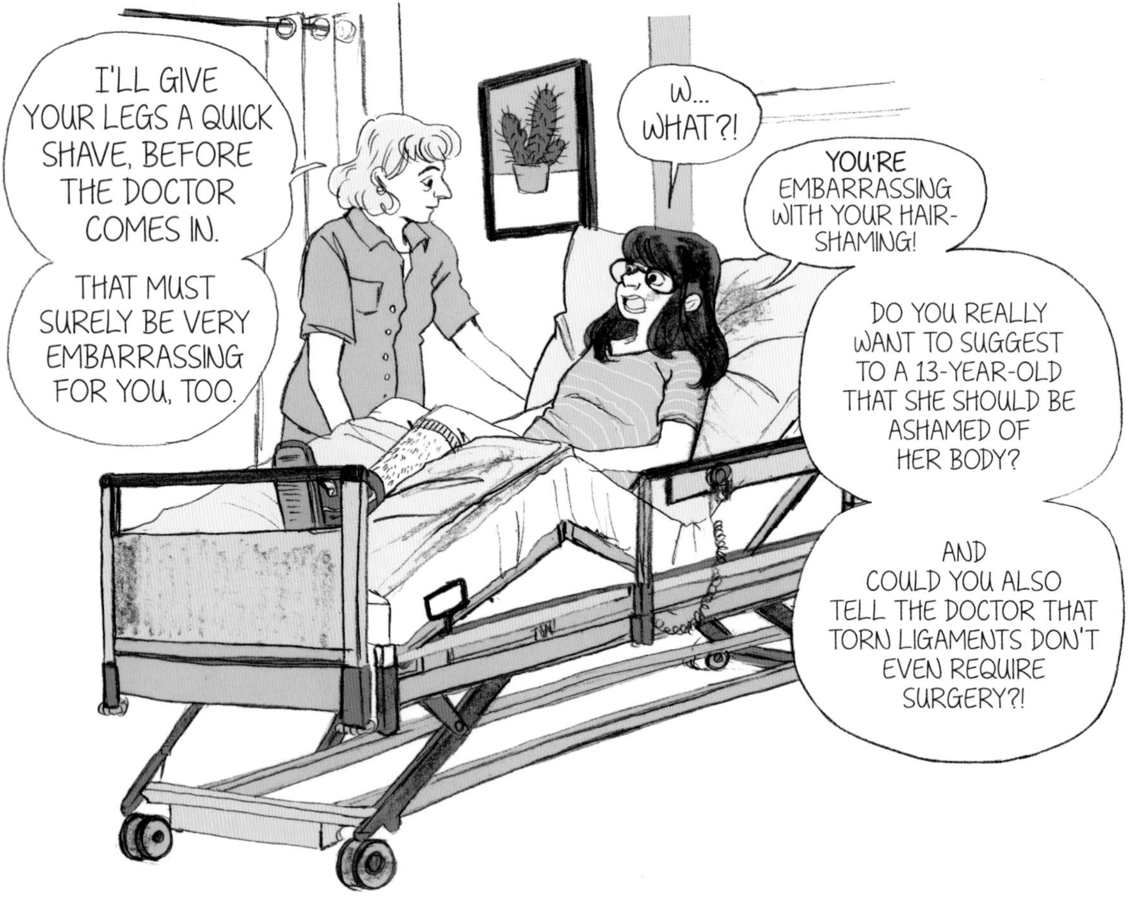
I'LL GIVE YOUR LEGS A QUICK SHAVE, BEFORE THE DOCTOR COMES IN.
THAT MUST SURELY BE VERY EMBARRASSING FOR YOU, TOO.
W... WHAT?!
YOU'RE EMBARRASSING WITH YOUR HAIR-SHAMING!
DO YOU REALLY WANT TO SUGGEST TO A 13-YEAR-OLD THAT SHE SHOULD BE ASHAMED OF HER BODY?
AND COULD YOU ALSO TELL THE DOCTOR THAT TORN LIGAMENTS DON'T EVEN REQUIRE SURGERY?!

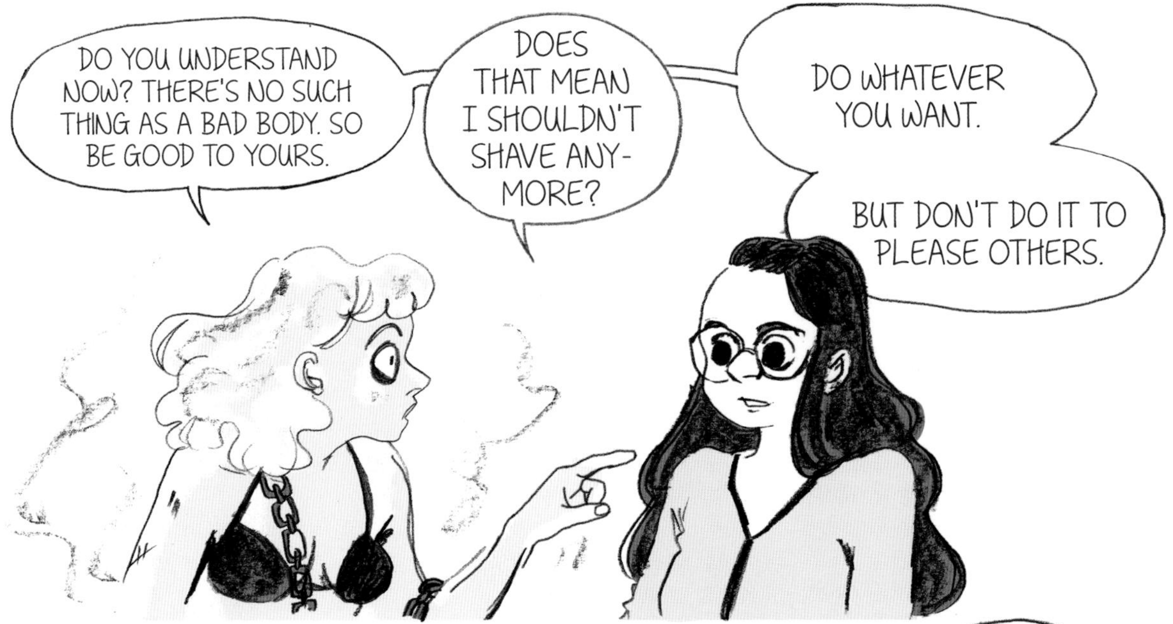
DO YOU UNDERSTAND NOW? THERE'S NO SUCH THING AS A BAD BODY. SO BE GOOD TO YOURS.
DOES THAT MEAN I SHOULDN'T SHAVE ANY-MORE?
DO WHATEVER YOU WANT.
BUT DON'T DO IT TO PLEASE OTHERS.

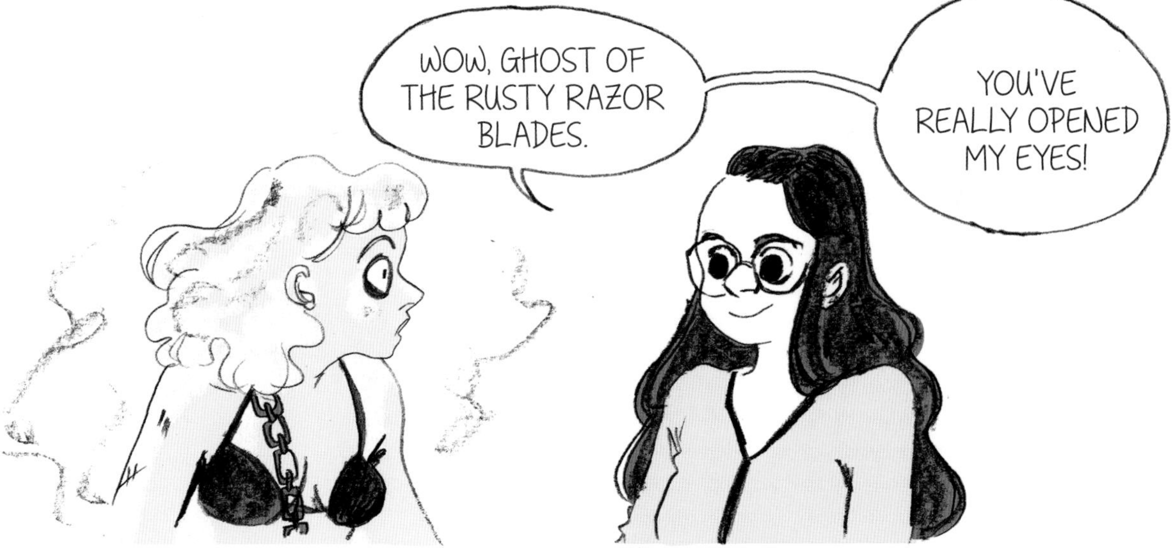
WOW, GHOST OF THE RUSTY RAZOR BLADES.
YOU'VE REALLY OPENED MY EYES!

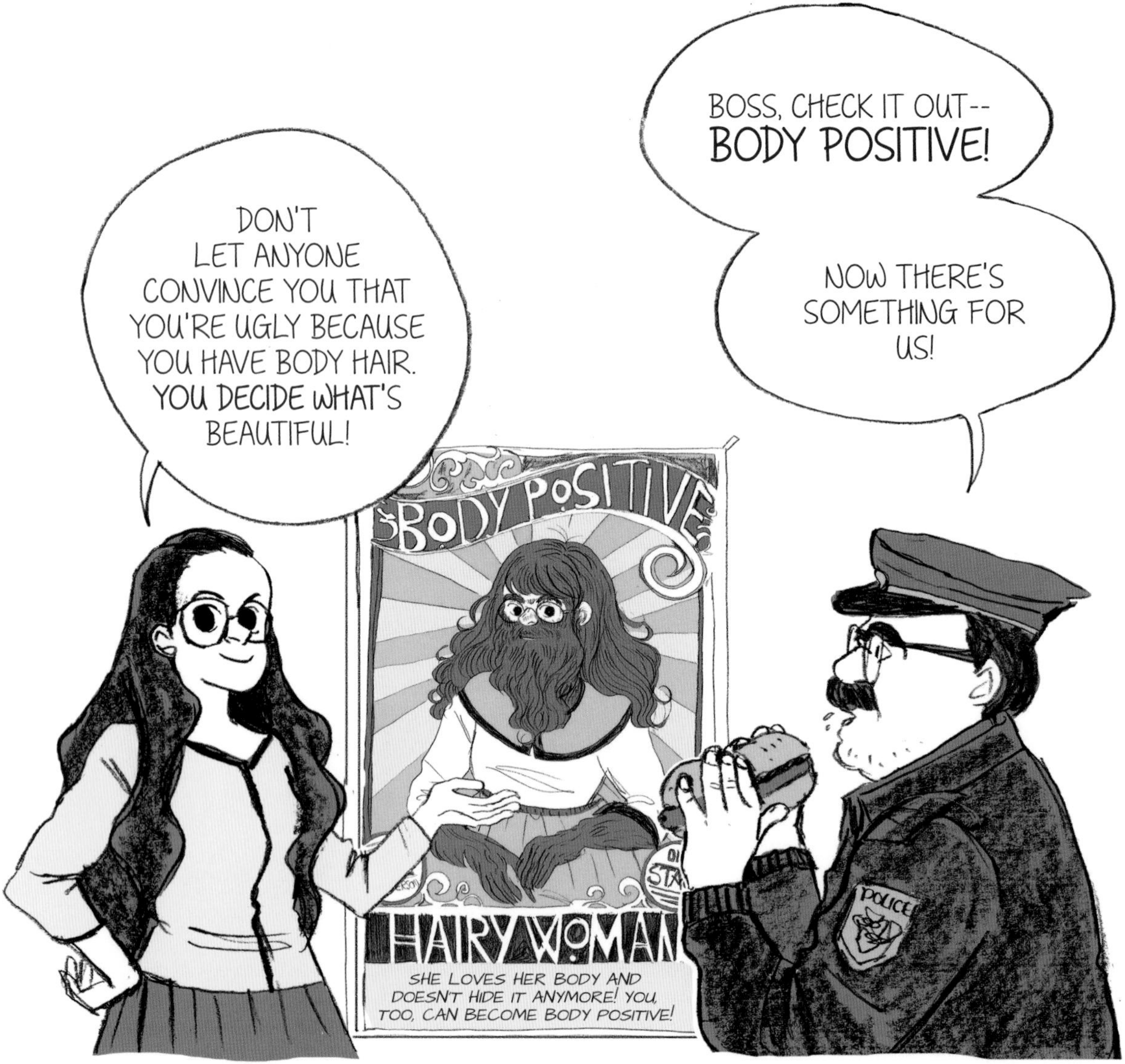
DON'T LET ANYONE CONVINCE YOU THAT YOU'RE UGLY BECAUSE YOU HAVE BODY HAIR. YOU DECIDE WHAT'S BEAUTIFUL!
BOSS, CHECK IT OUT-- BODY POSITIVE!
NOW THERE'S SOMETHING FOR US!
BODY POSITIVE
HAIRY WOMAN
SHE LOVES HER BODY AND DOESN'T HIDE IT ANYMORE! YOU, TOO, CAN BECOME BODY POSITIVE!
POLICE

The Baby Chainsaw Massacre

So, imagine this--you're in a fancy café. Suddenly, a piece of cake jumps out at you. Until then, you didn't have any idea that you wanted one, but now the chocolate temptation beckons to you. The cake looks expensive, no question, but you'll only know after the fact whether it was worth the price. And now it's sitting there, and you can't decide. I call this the **Cake Principle**.

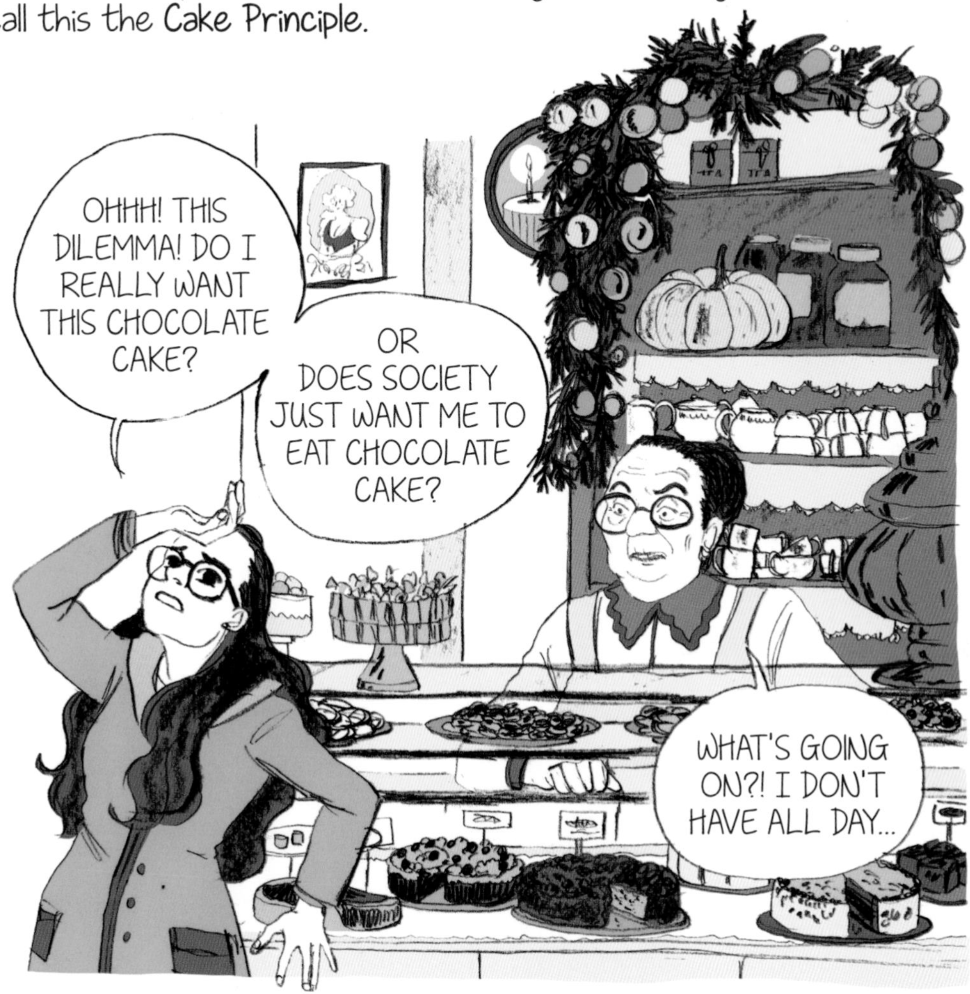
OHHH! THIS DILEMMA! DO I REALLY WANT THIS CHOCOLATE CAKE?
OR DOES SOCIETY JUST WANT ME TO EAT CHOCOLATE CAKE?
WHAT'S GOING ON?! I DON'T HAVE ALL DAY...

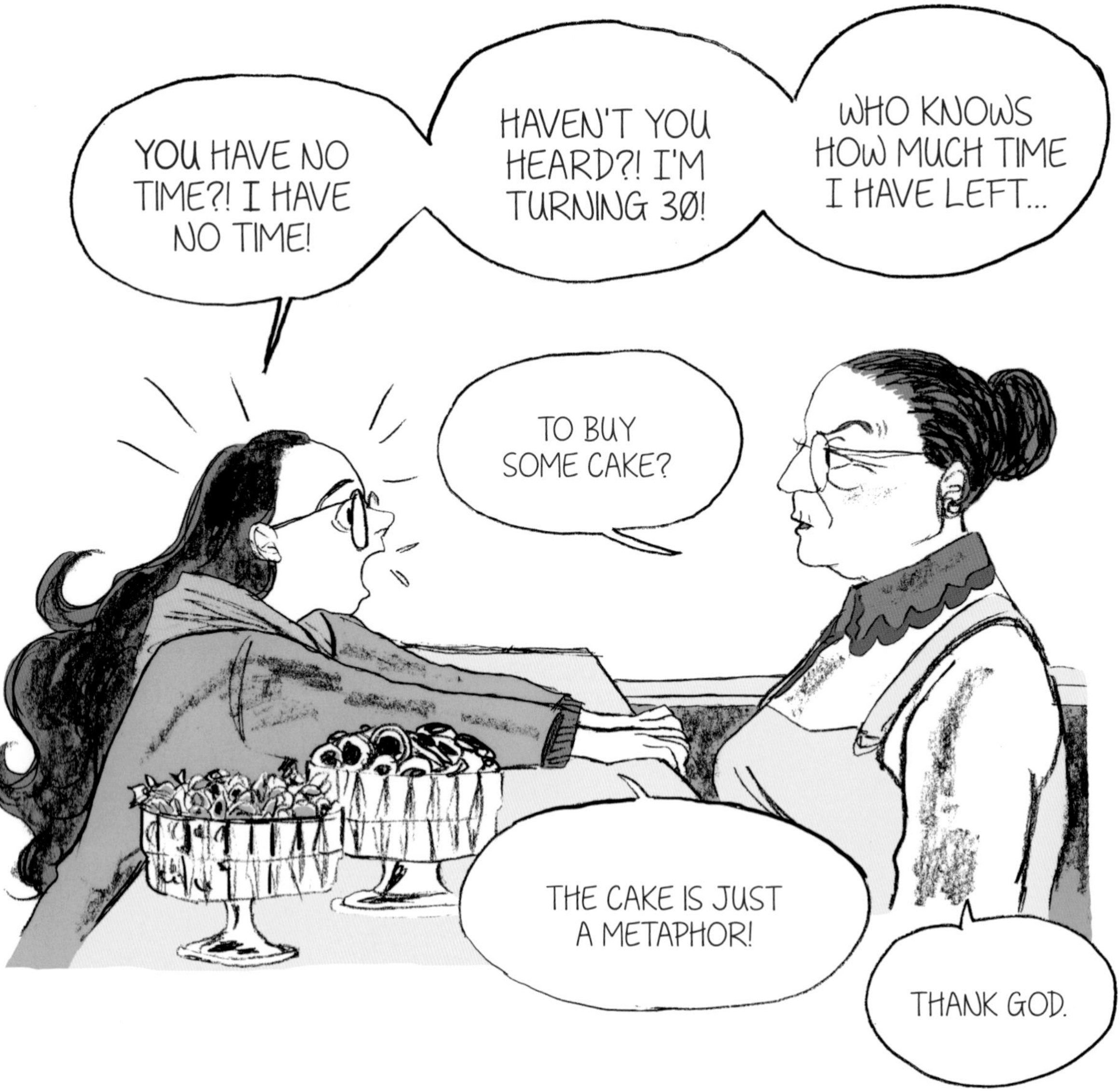
YOU HAVE NO TIME?! I HAVE NO TIME!
HAVEN'T YOU HEARD?! I'M TURNING 30!
WHO KNOWS HOW MUCH TIME I HAVE LEFT...
TO BUY SOME CAKE?
THE CAKE IS JUST A METAPHOR!
THANK GOD.

You see how hard it is for me to decide on a piece of cake. How am I supposed to come to a conclusion regarding much more sensitive topics? Funnily enough, it's the sensitive topics that other people always want to discuss. That's the **Bridget Jones Principle.***

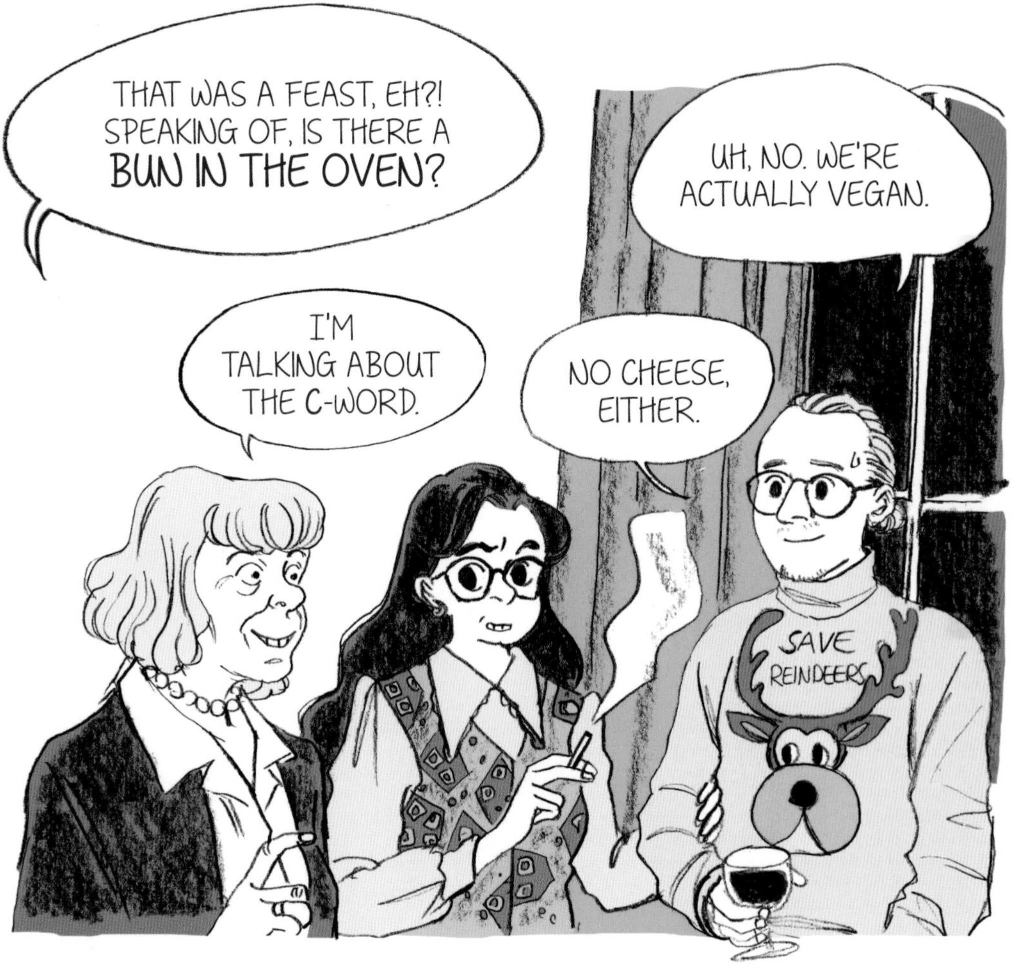
THAT WAS A FEAST, EH?! SPEAKING OF, IS THERE A BUN IN THE OVEN?
UH, NO. WE'RE ACTUALLY VEGAN.
I'M TALKING ABOUT THE C-WORD.
NO CHEESE, EITHER.
SAVE REINDEERS

*It comes right after the Cake Principle.

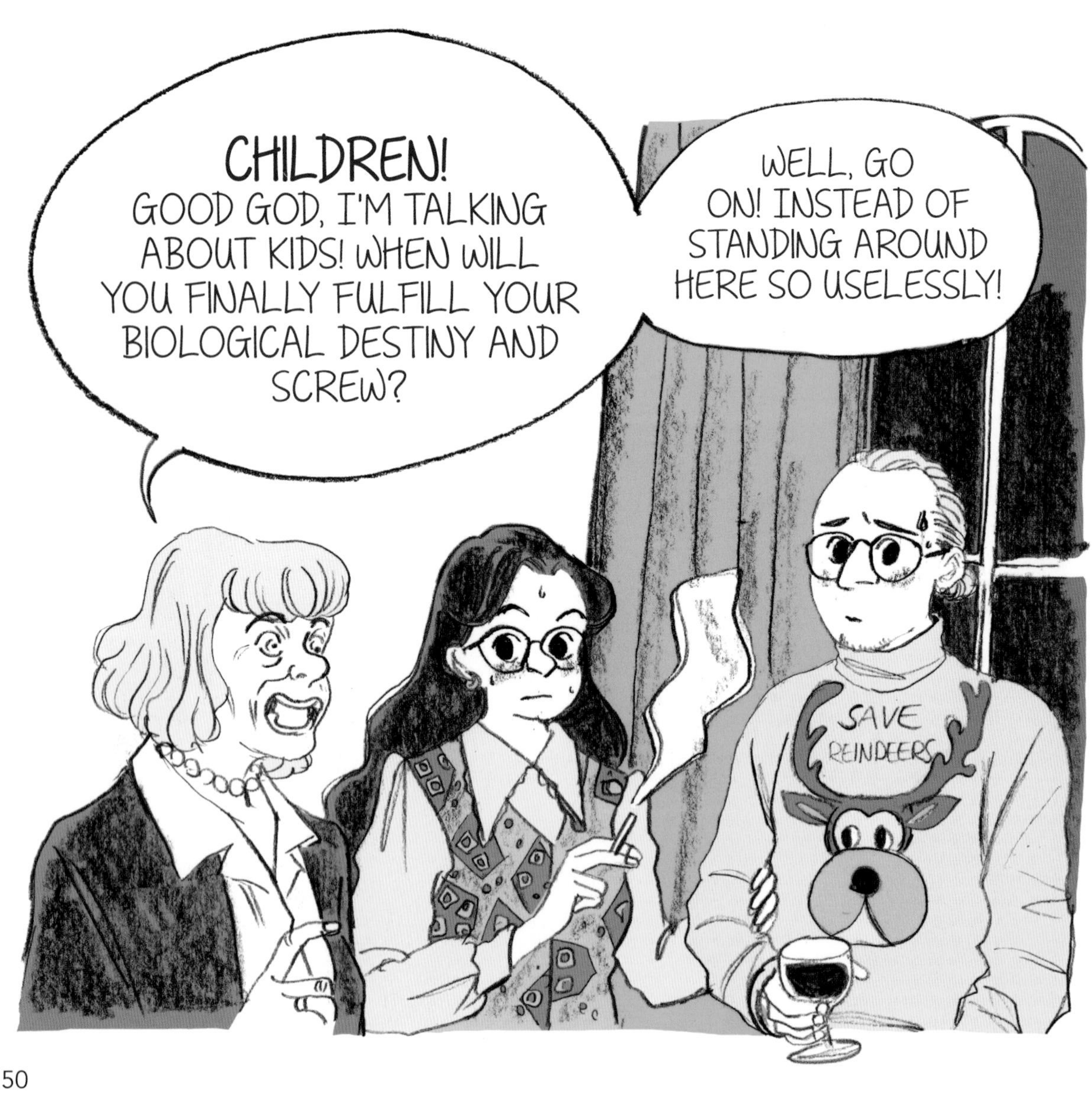
CHILDREN! GOOD GOD, I'M TALKING ABOUT KIDS! WHEN WILL YOU FINALLY FULFILL YOUR BIOLOGICAL DESTINY AND SCREW?
WELL, GO ON! INSTEAD OF STANDING AROUND HERE SO USELESSLY!
SAVE REINDEERS

And suddenly, there it is--the elephant in the room.

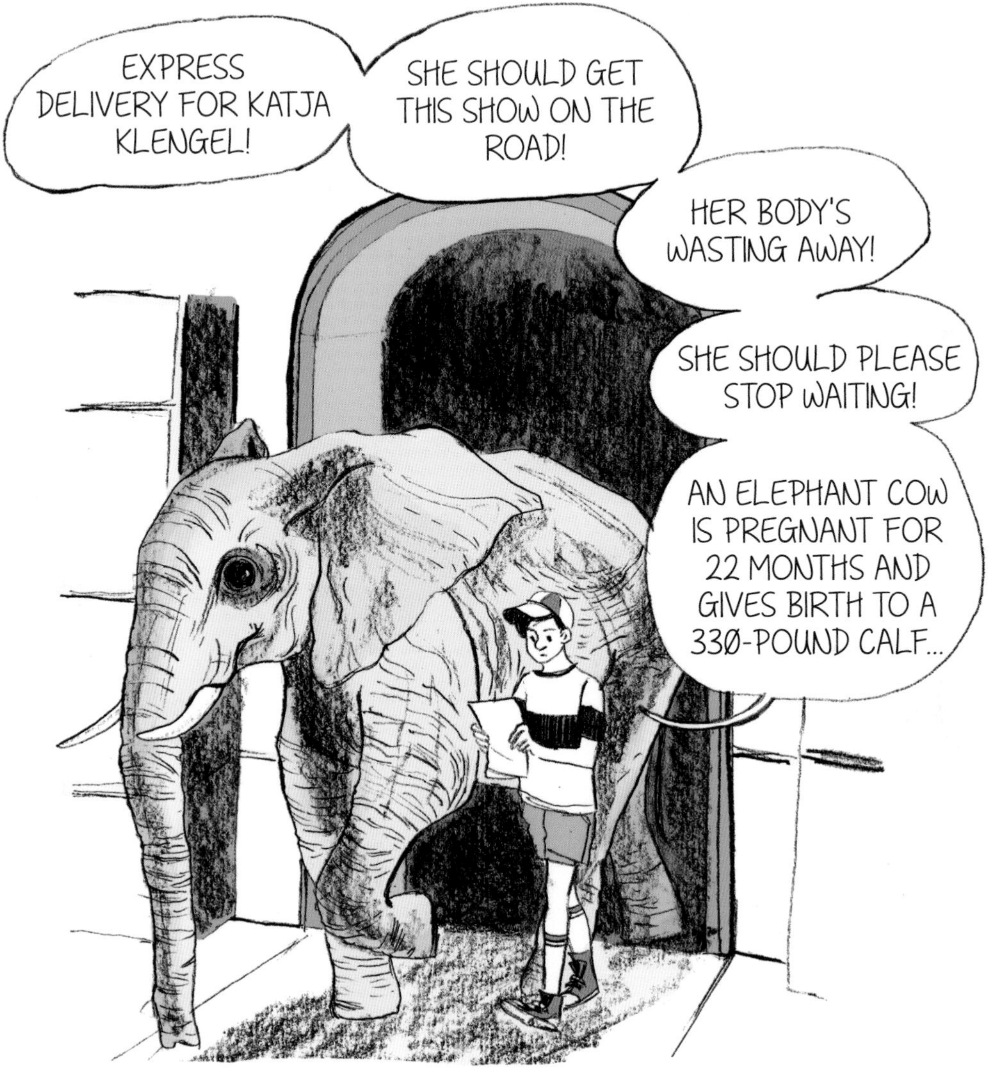
EXPRESS DELIVERY FOR KATJA KLENGEL!
SHE SHOULD GET THIS SHOW ON THE ROAD!
HER BODY'S WASTING AWAY!
SHE SHOULD PLEASE STOP WAITING!
AN ELEPHANT COW IS PREGNANT FOR 22 MONTHS AND GIVES BIRTH TO A 33Ø-POUND CALF...

I think kids are super, honestly! I love kids! Recently, I actually spotted the ideal child in the subway wearing a Ravenclaw hoodie, with a book in hand (of course), bright red curls and freckles, a bit nerdy--what else could I want?!

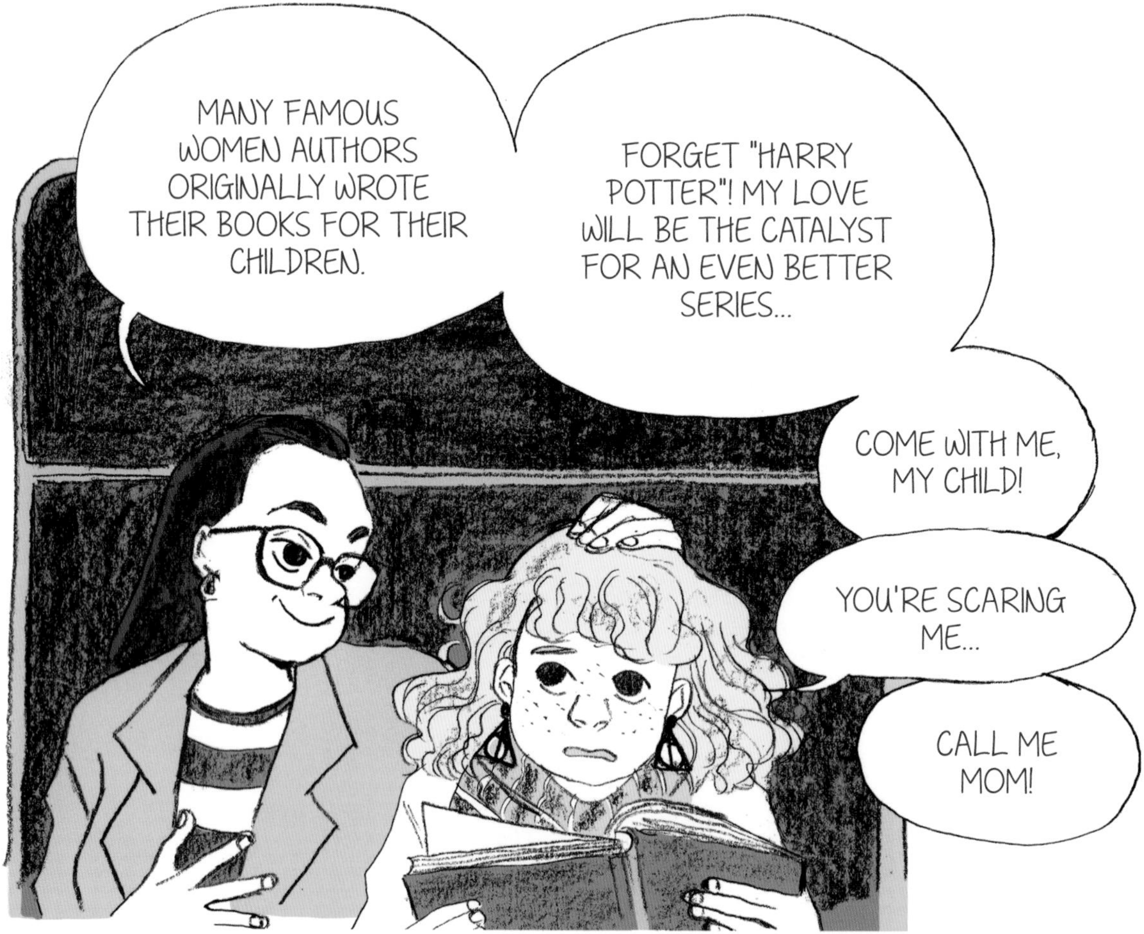
MANY FAMOUS WOMEN AUTHORS ORIGINALLY WROTE THEIR BOOKS FOR THEIR CHILDREN.
FORGET "HARRY POTTER"! MY LOVE WILL BE THE CATALYST FOR AN EVEN BETTER SERIES...
COME WITH ME, MY CHILD!
YOU'RE SCARING ME...
CALL ME MOM!

But to have kids myself?! I don't know if I'm ready yet. I have the feeling that I needed all of my twenties to figure out what I want, and especially what I don't want. Or, more accurately, **who** I don't want...

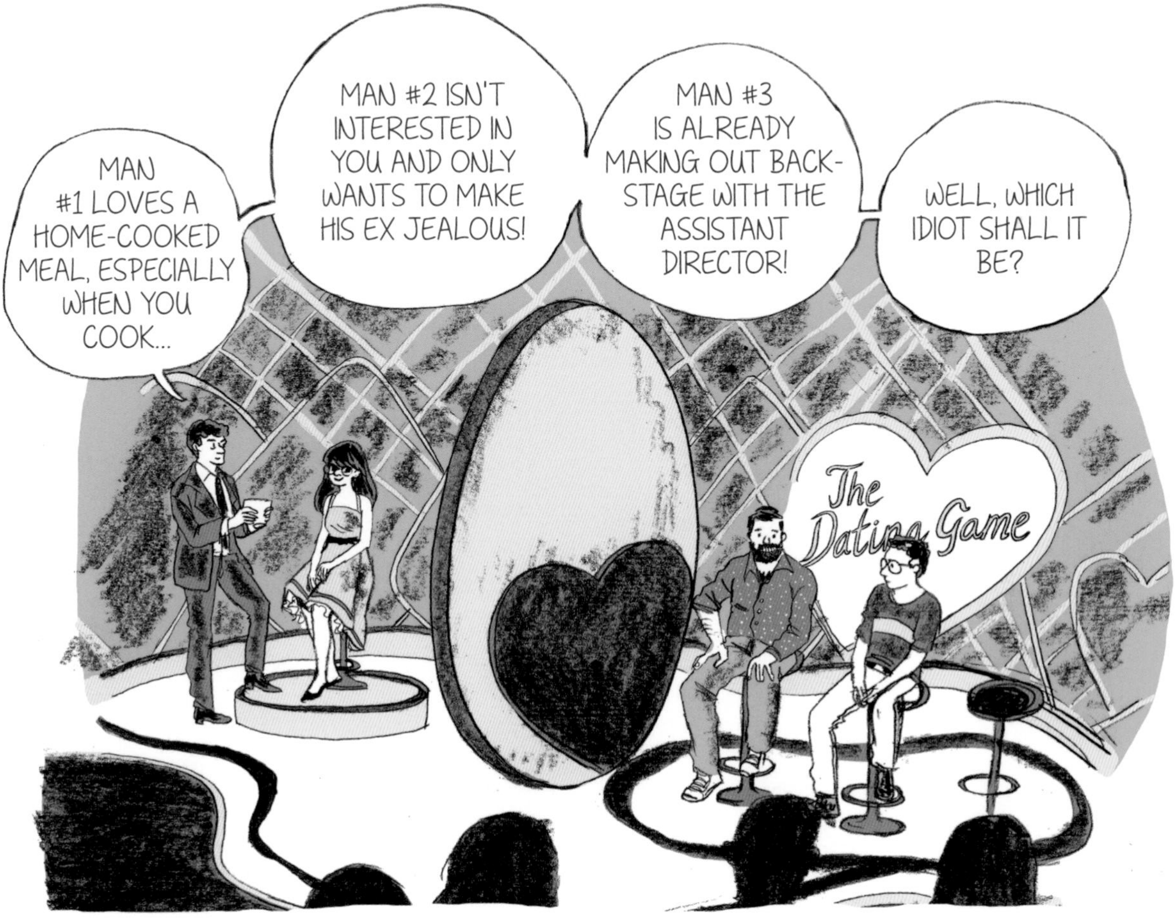
MAN #1 LOVES A HOME-COOKED MEAL, ESPECIALLY WHEN YOU COOK...
MAN #2 ISN'T INTERESTED IN YOU AND ONLY WANTS TO MAKE HIS EX JEALOUS!
MAN #3 IS ALREADY MAKING OUT BACK-STAGE WITH THE ASSISTANT DIRECTOR!
WELL, WHICH IDIOT SHALL IT BE?
The Dating Game

Now it's about me, about what I want! It's about who I am. I'm getting to know myself, and I'm enjoying myself. I must say: I'm the best date I've ever had!

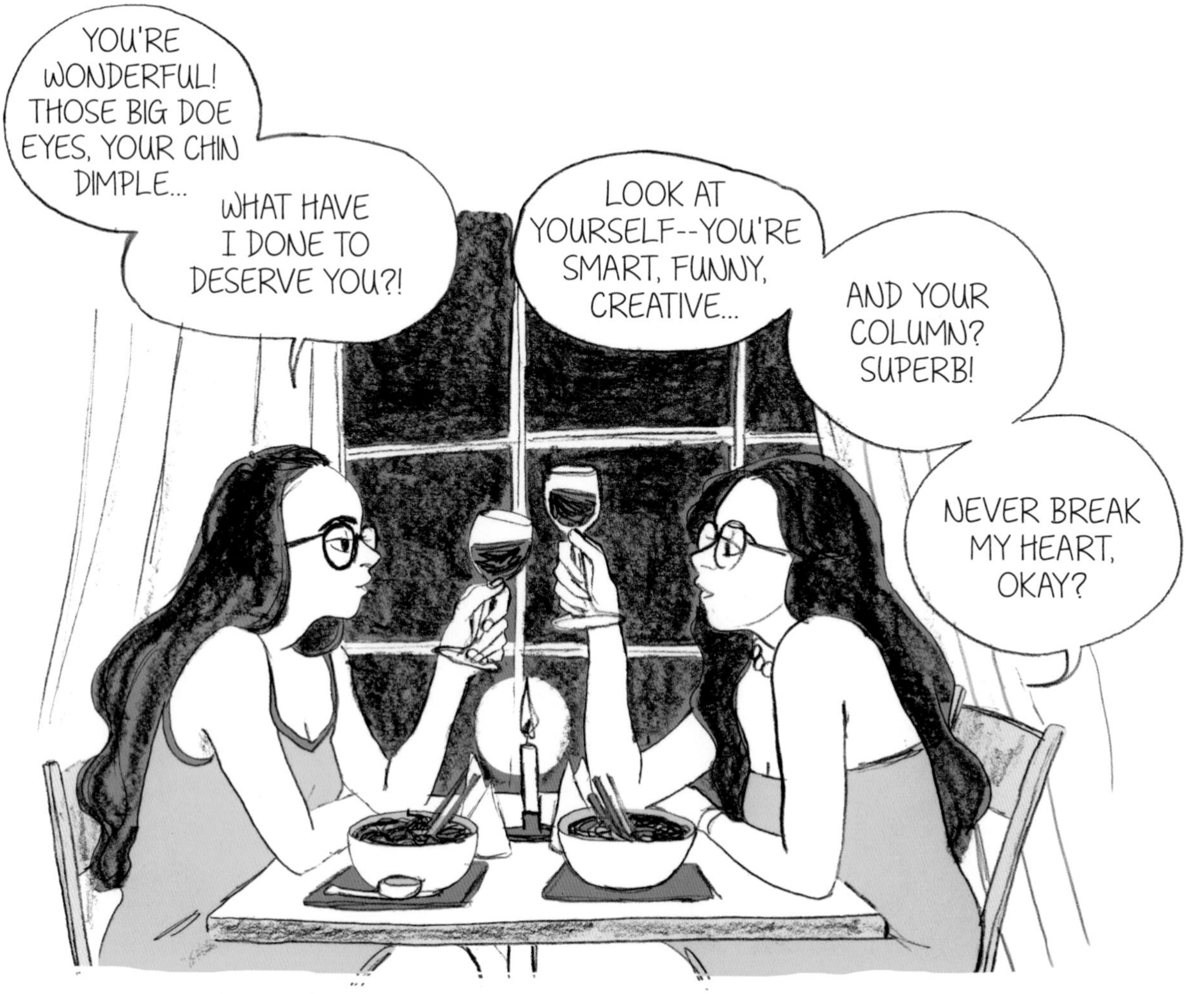
YOU'RE WONDERFUL! THOSE BIG DOE EYES, YOUR CHIN DIMPLE...
WHAT HAVE I DONE TO DESERVE YOU?!
LOOK AT YOURSELF--YOU'RE SMART, FUNNY, CREATIVE...
AND YOUR COLUMN? SUPERB!
NEVER BREAK MY HEART, OKAY?

I'm afraid I won't have any more time for myself once a child is here. But a friend who already has kids told me--

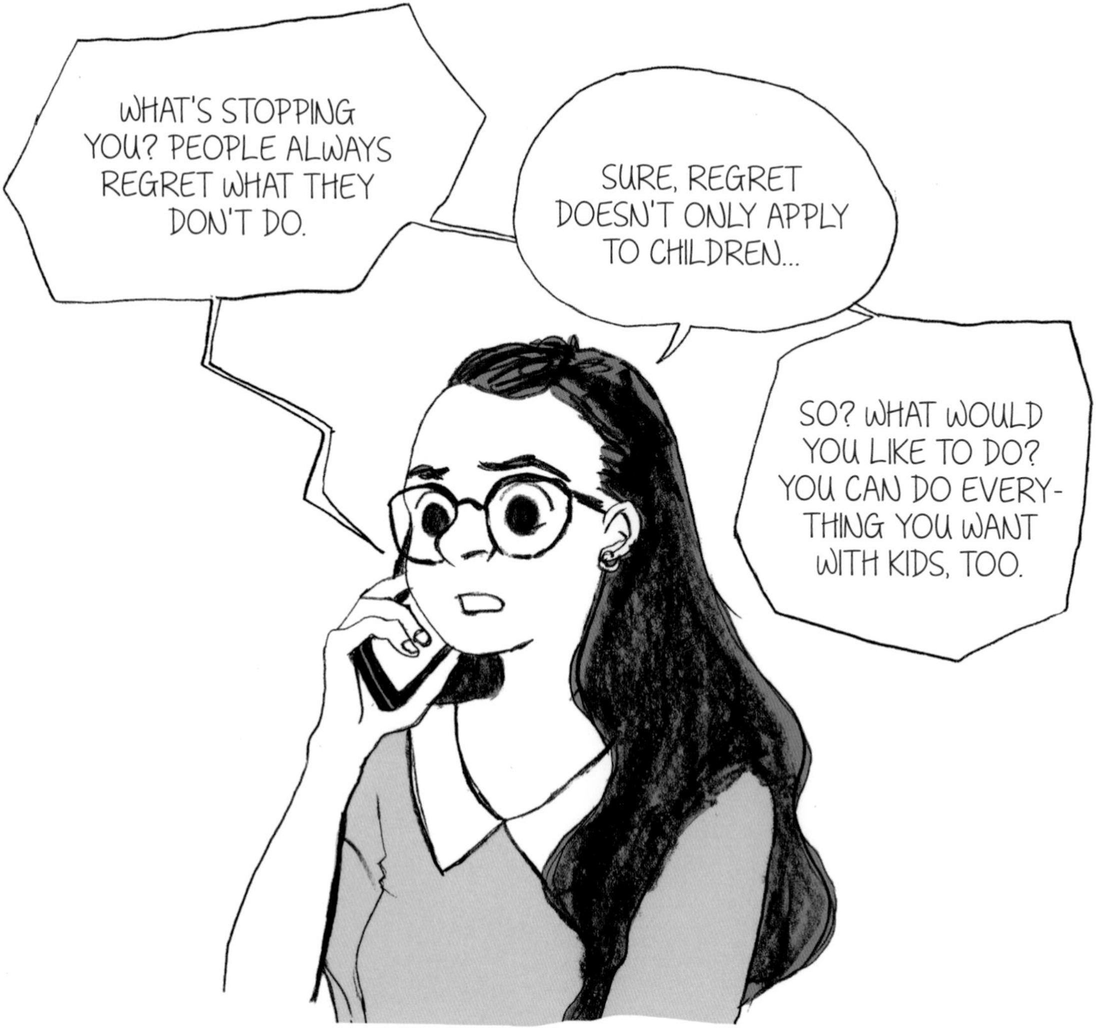
WHAT'S STOPPING YOU? PEOPLE ALWAYS REGRET WHAT THEY DON'T DO.
SURE, REGRET DOESN'T ONLY APPLY TO CHILDREN...
SO? WHAT WOULD YOU LIKE TO DO? YOU CAN DO EVERY-THING YOU WANT WITH KIDS, TOO.

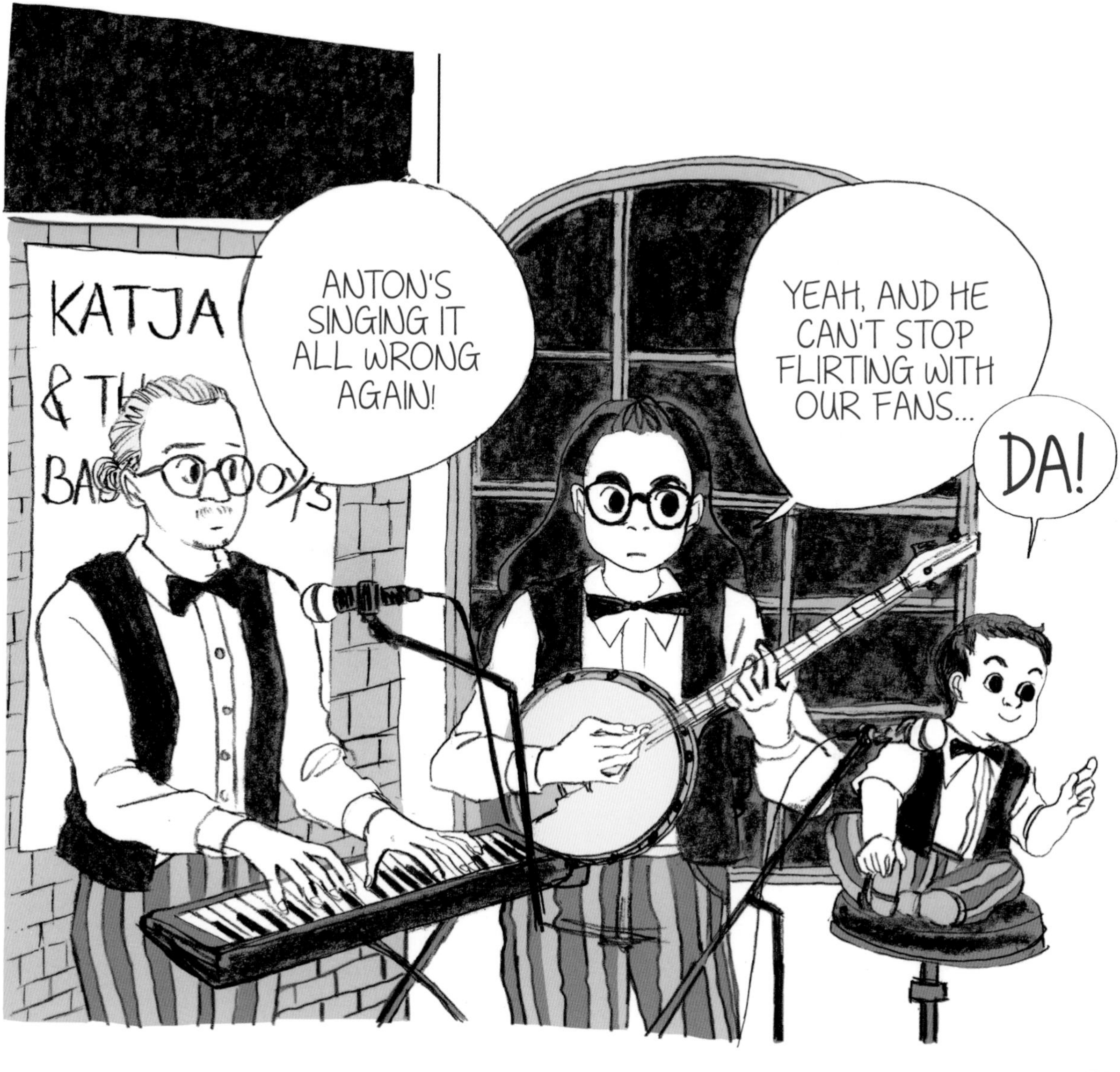
KATJA
&
ANTON'S SINGING IT ALL WRONG AGAIN!
YEAH, AND HE CAN'T STOP FLIRTING WITH OUR FANS...
DA!

And what about financial concerns? I'm a student and I'm still dependent on my parents. How is that supposed to work?

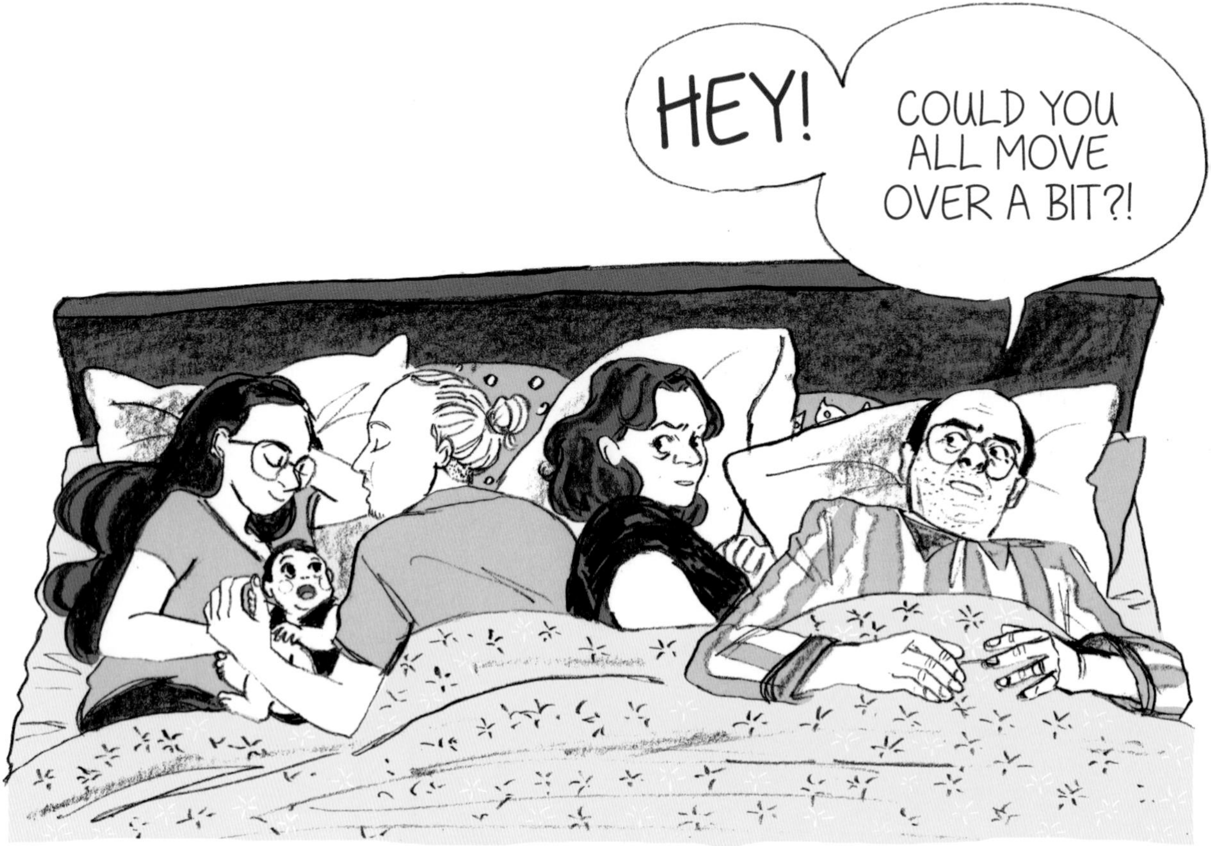
HEY!
COULD YOU ALL MOVE OVER A BIT?!

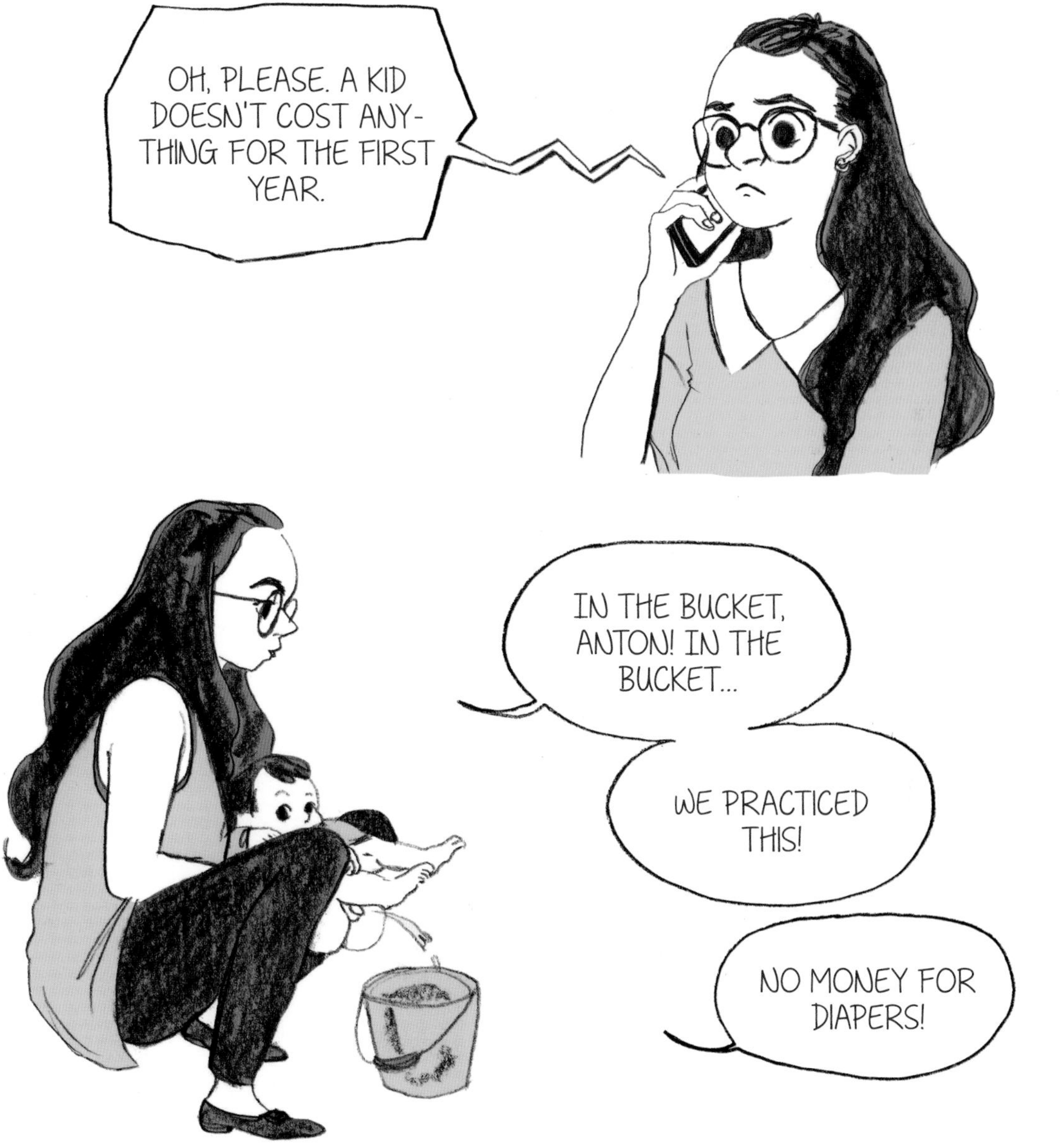
OH, PLEASE. A KID DOESN'T COST ANY-THING FOR THE FIRST YEAR.
IN THE BUCKET, ANTON! IN THE BUCKET...
WE PRACTICED THIS!
NO MONEY FOR DIAPERS!

And besides that--do I want to bring kids into this world? A world in which crazy, narcissistic, disturbed people do racist, homophobic, misogynistic shit and threaten to bomb everything into space?

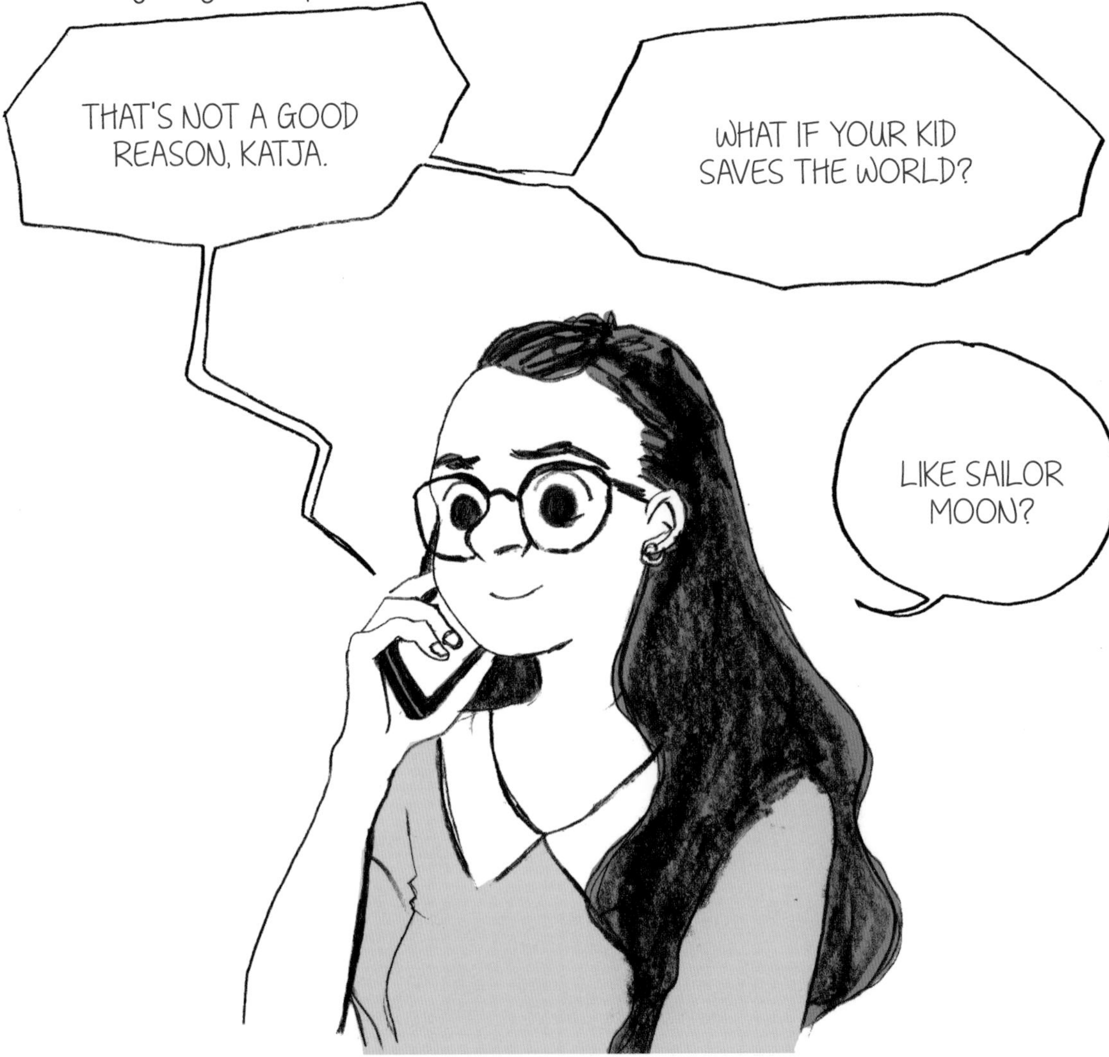
THAT'S NOT A GOOD REASON, KATJA.
WHAT IF YOUR KID SAVES THE WORLD?
LIKE SAILOR MOON?

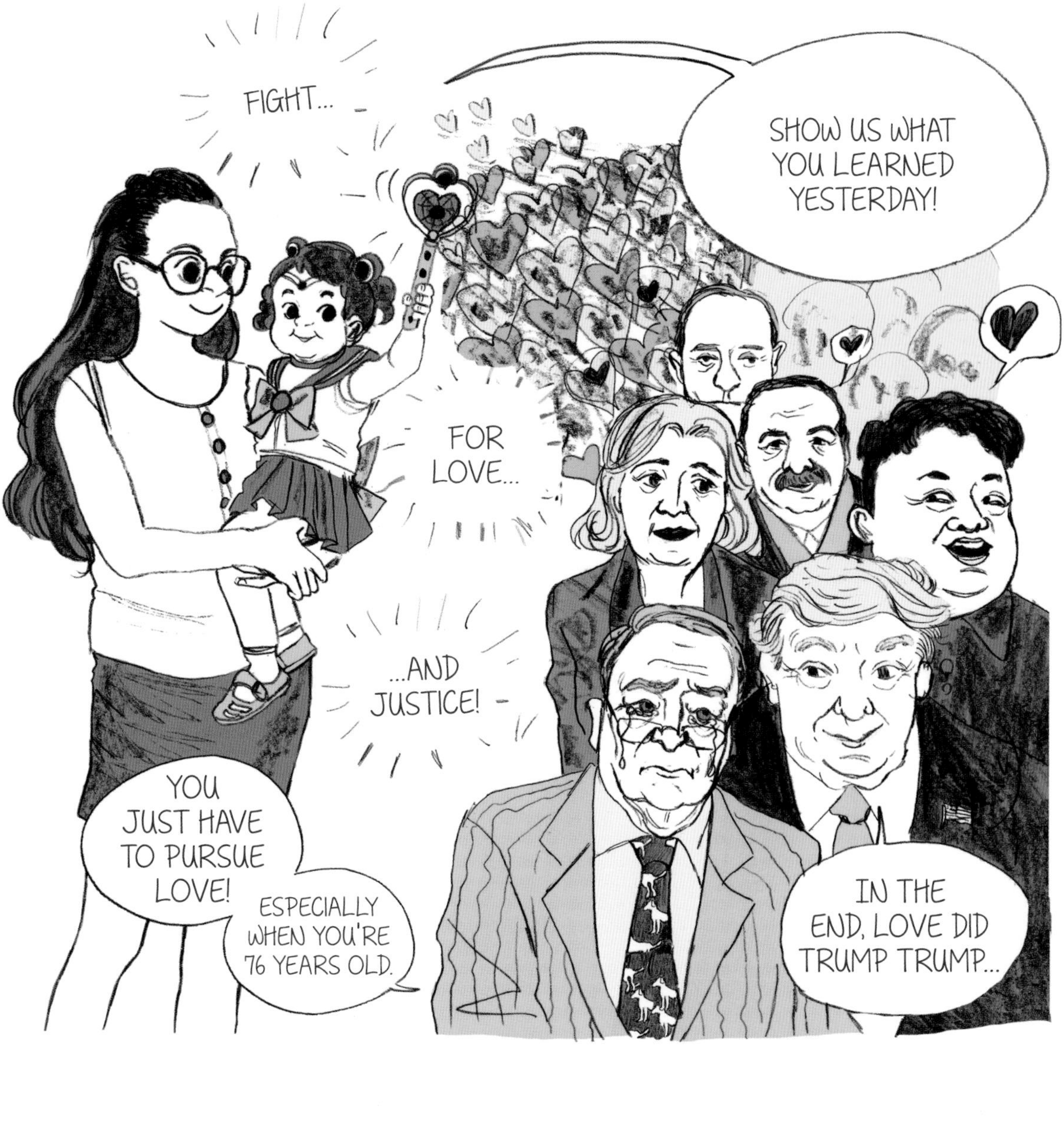
FIGHT...
SHOW US WHAT YOU LEARNED YESTERDAY!
FOR LOVE...
...AND JUSTICE!
YOU JUST HAVE TO PURSUE LOVE!
ESPECIALLY WHEN YOU'RE 76 YEARS OLD.
IN THE END, LOVE DID TRUMP TRUMP...

And what about the birth itself? I so rarely hear an "it went perfectly!" anecdote. All the stories are **horrible**!

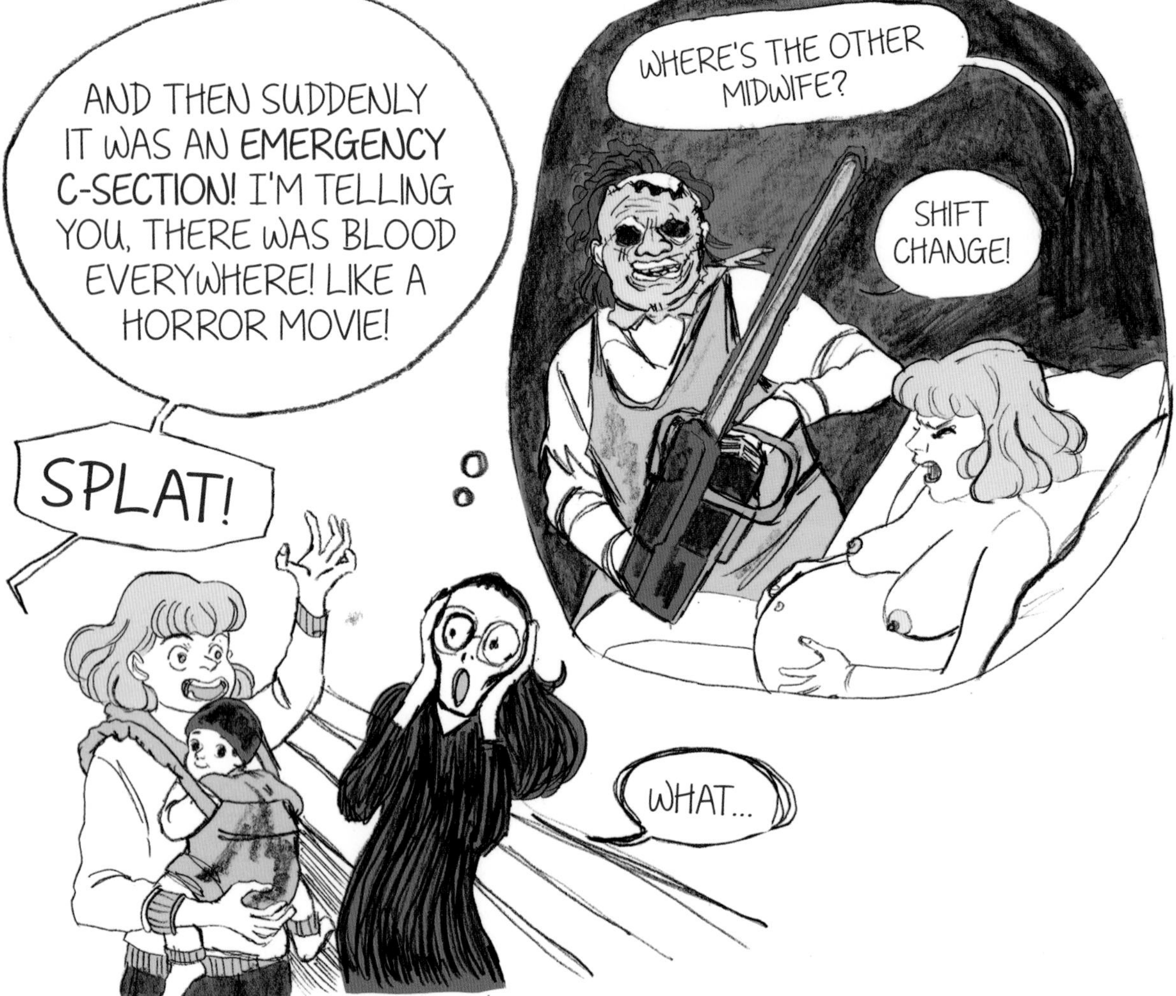

AND THEN SUDDENLY IT WAS AN EMERGENCY C-SECTION! I'M TELLING YOU, THERE WAS BLOOD EVERYWHERE! LIKE A HORROR MOVIE!
SPLAT!
WHERE'S THE OTHER MIDWIFE?
SHIFT CHANGE!
WHAT...

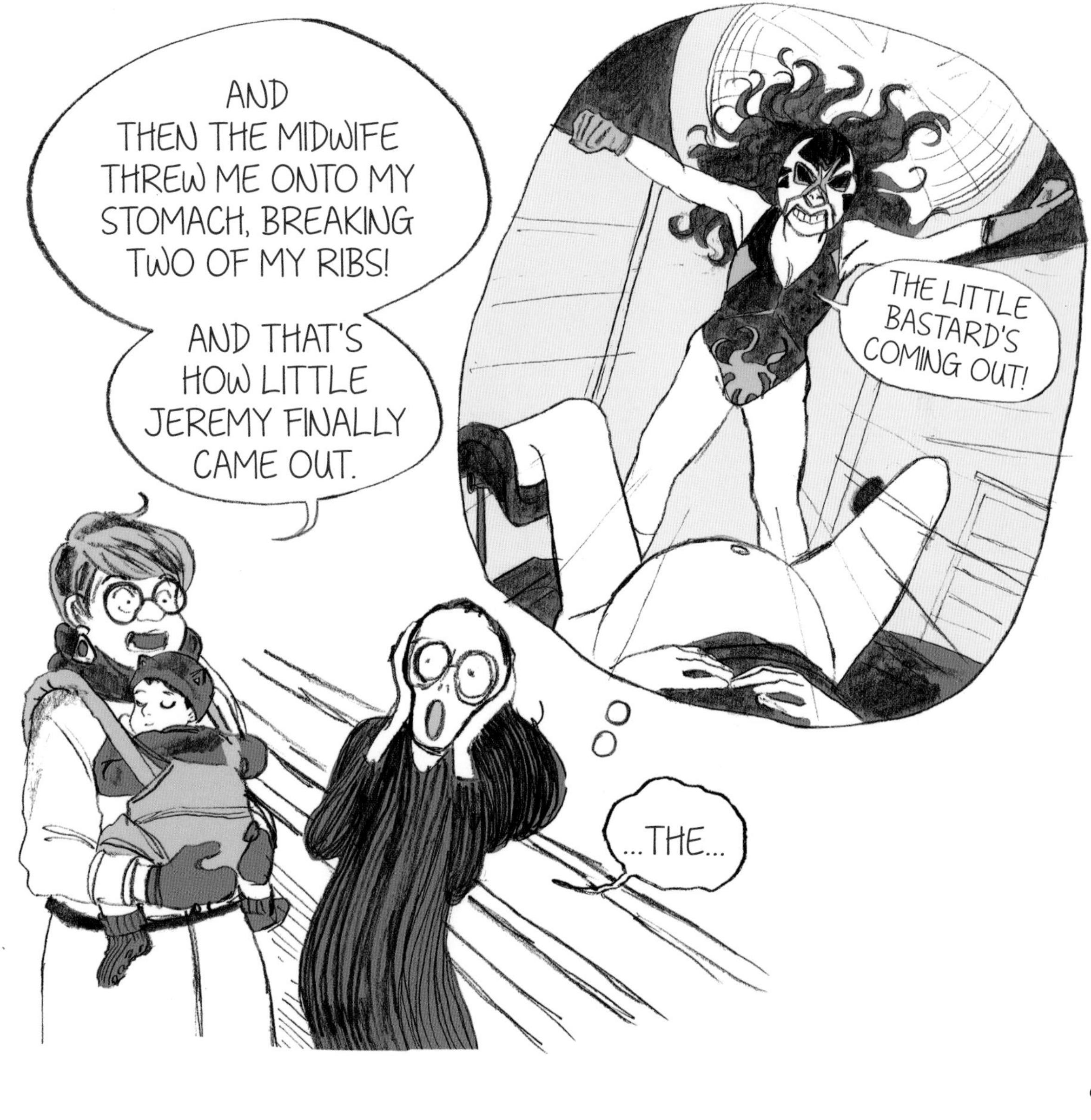
AND
THEN THE MIDWIFE
THREW ME ONTO MY
STOMACH, BREAKING
TWO OF MY RIBS!
AND THAT'S
HOW LITTLE
JEREMY FINALLY
CAME OUT.
THE LITTLE
BASTARD'S
COMING OUT!
...THE...

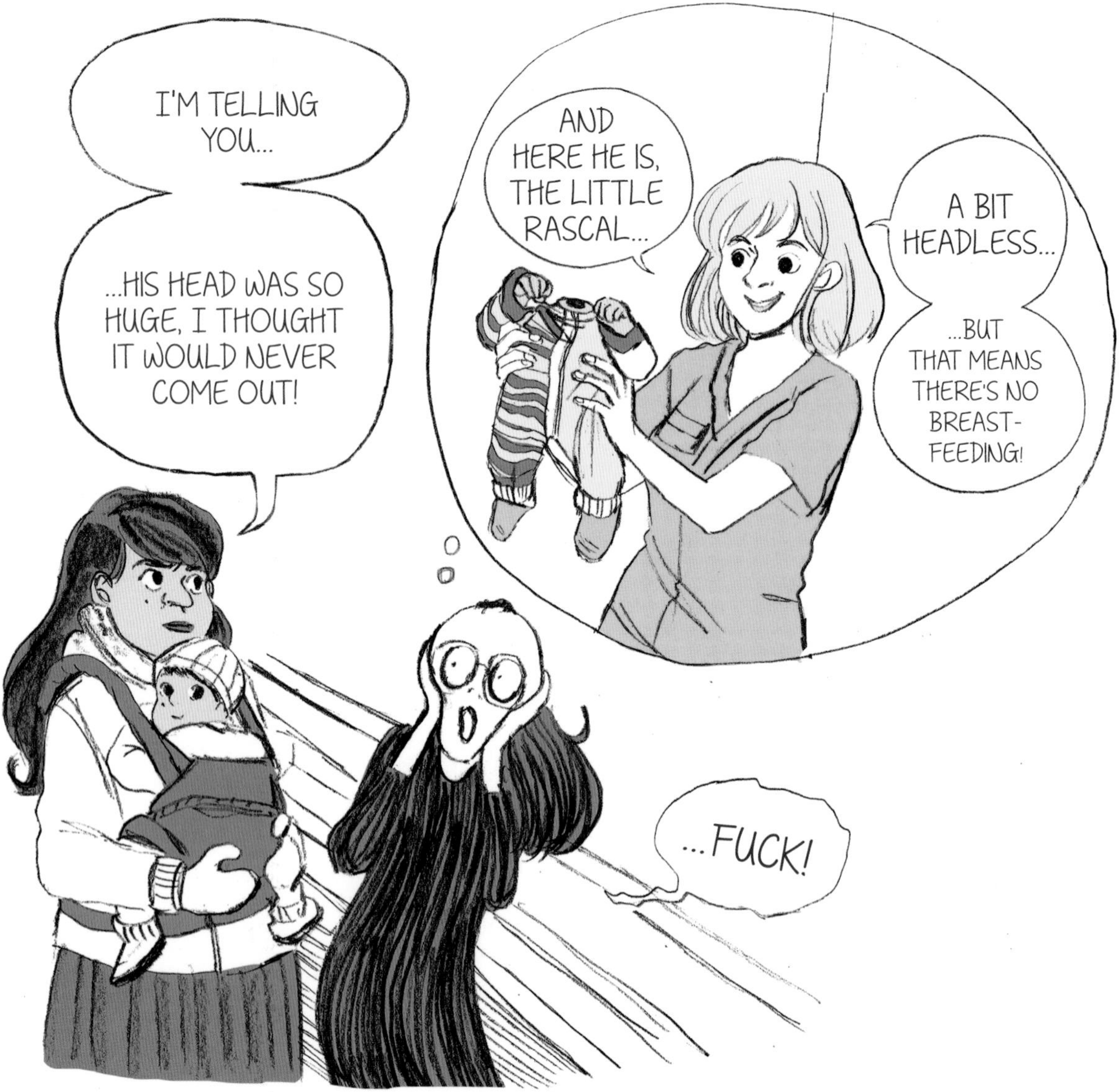
I'M TELLING YOU...
...HIS HEAD WAS SO HUGE, I THOUGHT IT WOULD NEVER COME OUT!
AND HERE HE IS, THE LITTLE RASCAL...
A BIT HEADLESS...
...BUT THAT MEANS THERE'S NO BREAST-FEEDING!
...FUCK!

I had never imagined birth to be so grisly. All these stories, but everyone still says: "YOU HAVE TO DO IT, TOO!" Shouldn't birth be a wonderful and natural event? A short and pain-free experience that happens at home, in your own comfort zone, instead of at a clinical hospital?

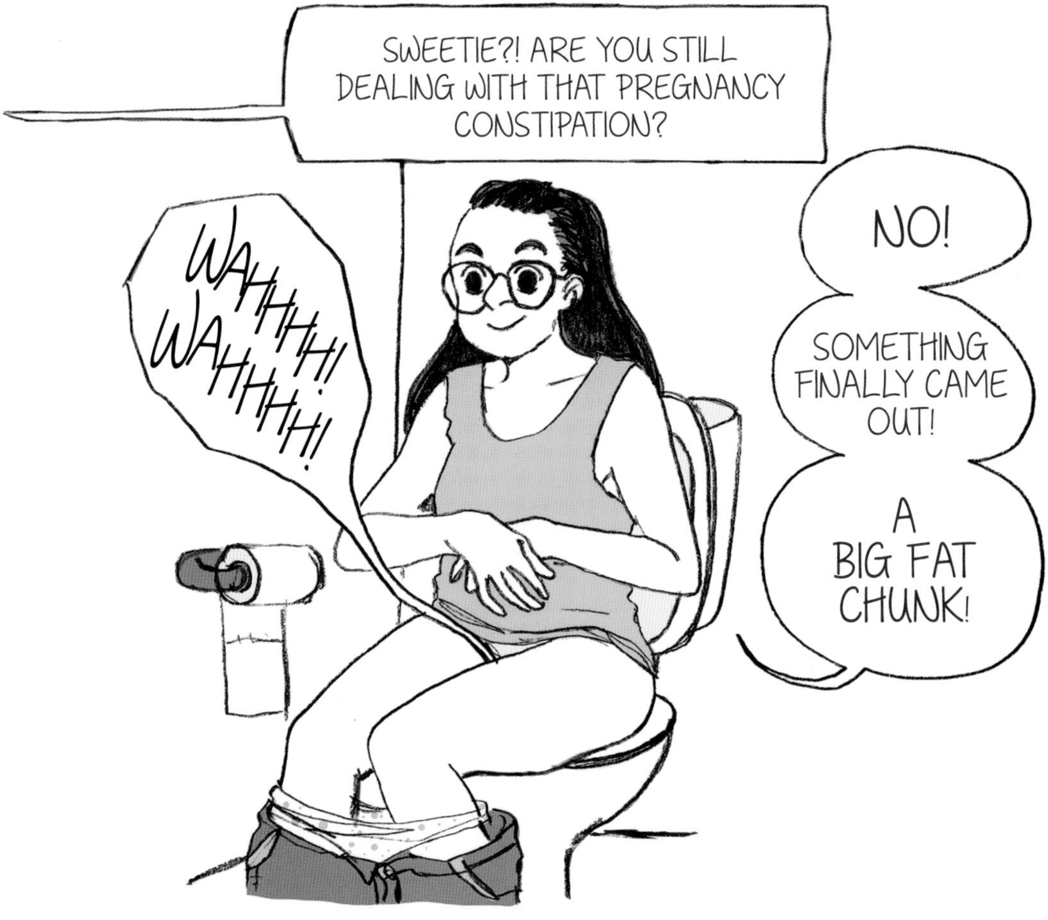
SWEETIE?! ARE YOU STILL DEALING WITH THAT PREGNANCY CONSTIPATION?
NO!
SOMETHING FINALLY CAME OUT!
A BIG FAT CHUNK!
WAHHHH! WAHHHHH!

Allow me to be a little freaked out by the whole topic of kids. It's hard enough to deliberately choose something, especially when you're being pressured from all sides. So let me do a bit of arguing and doubting. It will all work out in the end. And until then--

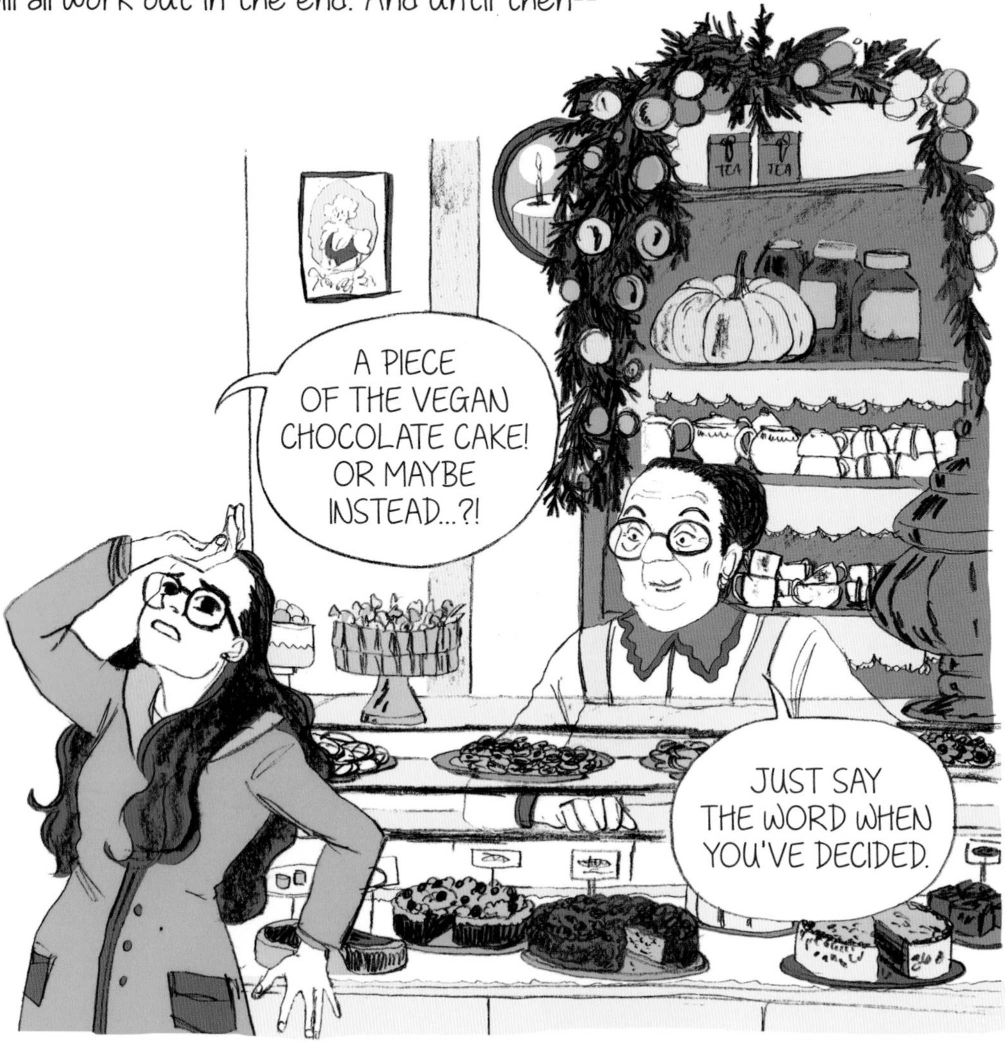
A PIECE OF THE VEGAN CHOCOLATE CAKE! OR MAYBE INSTEAD...?!
JUST SAY THE WORD WHEN YOU'VE DECIDED.

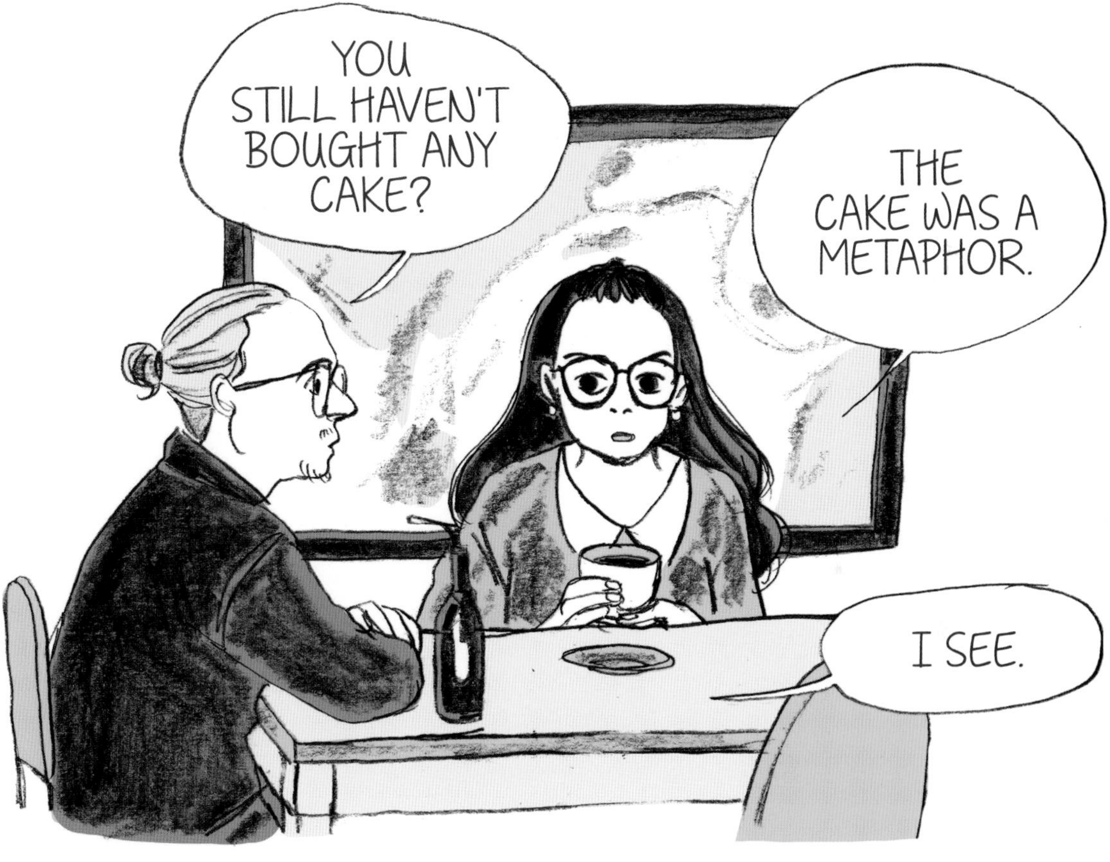
YOU STILL HAVEN'T BOUGHT ANY CAKE?
THE CAKE WAS A METAPHOR.
I SEE.

Superheroine with Red Wine

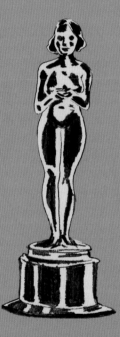

When I make comics, I can formulate thoughts that don't occur to me in real time. To be totally honest, in unexpected situations, I often lack the courage to react and say something. For example, when someone's unfriendly or awkwardly hits on me--

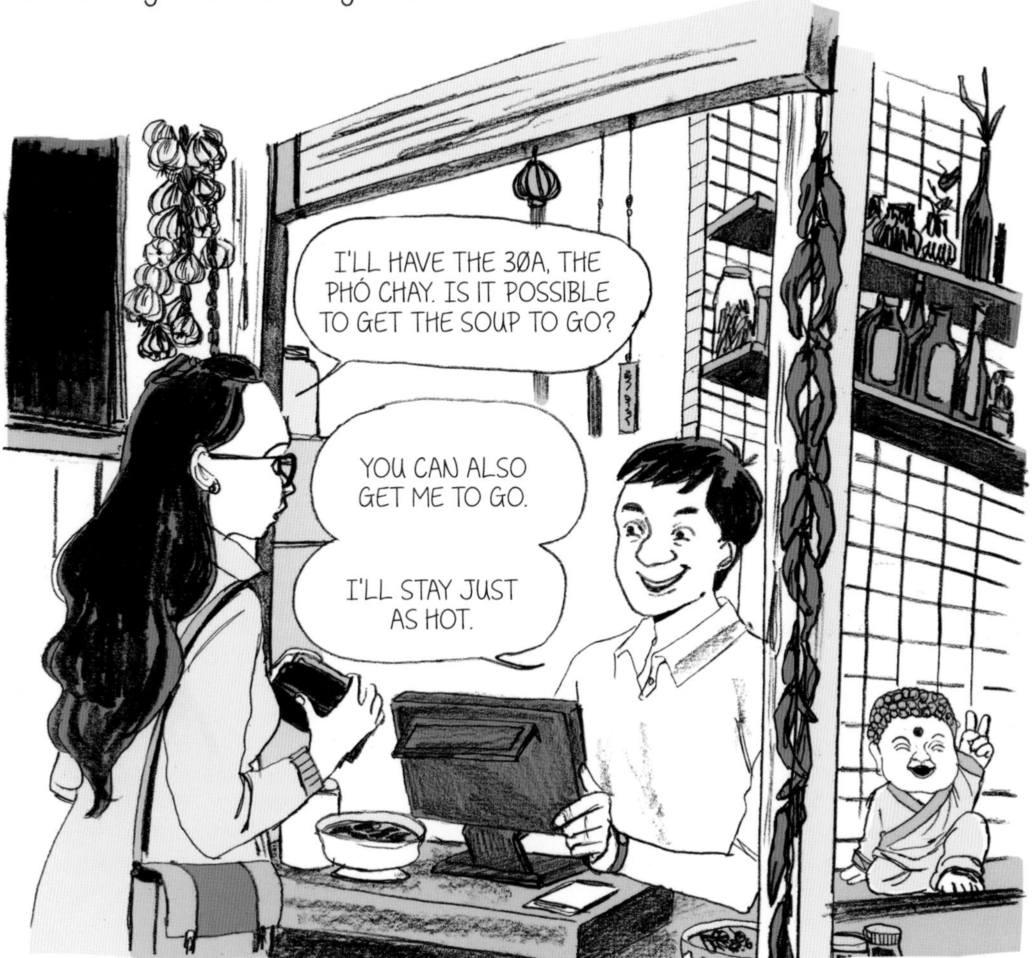
I'LL HAVE THE 30A, THE PHÓ CHAY. IS IT POSSIBLE TO GET THE SOUP TO GO?
YOU CAN ALSO GET ME TO GO.
I'LL STAY JUST AS HOT.

You know that feeling? Your heart speeds up, your chest tightens, and no discernible thoughts appear. In this moment I wanted to say something tough and pithy. But instead--

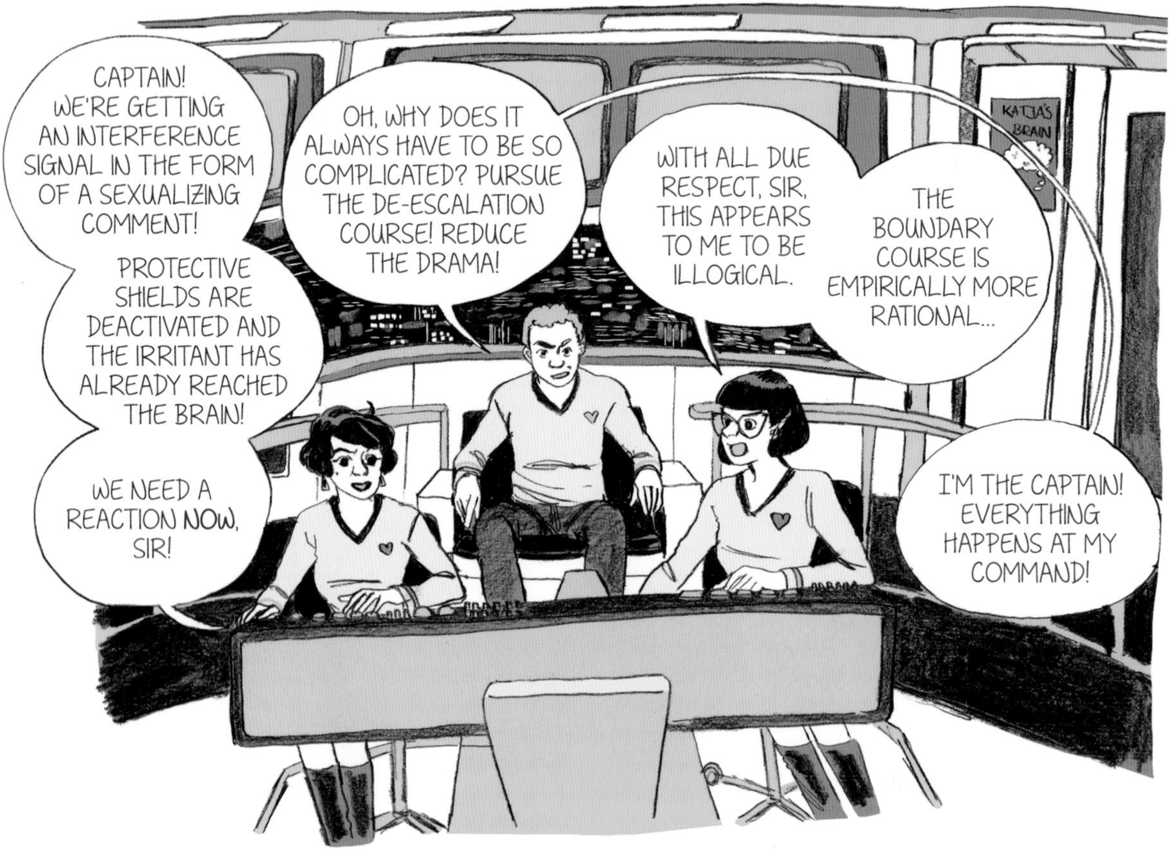
CAPTAIN! WE'RE GETTING AN INTERFERENCE SIGNAL IN THE FORM OF A SEXUALIZING COMMENT!
PROTECTIVE SHIELDS ARE DEACTIVATED AND THE IRRITANT HAS ALREADY REACHED THE BRAIN!
WE NEED A REACTION **NOW**, SIR!
OH, WHY DOES IT ALWAYS HAVE TO BE SO COMPLICATED? PURSUE THE DE-ESCALATION COURSE! REDUCE THE DRAMA!
WITH ALL DUE RESPECT, SIR, THIS APPEARS TO ME TO BE ILLOGICAL.
THE BOUNDARY COURSE IS EMPIRICALLY MORE RATIONAL...
KATJA'S BRAIN
I'M THE CAPTAIN! EVERYTHING HAPPENS AT MY COMMAND!

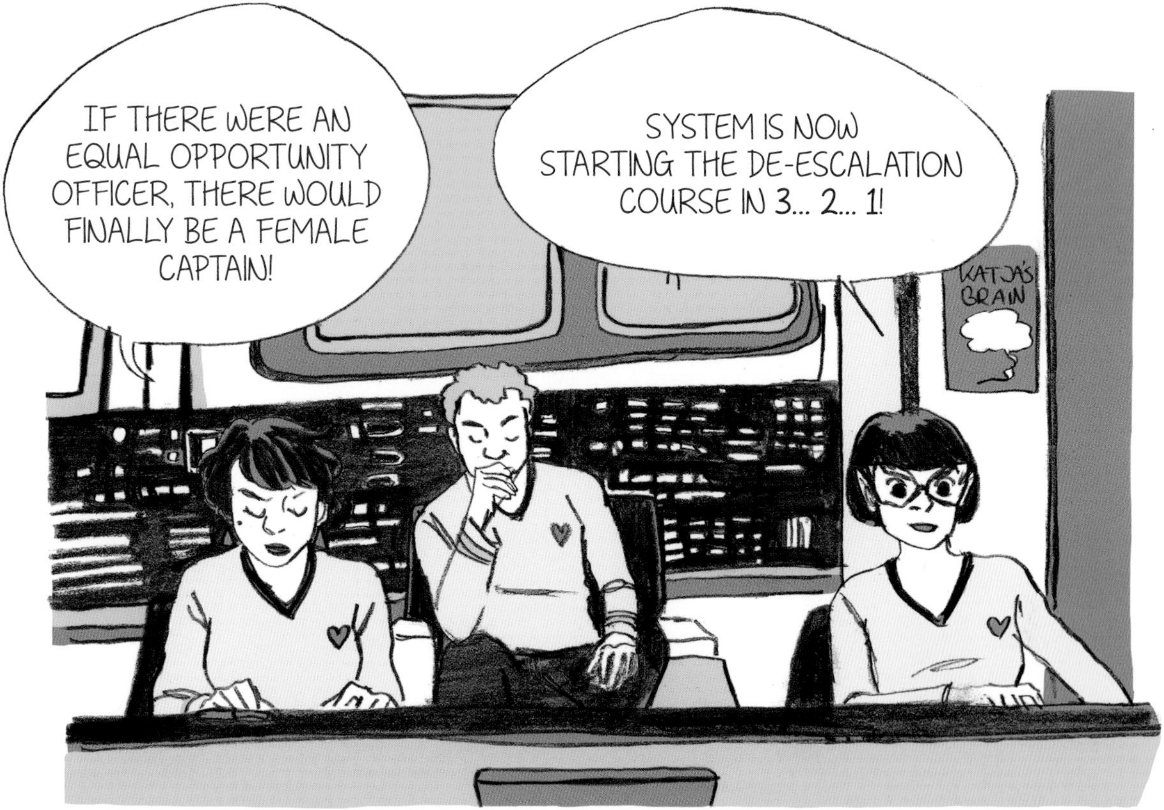
IF THERE WERE AN EQUAL OPPORTUNITY OFFICER, THERE WOULD FINALLY BE A FEMALE CAPTAIN!
SYSTEM IS NOW STARTING THE DE-ESCALATION COURSE IN 3... 2... 1!
KATJA'S BRAIN

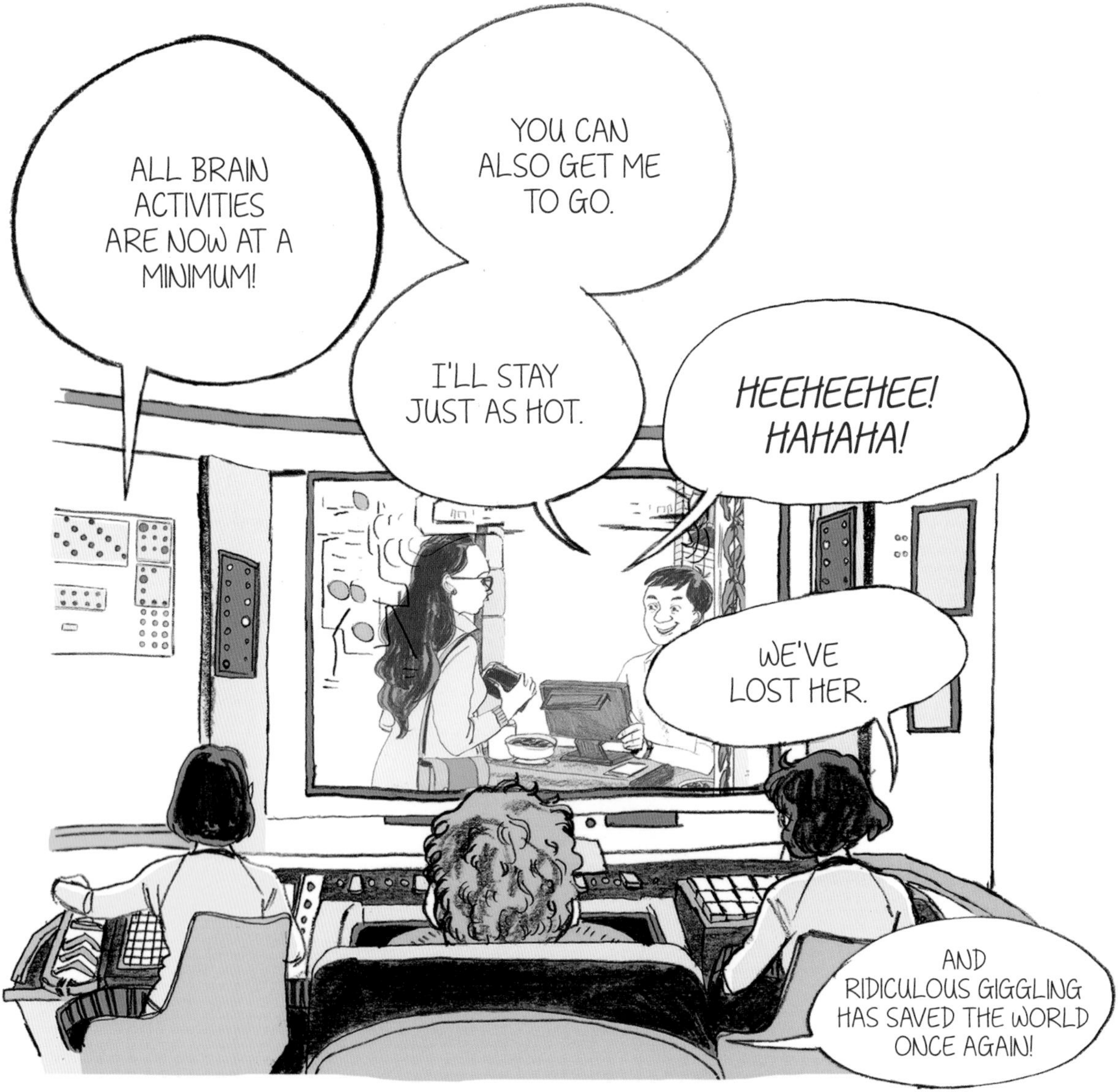
ALL BRAIN ACTIVITIES ARE NOW AT A MINIMUM!
YOU CAN ALSO GET ME TO GO.
I'LL STAY JUST AS HOT.
HEEHEEHEE! HAHAHA!
WE'VE LOST HER.
AND RIDICULOUS GIGGLING HAS SAVED THE WORLD ONCE AGAIN!

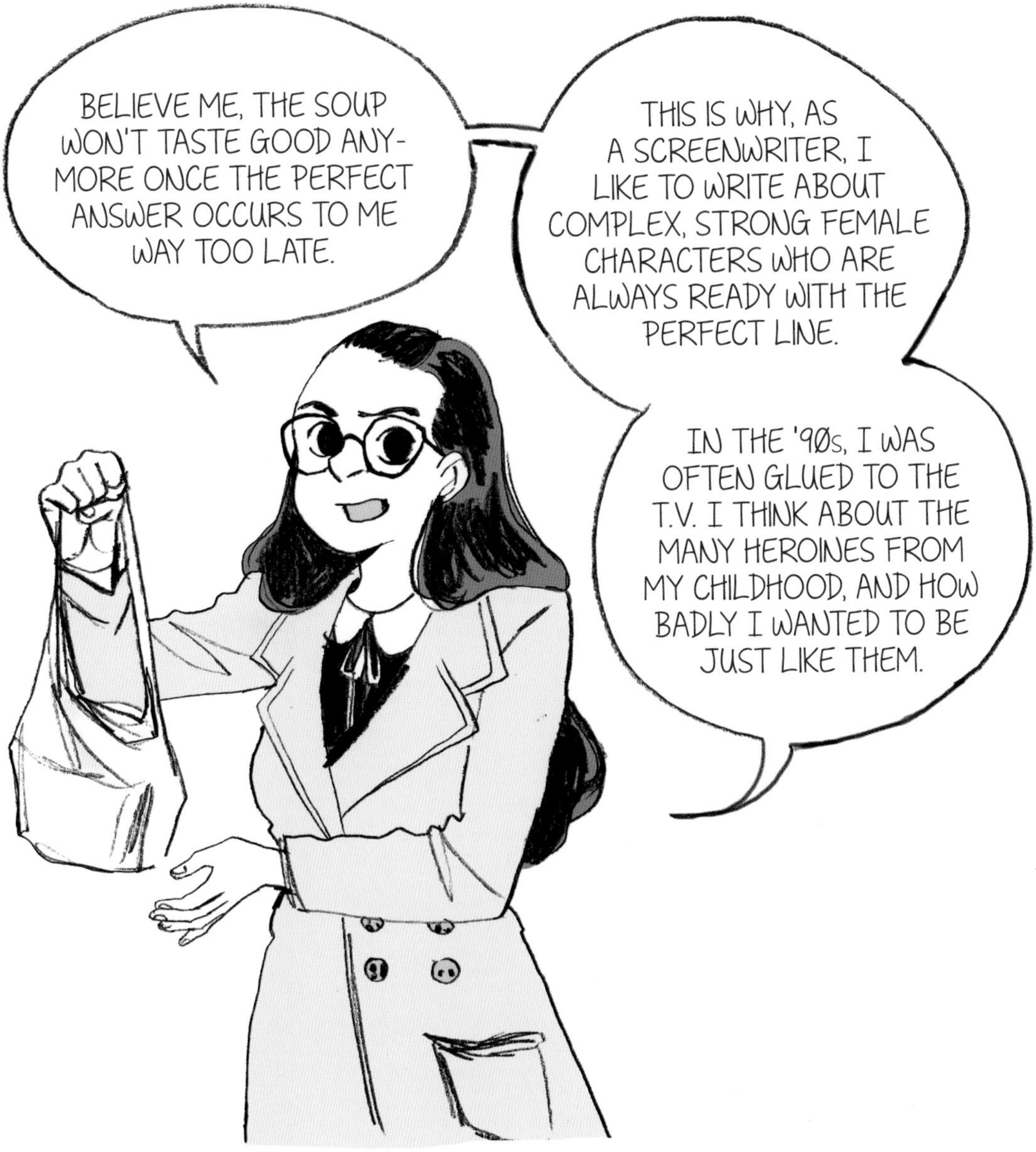
BELIEVE ME, THE SOUP WON'T TASTE GOOD ANY-MORE ONCE THE PERFECT ANSWER OCCURS TO ME WAY TOO LATE.
THIS IS WHY, AS A SCREENWRITER, I LIKE TO WRITE ABOUT COMPLEX, STRONG FEMALE CHARACTERS WHO ARE ALWAYS READY WITH THE PERFECT LINE.
IN THE '90s, I WAS OFTEN GLUED TO THE T.V. I THINK ABOUT THE MANY HEROINES FROM MY CHILDHOOD, AND HOW BADLY I WANTED TO BE JUST LIKE THEM.

Oh, how intensely I wished I could be just a little bit like Buffy. She's in high school, but at night she hunts vampires. And not only does she look wildly cool while she does it--she's always ready with the wittiest lines whenever anyone fucks with her. Like this--

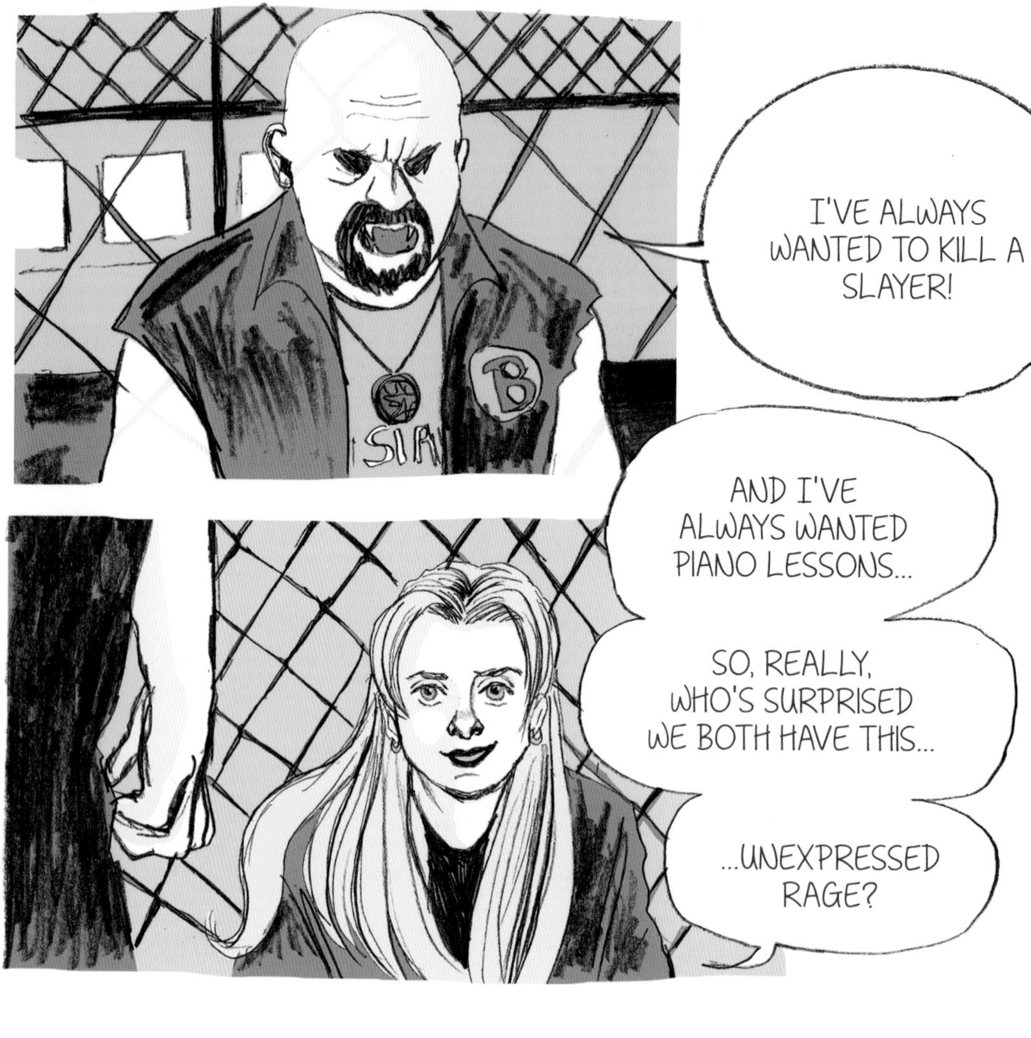

I'VE ALWAYS WANTED TO KILL A SLAYER!
SIR
AND I'VE ALWAYS WANTED PIANO LESSONS...
SO, REALLY, WHO'S SURPRISED WE BOTH HAVE THIS...
...UNEXPRESSED RAGE?

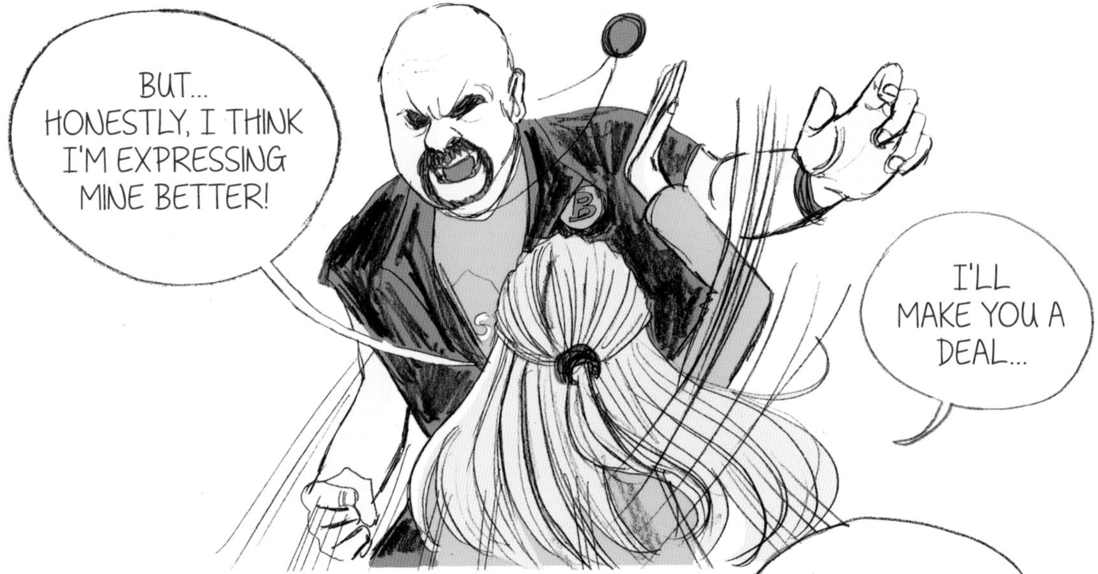
BUT... HONESTLY, I THINK I'M EXPRESSING MINE BETTER!
I'LL MAKE YOU A DEAL...

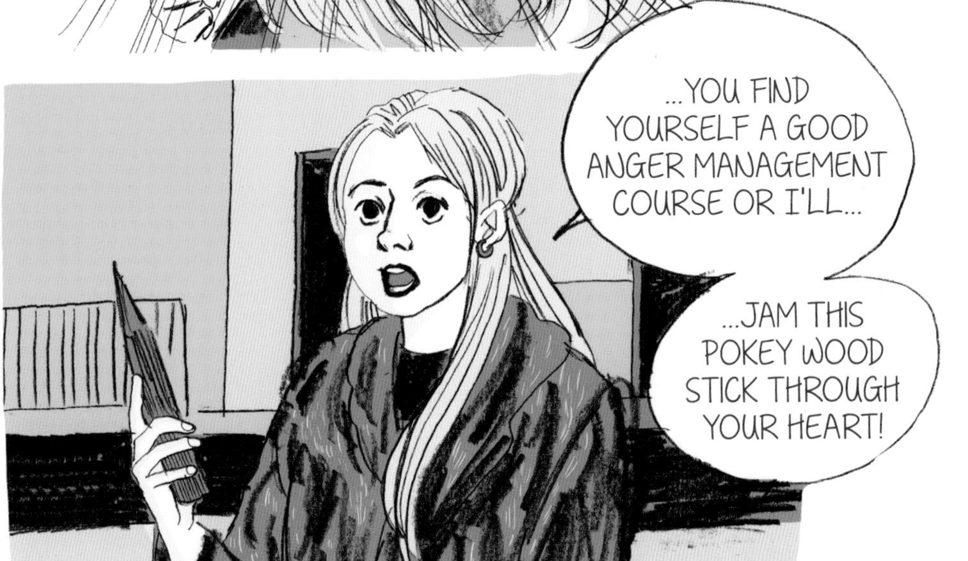
...YOU FIND YOURSELF A GOOD ANGER MANAGEMENT COURSE OR I'LL...
...JAM THIS POKEY WOOD STICK THROUGH YOUR HEART!

I'm telling you--the '90s were full of inspiring T.V. heroines. For example, Princess Fantaghirò. She doesn't want to be a princess at all. She wants to be free and fight! And so she cuts her hair, dresses like a man, and duels her (sexy) enemy in order to save her father's kingdom (and to overcome her daddy issues).

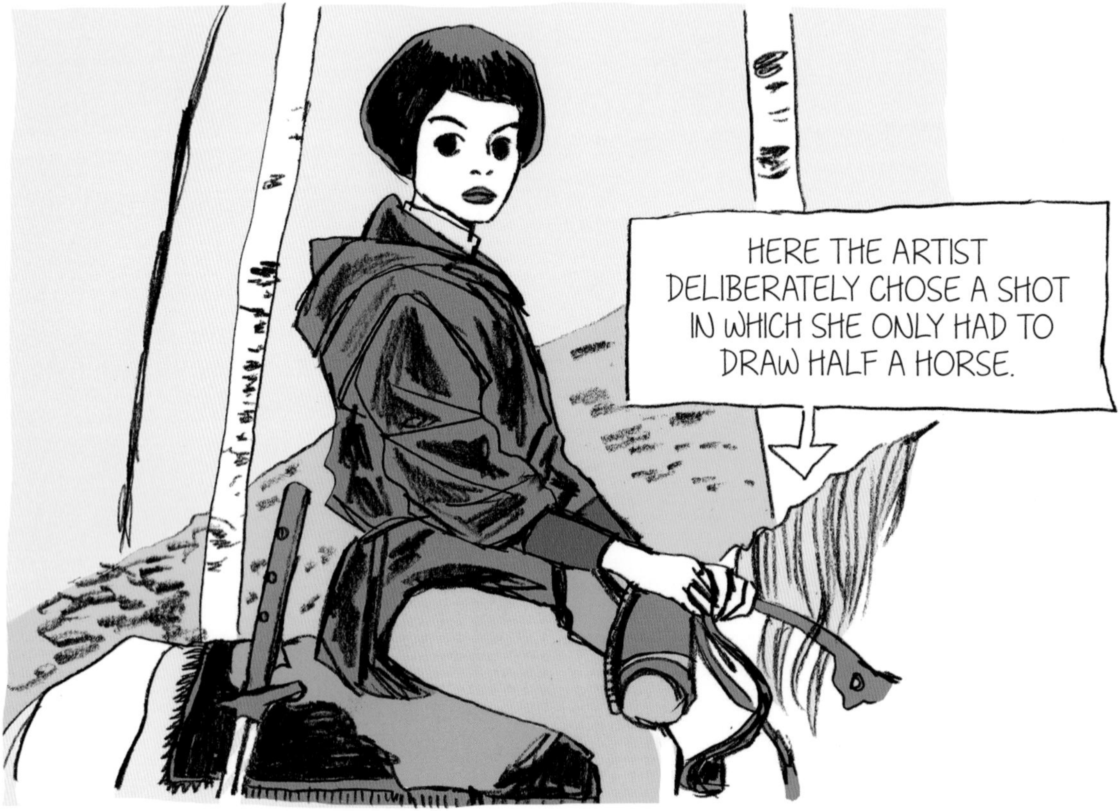
HERE THE ARTIST DELIBERATELY CHOSE A SHOT IN WHICH SHE ONLY HAD TO DRAW HALF A HORSE.

I found it so revolutionary that I ~~stole~~ adapted the whole story for a play. My woodworking teacher made me a sword for it and my mom crafted a castle out of moving boxes. But on the day of the premiere, the male actors, of all people, called the play into question...

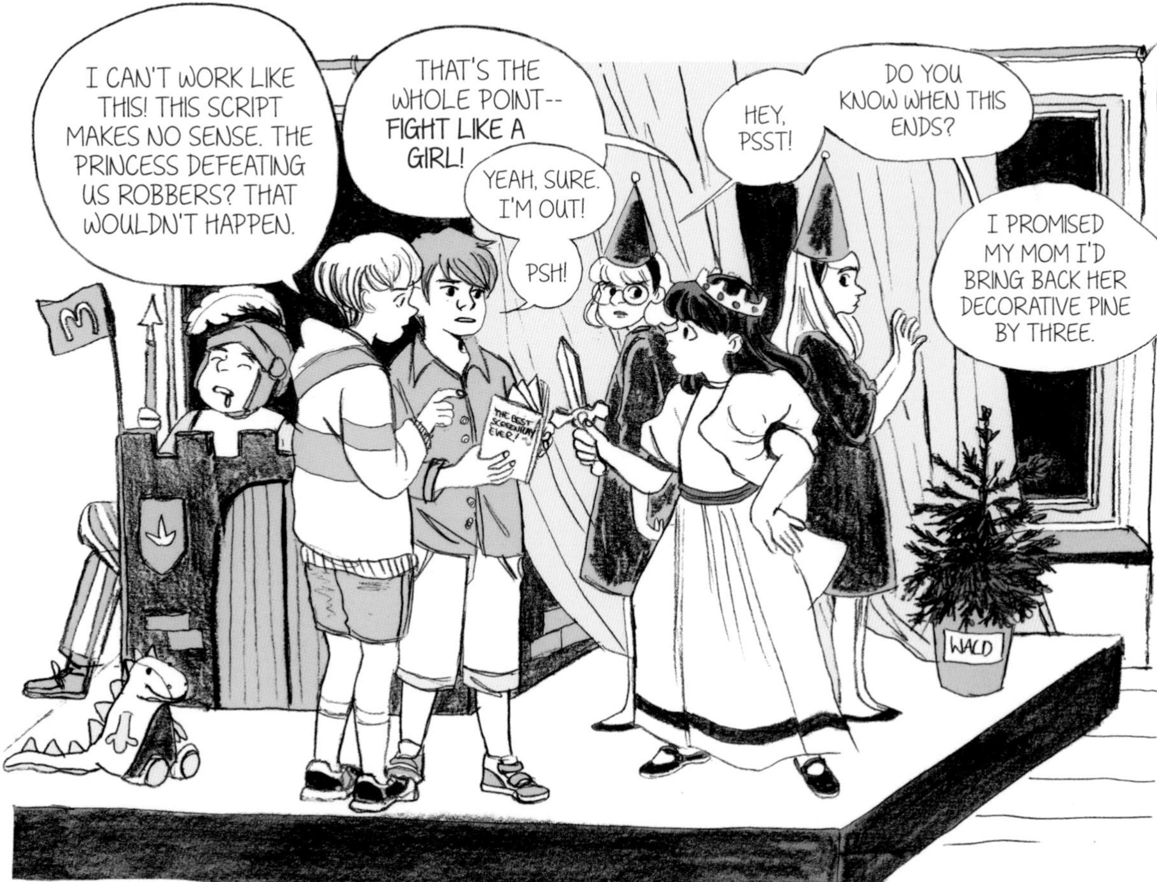
I CAN'T WORK LIKE THIS! THIS SCRIPT MAKES NO SENSE. THE PRINCESS DEFEATING US ROBBERS? THAT WOULDN'T HAPPEN.
THAT'S THE WHOLE POINT-- **FIGHT LIKE A GIRL!**
YEAH, SURE. I'M OUT!
PSH!
THE BEST SCREENPLAY EVER!
HEY, PSST!
DO YOU KNOW WHEN THIS ENDS?
I PROMISED MY MOM I'D BRING BACK HER DECORATIVE PINE BY THREE.
WALD

In the end, I had to improvise with the remaining actresses. It was the most successful play ever put on at a German elementary school. To this day, fans still call to congratulate me.

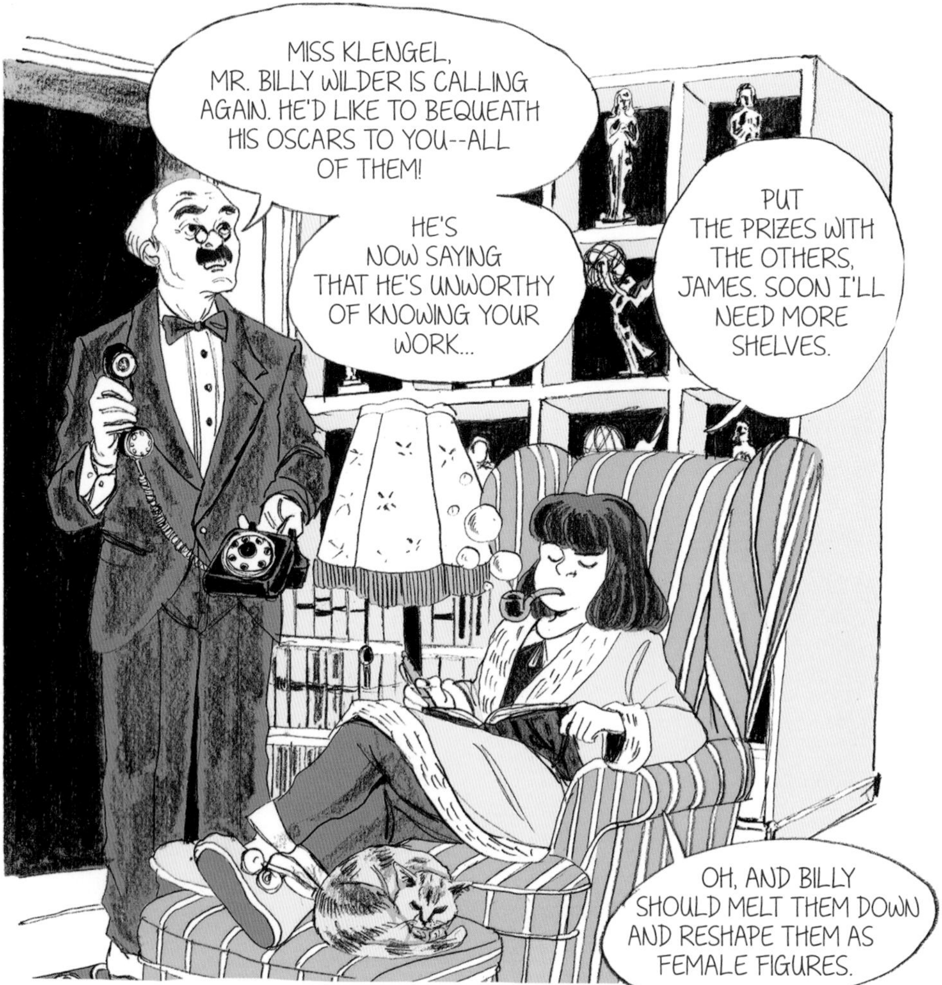
MISS KLENGEL, MR. BILLY WILDER IS CALLING AGAIN. HE'D LIKE TO BEQUEATH HIS OSCARS TO YOU--ALL OF THEM!
HE'S NOW SAYING THAT HE'S UNWORTHY OF KNOWING YOUR WORK...
PUT THE PRIZES WITH THE OTHERS, JAMES. SOON I'LL NEED MORE SHELVES.
OH, AND BILLY SHOULD MELT THEM DOWN AND RESHAPE THEM AS FEMALE FIGURES.

My favorite heroine was Sailor Moon. Sailor Moon draws magic powers from the moon, wears a sailor outfit, and fights demons. She fights with other women warriors by her side, and they all gave me the sense that, well... women have power! More than that, the television series also conveyed that love isn't necessarily bound to a particular gender. One can simply love a person for who they are. There were even character transformations that made women out of men. It was never an issue. It just was.

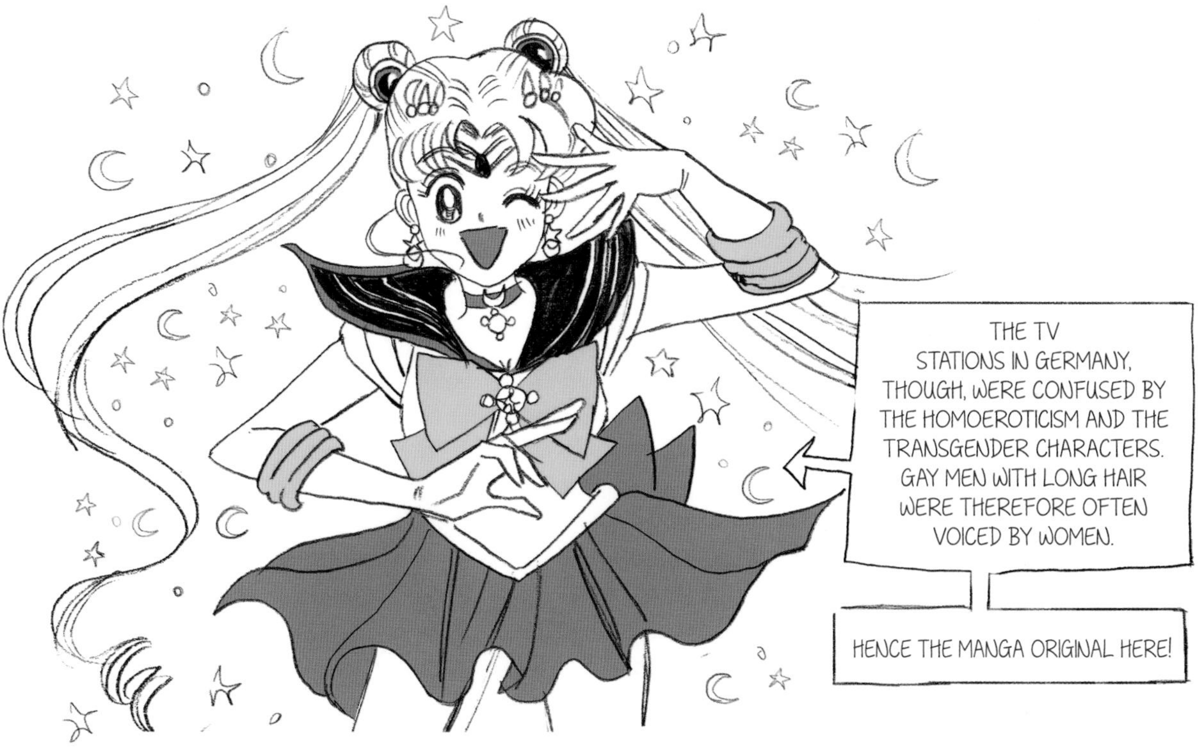
THE TV STATIONS IN GERMANY, THOUGH, WERE CONFUSED BY THE HOMOEROTICISM AND THE TRANSGENDER CHARACTERS. GAY MEN WITH LONG HAIR WERE THEREFORE OFTEN VOICED BY WOMEN.
HENCE THE MANGA ORIGINAL HERE!

Of course, I always wanted to be a sailor-warrior. But it always failed... because of the costume.

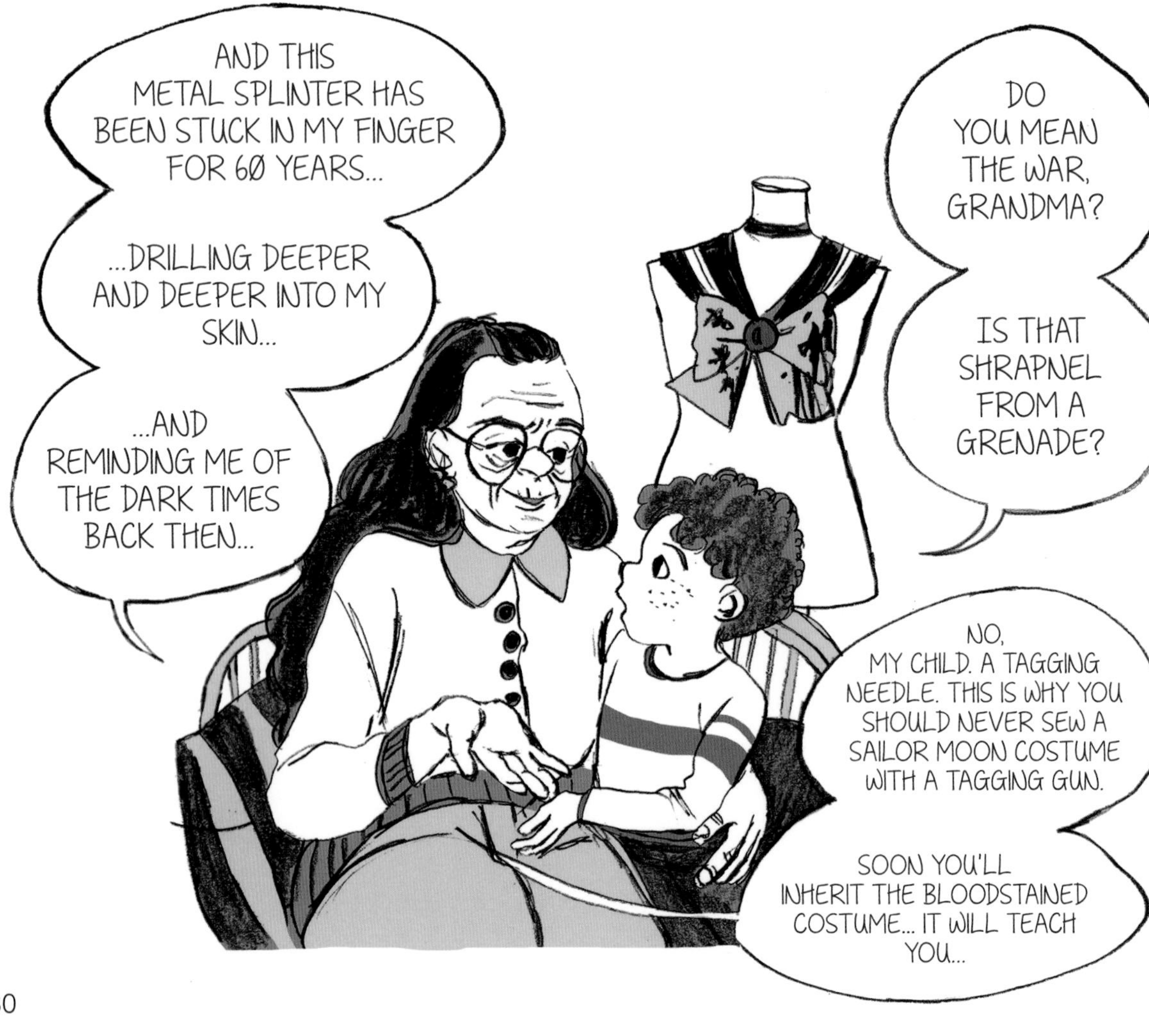
AND THIS METAL SPLINTER HAS BEEN STUCK IN MY FINGER FOR 60 YEARS...
...DRILLING DEEPER AND DEEPER INTO MY SKIN...
...AND REMINDING ME OF THE DARK TIMES BACK THEN...
DO YOU MEAN THE WAR, GRANDMA?
IS THAT SHRAPNEL FROM A GRENADE?
NO, MY CHILD. A TAGGING NEEDLE. THIS IS WHY YOU SHOULD NEVER SEW A SAILOR MOON COSTUME WITH A TAGGING GUN.
SOON YOU'LL INHERIT THE BLOODSTAINED COSTUME... IT WILL TEACH YOU...

There were still more heroines I admired--Lady Oscar, Utena, The Powerpuff Girls, Ronja Räubertochter, Helga Pataki from "Hey Arnold!," Anne of Green Gables, Clarissa (explains it all), Umi from "Magic Knight Rayearth," and many others... I'm truly glad that these heroines existed--even though they were fictional, they were my guides. In "real life," heroines were rare. If you look up the word "heroine," Wikipedia seems confused...

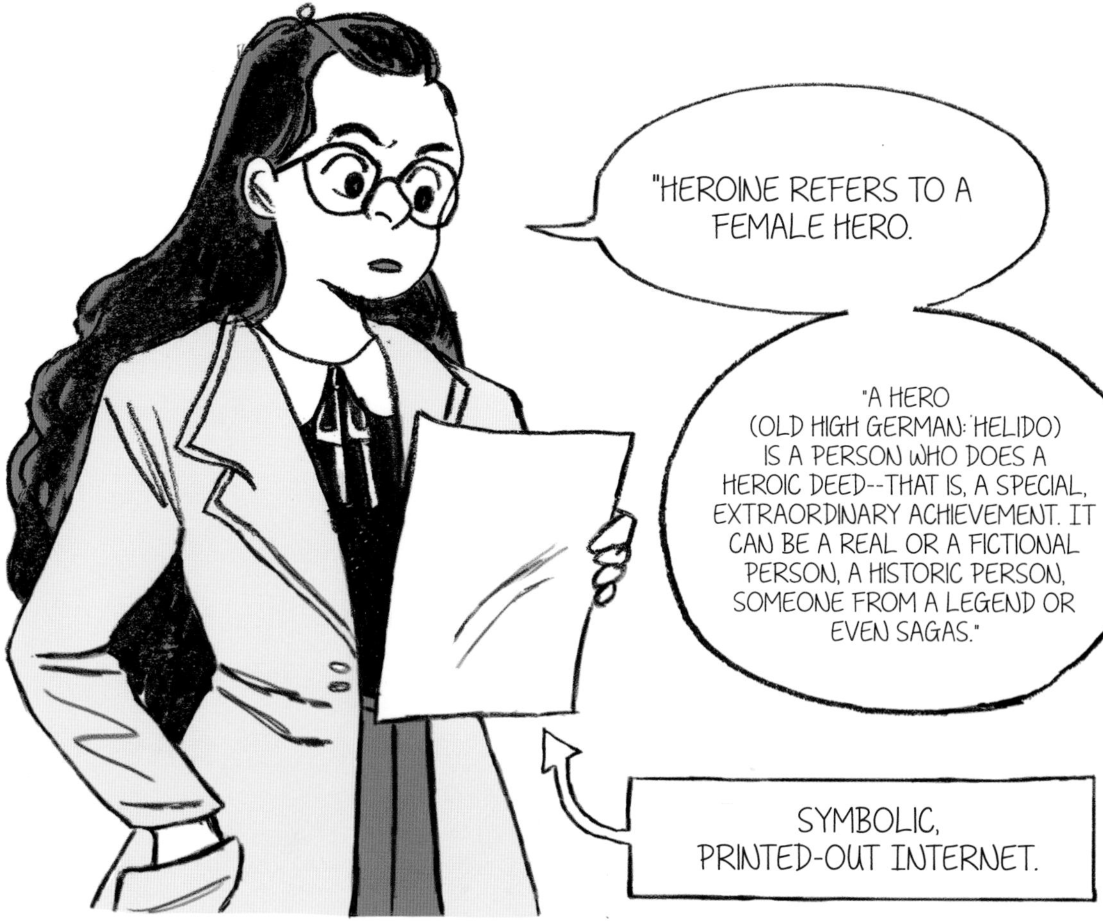
"HEROINE REFERS TO A FEMALE HERO.
"A HERO (OLD HIGH GERMAN: HELIDO) IS A PERSON WHO DOES A HEROIC DEED--THAT IS, A SPECIAL, EXTRAORDINARY ACHIEVEMENT. IT CAN BE A REAL OR A FICTIONAL PERSON, A HISTORIC PERSON, SOMEONE FROM A LEGEND OR EVEN SAGAS."
SYMBOLIC, PRINTED-OUT INTERNET.

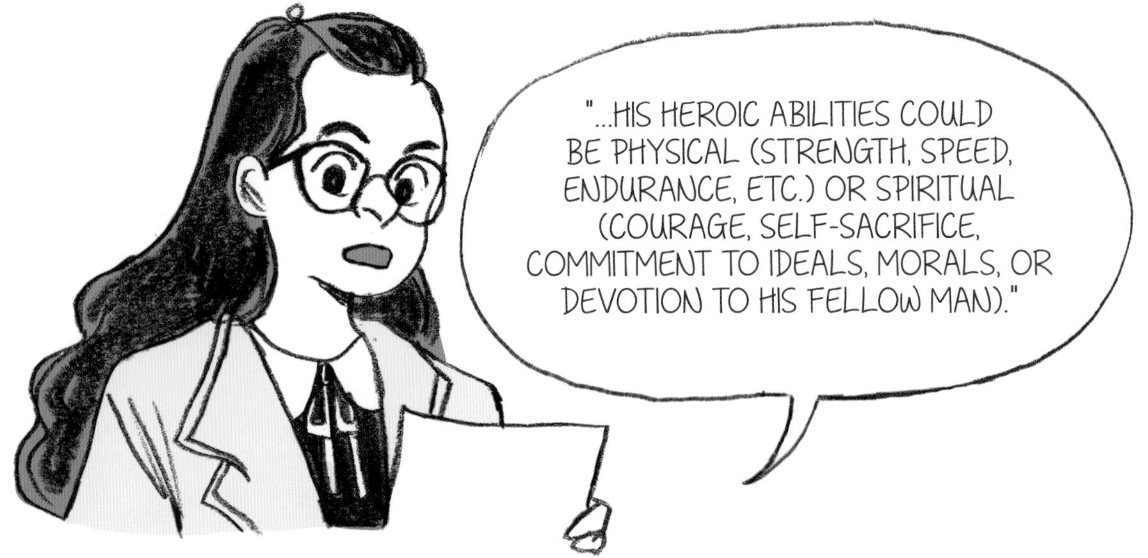
"...HIS HEROIC ABILITIES COULD BE PHYSICAL (STRENGTH, SPEED, ENDURANCE, ETC.) OR SPIRITUAL (COURAGE, SELF-SACRIFICE, COMMITMENT TO IDEALS, MORALS, OR DEVOTION TO HIS FELLOW MAN)."

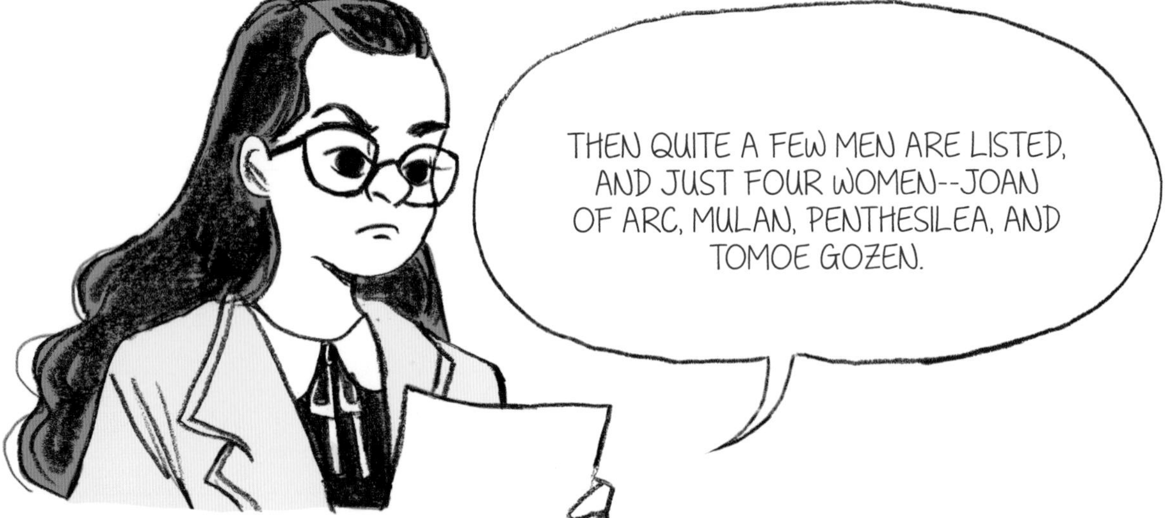
THEN QUITE A FEW MEN ARE LISTED, AND JUST FOUR WOMEN--JOAN OF ARC, MULAN, PENTHESILEA, AND TOMOE GOZEN.

Where are the heroines besides Joan of Arc? It can't be that the virgin from Orleans is the only one that people remember. She's a heroine who has nothing to do with my world, who feels foreign to me. People, there are other great women who should have been burned at the stake...

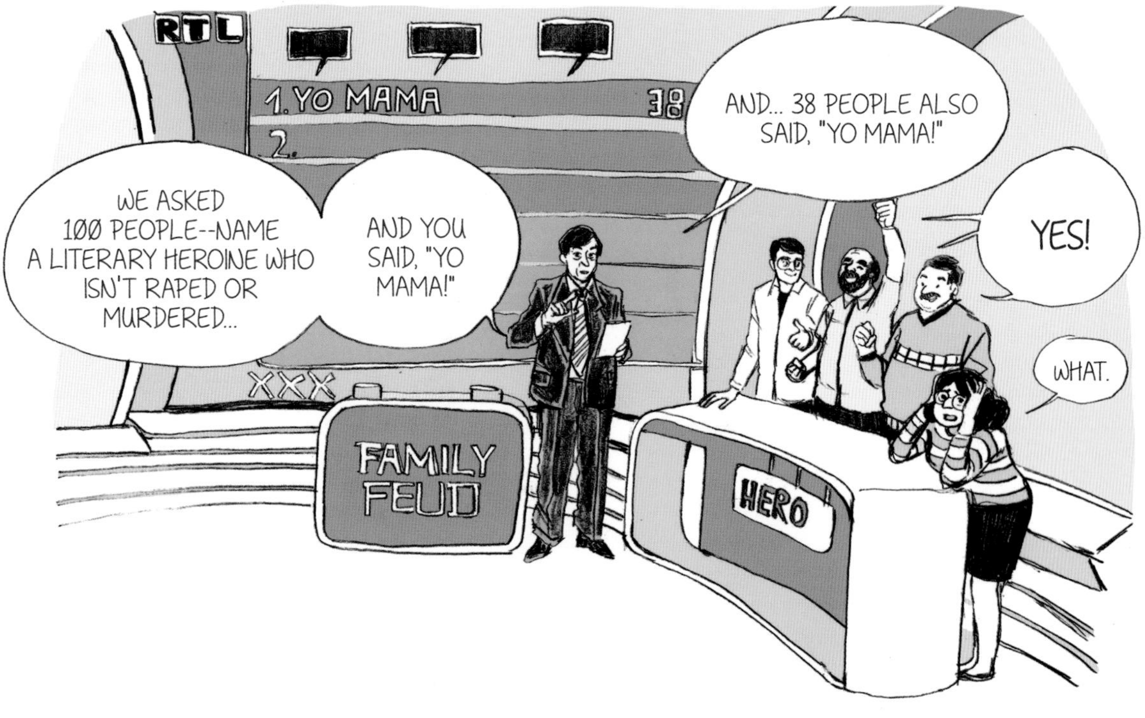
RTL
1. YO MAMA
38
2.
WE ASKED 100 PEOPLE--NAME A LITERARY HEROINE WHO ISN'T RAPED OR MURDERED...
AND YOU SAID, "YO MAMA!"
AND... 38 PEOPLE ALSO SAID, "YO MAMA!"
YES!
WHAT.
FAMILY FEUD
HERO

It's not that these heroines didn't exist. They were withheld from us. There were the male paragons that characterized my school years: Zeus, Thor, and Heracles in mythology; Schiller, Shakespeare, and Fontane in German and English classes; Chagall, Dalí, and Kandinsky in art... etc. My friend Yael recognized it back then and started a school petition for us to read more literature by women. I call that heroine-like!

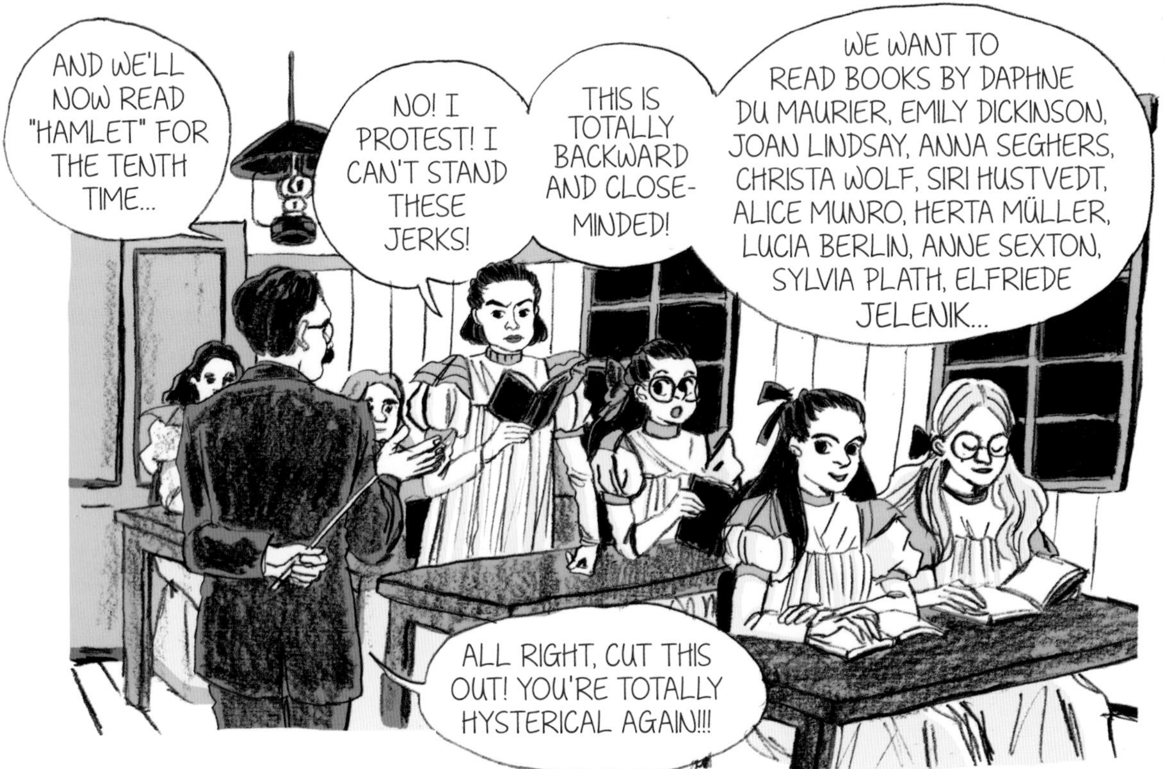
AND WE'LL NOW READ "HAMLET" FOR THE TENTH TIME...
NO! I PROTEST! I CAN'T STAND THESE JERKS!
THIS IS TOTALLY BACKWARD AND CLOSE-MINDED!
WE WANT TO READ BOOKS BY DAPHNE DU MAURIER, EMILY DICKINSON, JOAN LINDSAY, ANNA SEGHERS, CHRISTA WOLF, SIRI HUSTVEDT, ALICE MUNRO, HERTA MÜLLER, LUCIA BERLIN, ANNE SEXTON, SYLVIA PLATH, ELFRIEDE JELENIK...
ALL RIGHT, CUT THIS OUT! YOU'RE TOTALLY HYSTERICAL AGAIN!!!

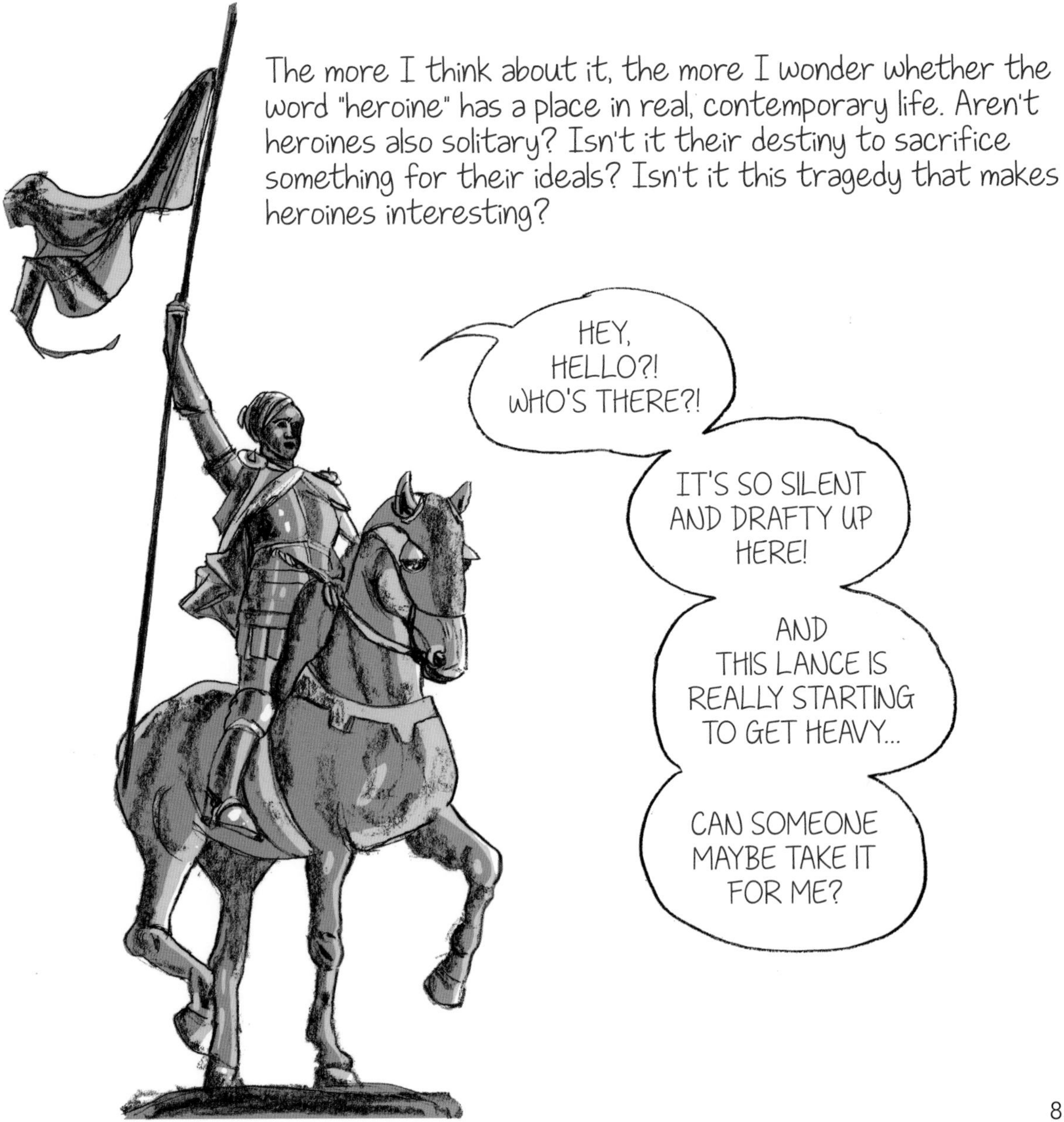

The more I think about it, the more I wonder whether the word "heroine" has a place in real, contemporary life. Aren't heroines also solitary? Isn't it their destiny to sacrifice something for their ideals? Isn't it this tragedy that makes heroines interesting?
HEY, HELLO?! WHO'S THERE?!
IT'S SO SILENT AND DRAFTY UP HERE!
AND THIS LANCE IS REALLY STARTING TO GET HEAVY...
CAN SOMEONE MAYBE TAKE IT FOR ME?

Aren't we making things too easy for ourselves then? In the end, do heroes only belong in books and on television?

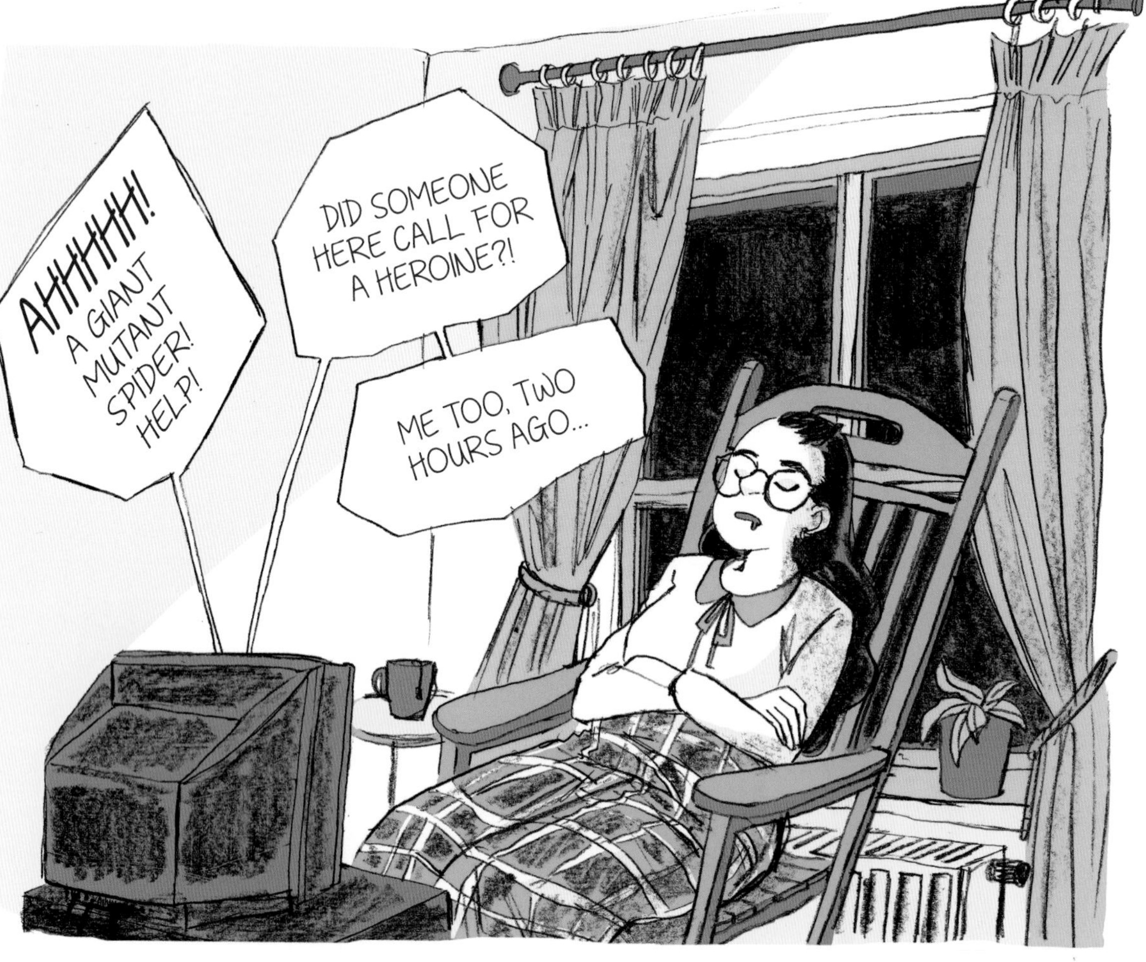
AHHHHH! A GIANT MUTANT SPIDER! HELP!
DID SOMEONE HERE CALL FOR A HEROINE?!
ME TOO, TWO HOURS AGO...

A friend describes an incident on the subway. A woman is being sexually harassed in a full subway car. She's being pressured by a man to get off the car and have sex with him. The woman agrees. She goes to the door. He gets off. The door closes, and he realizes that she's staying inside. The mob in the subway car applauds the heroine. But before, they were silent--nobody dared intervene. The solitary heroine, her cape waving in the wind. At home, she'll pour herself a glass of wine and wonder--

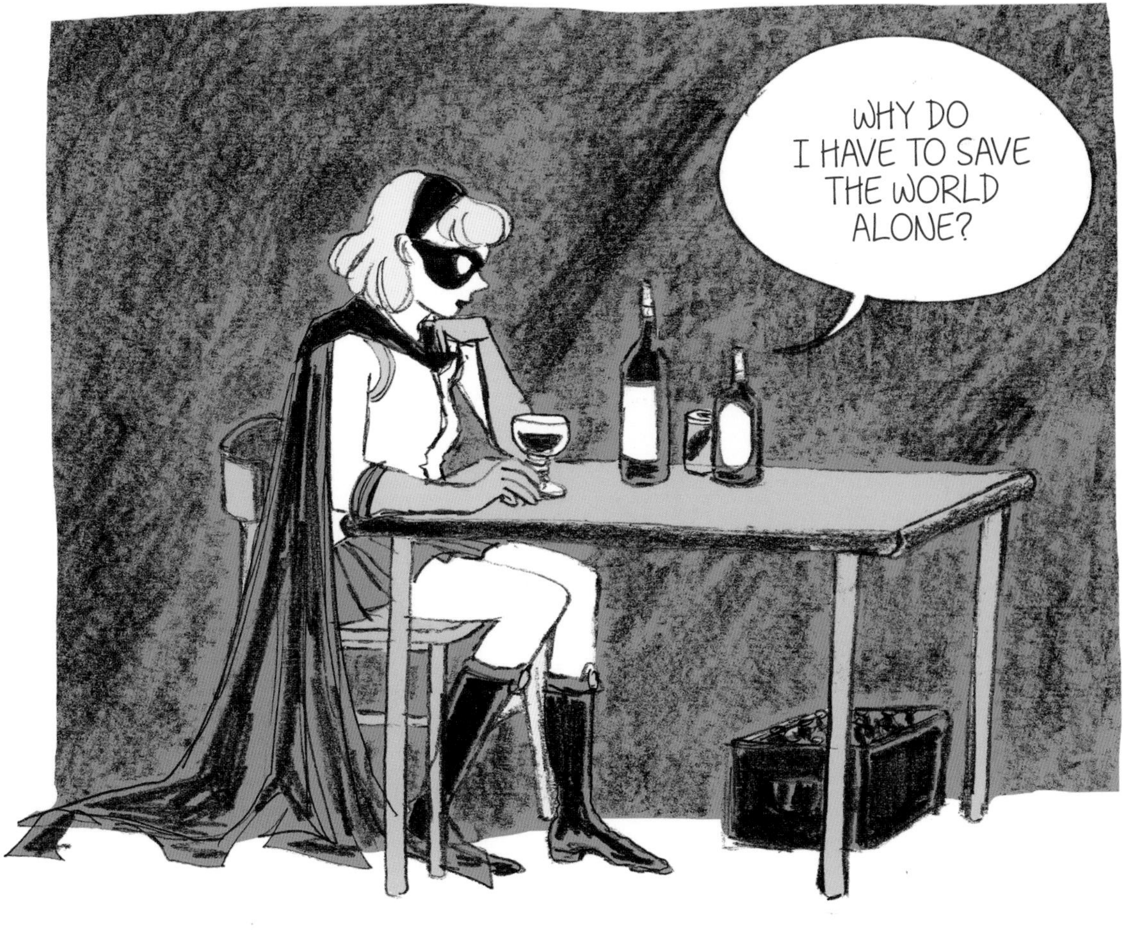
WHY DO I HAVE TO SAVE THE WORLD ALONE?

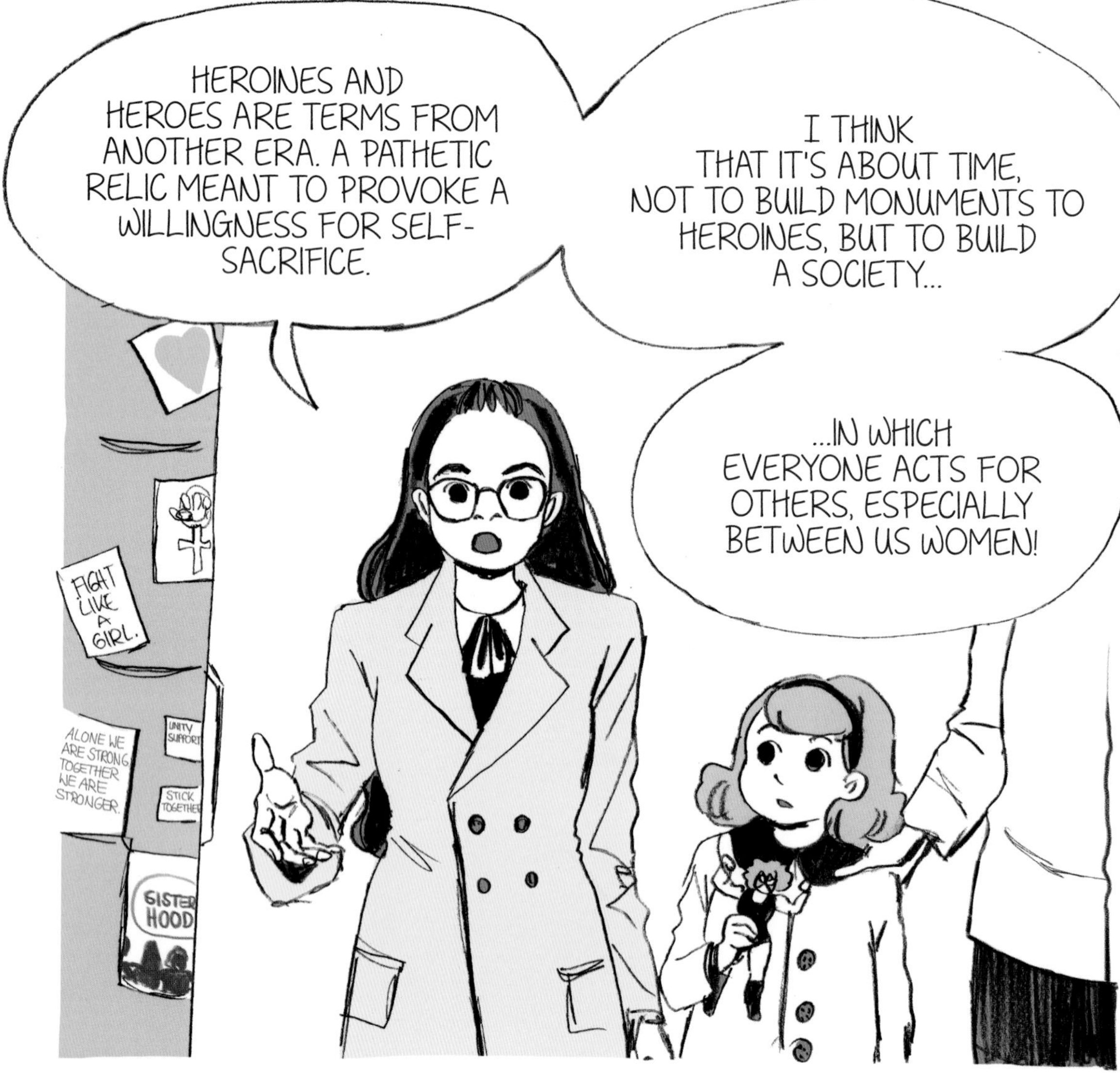
HEROINES AND HEROES ARE TERMS FROM ANOTHER ERA. A PATHETIC RELIC MEANT TO PROVOKE A WILLINGNESS FOR SELF-SACRIFICE.
I THINK THAT IT'S ABOUT TIME, NOT TO BUILD MONUMENTS TO HEROINES, BUT TO BUILD A SOCIETY...
...IN WHICH EVERYONE ACTS FOR OTHERS, ESPECIALLY BETWEEN US WOMEN!
FIGHT LIKE A GIRL.
ALONE WE ARE STRONG. TOGETHER WE ARE STRONGER.
UNITY SUPPORT
SISTERHOOD

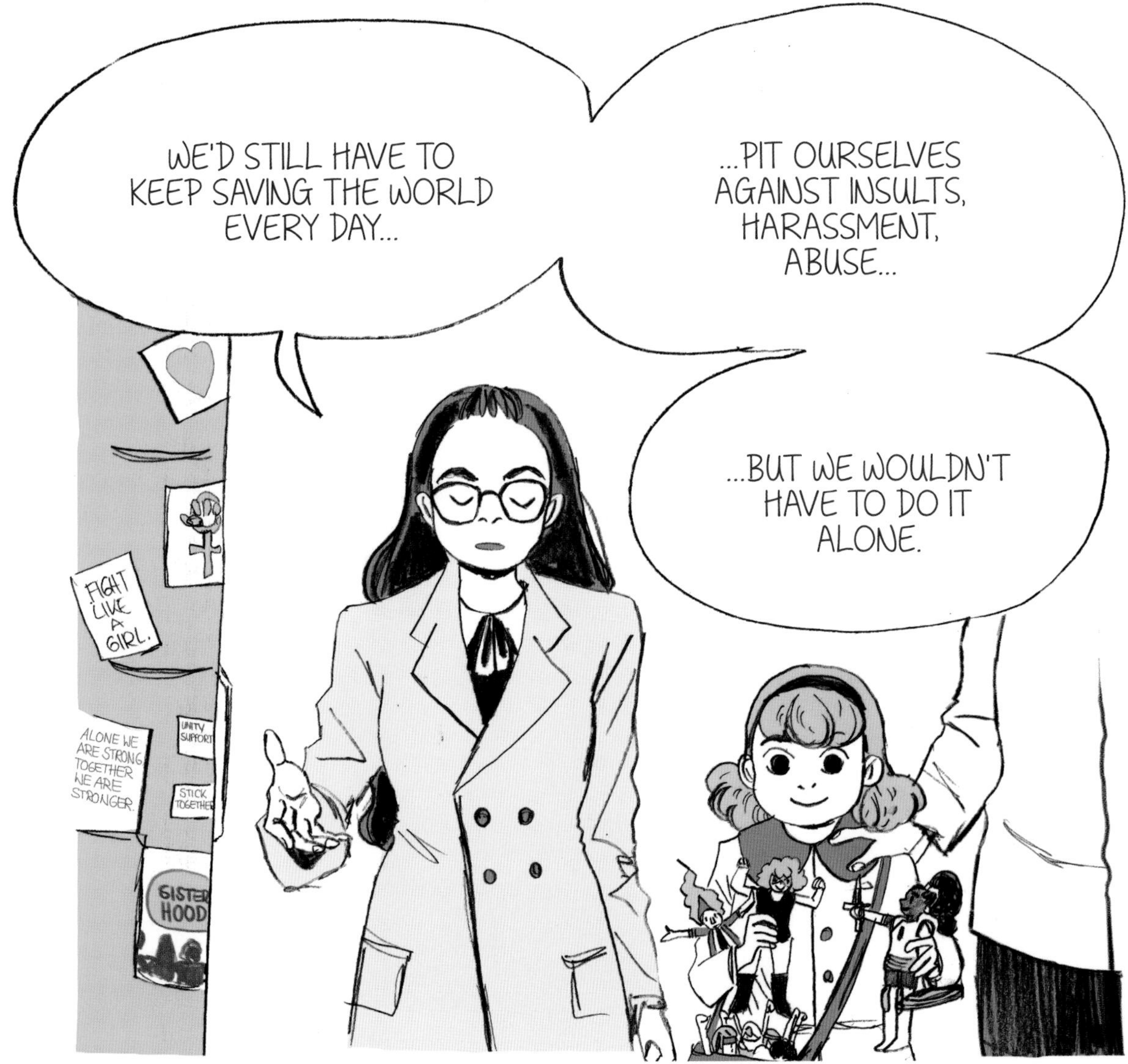
WE'D STILL HAVE TO KEEP SAVING THE WORLD EVERY DAY...
...PIT OURSELVES AGAINST INSULTS, HARASSMENT, ABUSE...
...BUT WE WOULDN'T HAVE TO DO IT ALONE.
FIGHT LIKE A GIRL.
ALONE WE ARE STRONG. TOGETHER WE ARE STRONGER.
UNITY SUPPORT
STICK TOGETHER

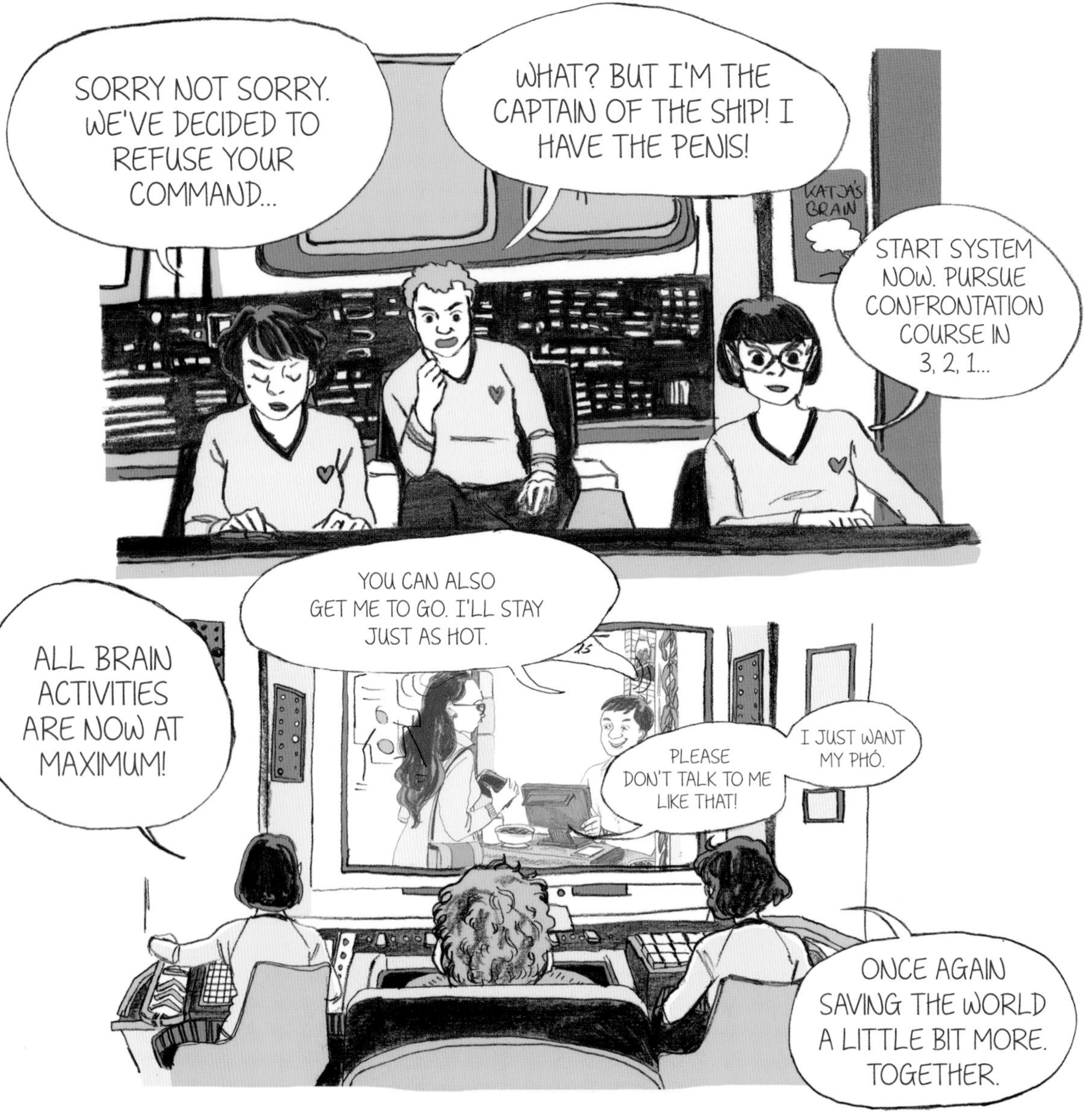
SORRY NOT SORRY. WE'VE DECIDED TO REFUSE YOUR COMMAND...
WHAT? BUT I'M THE CAPTAIN OF THE SHIP! I HAVE THE PENIS!
KATJA'S BRAIN
START SYSTEM NOW. PURSUE CONFRONTATION COURSE IN 3, 2, 1...
ALL BRAIN ACTIVITIES ARE NOW AT MAXIMUM!
YOU CAN ALSO GET ME TO GO. I'LL STAY JUST AS HOT.
PLEASE DON'T TALK TO ME LIKE THAT!
I JUST WANT MY PHÓ.
ONCE AGAIN SAVING THE WORLD A LITTLE BIT MORE. TOGETHER.

Together, be strong and act! And if a heroine has to sacrifice her life for a better world, then please let it be one that arouses empathy, strength, and courage, to be able to change something for the better. Please, not a woman who floats dead down the river or perishes at the hands of the patriarchy. Please, let it be a woman who is always ready with wisdom. Just like Buffy...

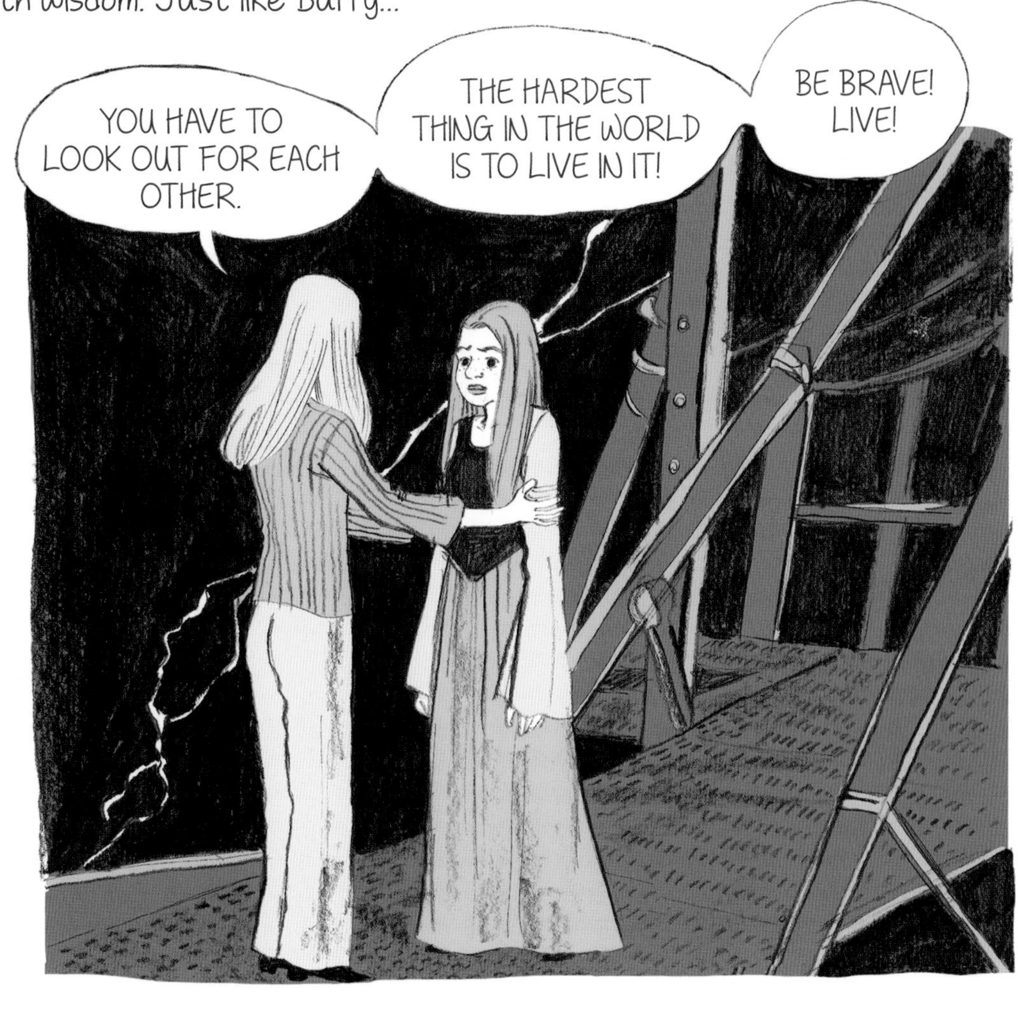
YOU HAVE TO LOOK OUT FOR EACH OTHER.
THE HARDEST THING IN THE WORLD IS TO LIVE IN IT!
BE BRAVE! LIVE!

Viva la Vulva!

It's hard to talk about women's genitals and desire when our sex organs are already made out to be something unspeakable. The fear of the... uh... whatsit starts in childhood--

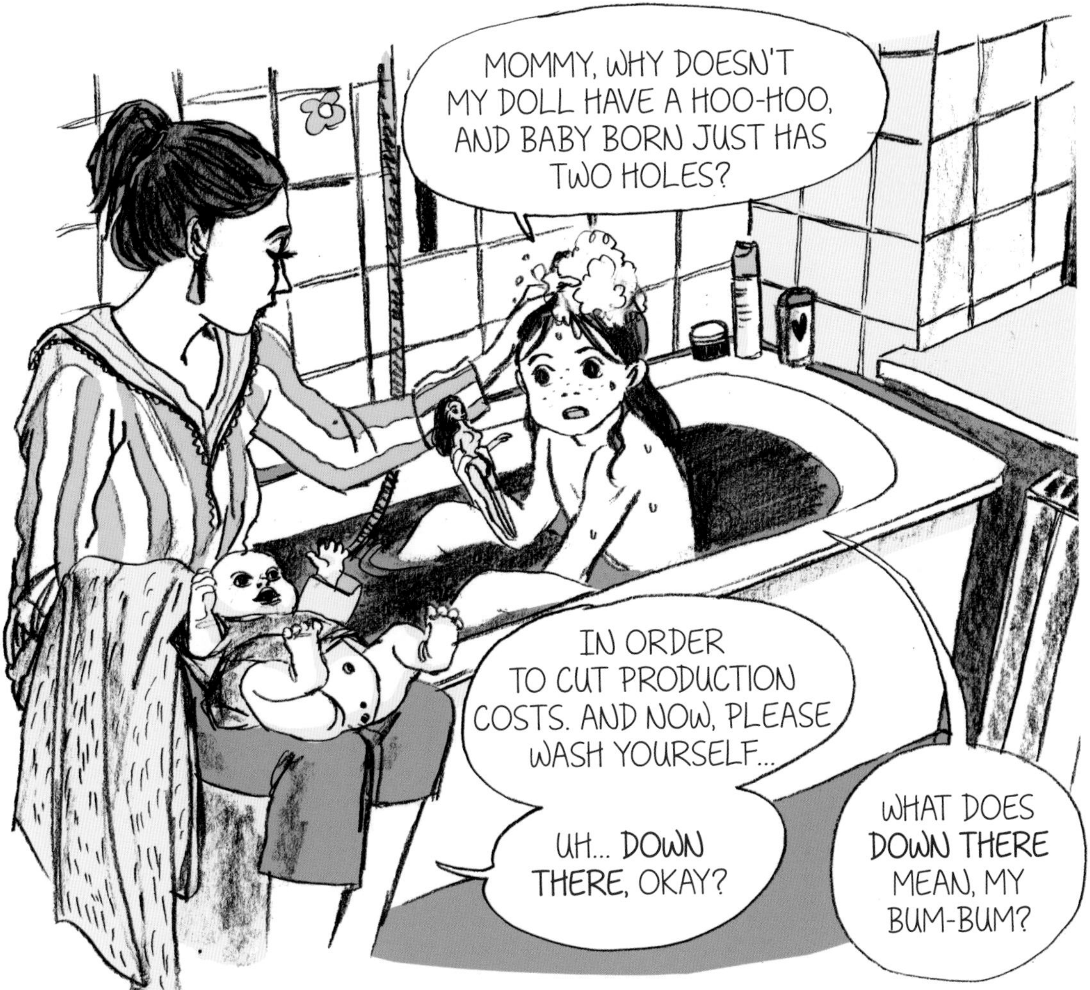
MOMMY, WHY DOESN'T MY DOLL HAVE A HOO-HOO, AND BABY BORN JUST HAS TWO HOLES?
IN ORDER TO CUT PRODUCTION COSTS. AND NOW, PLEASE WASH YOURSELF...
UH... **DOWN THERE**, OKAY?
WHAT DOES **DOWN THERE** MEAN, MY BUM-BUM?

I didn't understand yet that "down there" refers to a thing that should never be named, like a powerful, evil wizard or something.

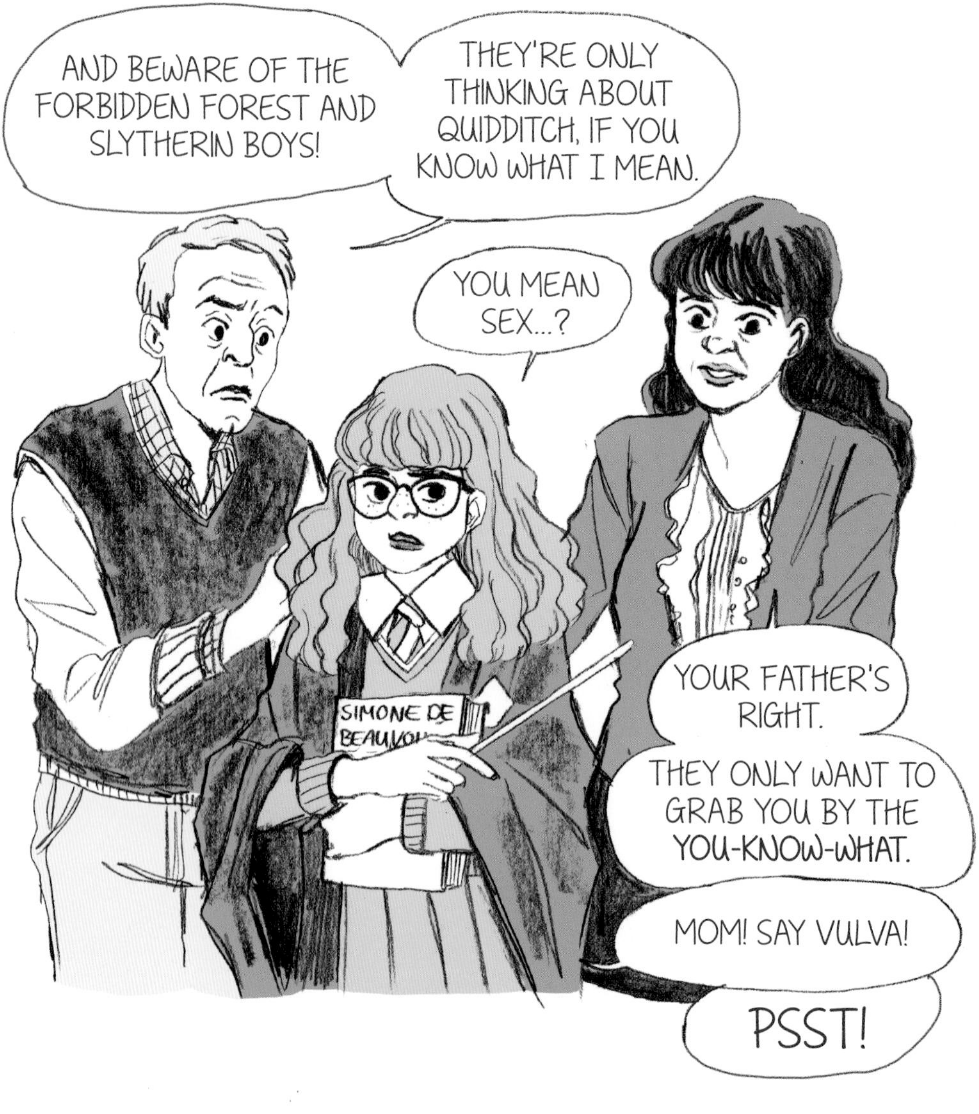
AND BEWARE OF THE FORBIDDEN FOREST AND SLYTHERIN BOYS!
THEY'RE ONLY THINKING ABOUT QUIDDITCH, IF YOU KNOW WHAT I MEAN.
YOU MEAN SEX...?
SIMONE DE BEAUVOI
YOUR FATHER'S RIGHT.
THEY ONLY WANT TO GRAB YOU BY THE YOU-KNOW-WHAT.
MOM! SAY VULVA!
PSST!

The fear of saying "vulva" isn't new. For a long time, the vulva was treated like it didn't exist. Women's lust isn't **supposed** to exist. For Sigmund Freud, the vagina was just a castrated penis, and therefore inferior. He asserted that girls would recognize the lack of a penis and then yearn for one. Abridged version: They develop "penis envy."

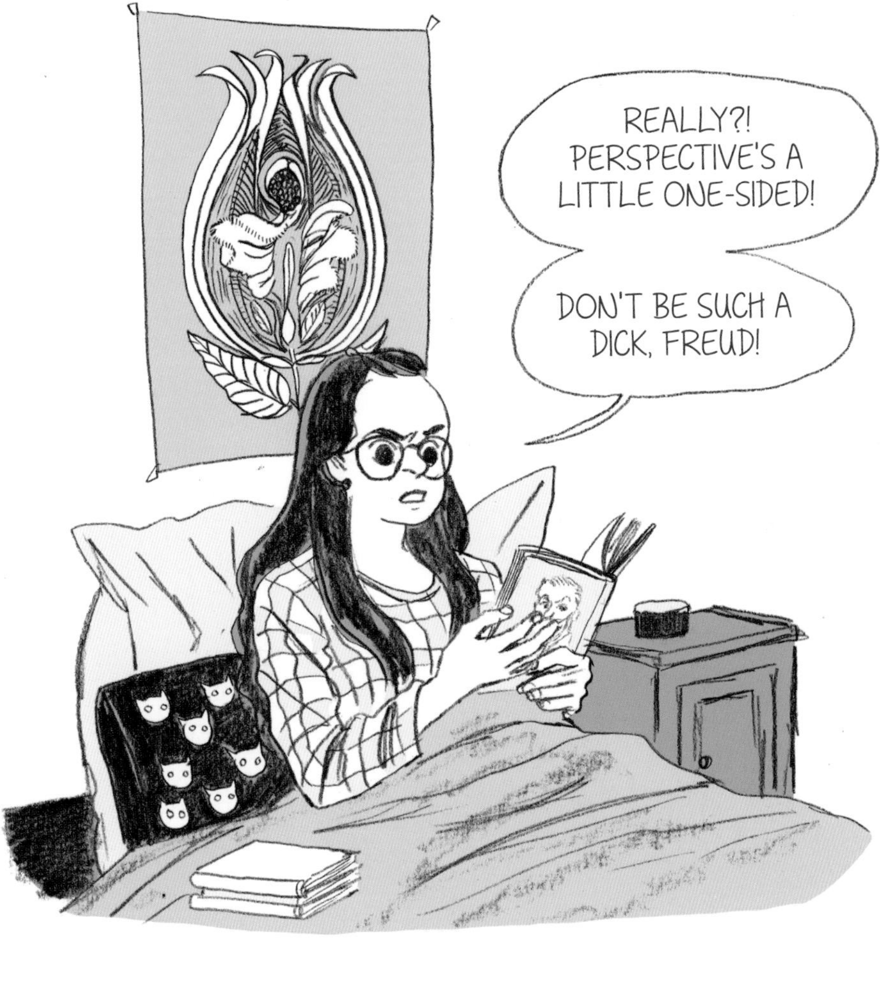
REALLY?! PERSPECTIVE'S A LITTLE ONE-SIDED!
DON'T BE SUCH A DICK, FREUD!

In 1900, though, the good man took it one step further: He coined the term "vagina dentata," a toothed vagina that threatened men with castration by ripping off their penises. I would sometimes imagine what it might have been like if Freud were in charge at a wizarding school.

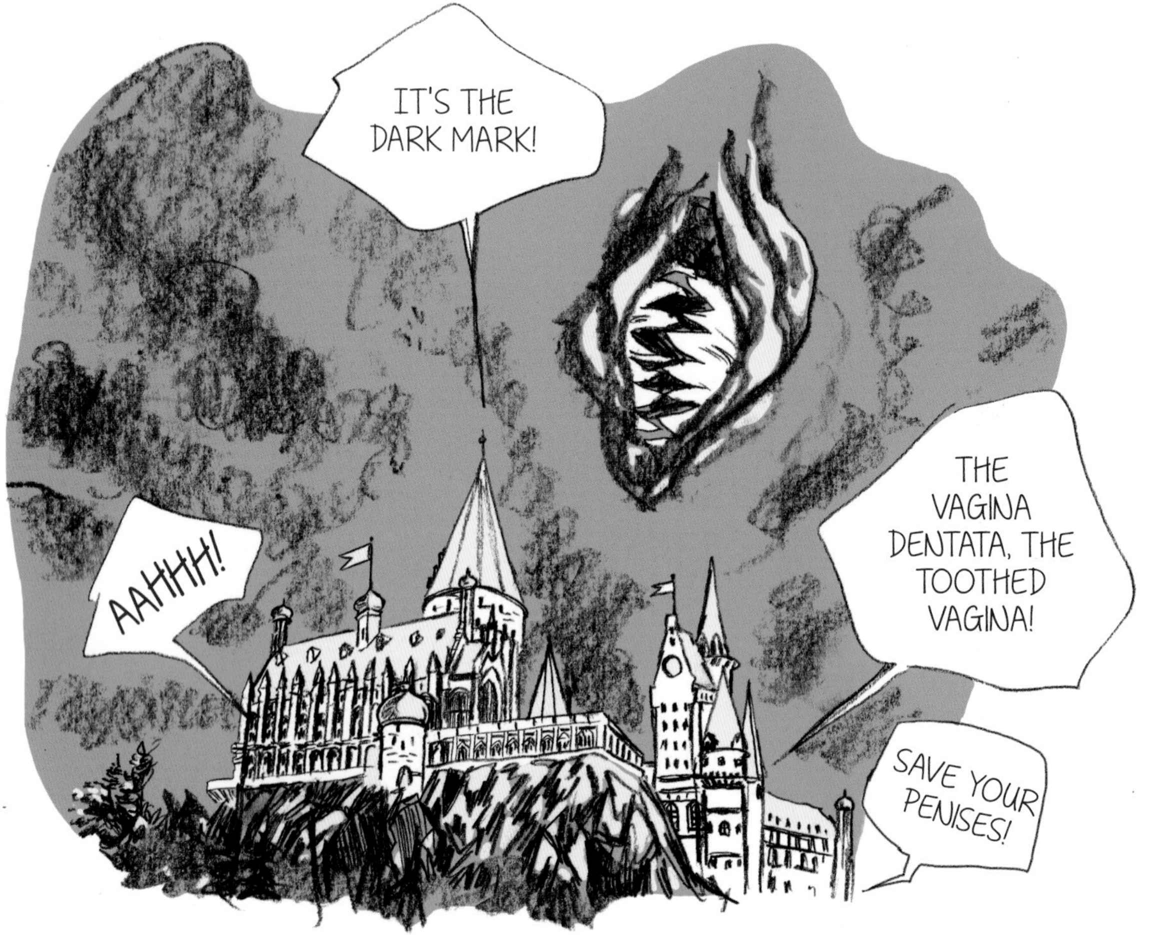
IT'S THE DARK MARK!
AAHHH!
THE VAGINA DENTATA, THE TOOTHED VAGINA!
SAVE YOUR PENISES!

The vagina dentata: evil, unspeakable, and good for scaring small children. I know this is a comic, but can you hear the sarcasm?

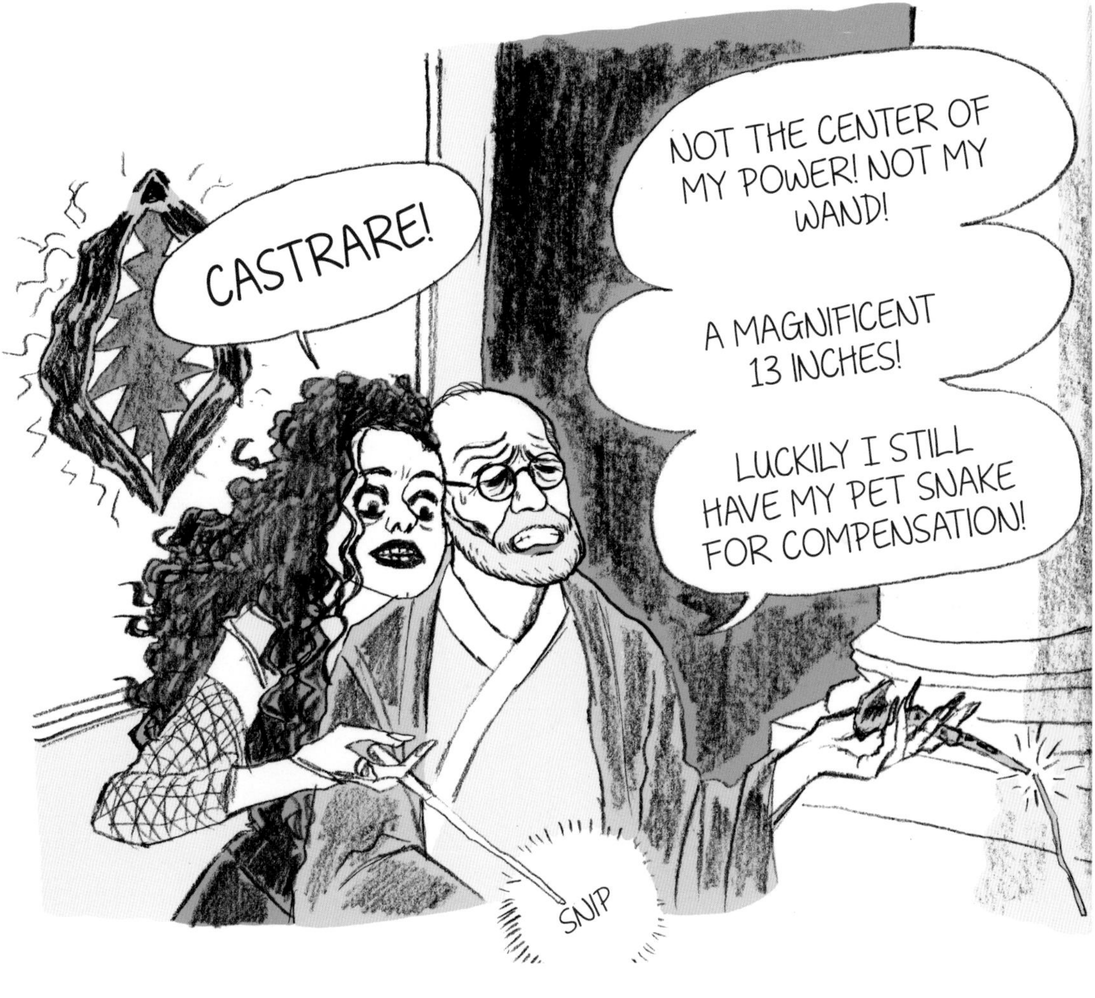

CASTRARE!
NOT THE CENTER OF MY POWER! NOT MY WAND!
A MAGNIFICENT 13 INCHES!
LUCKILY I STILL HAVE MY PET SNAKE FOR COMPENSATION!
SNIP

In these myths, women's sexuality is represented as threatening, and the woman is often penetrated against her will in order to pull out the dangerous teeth. But stories don't often stay just stories. Words shape reality.

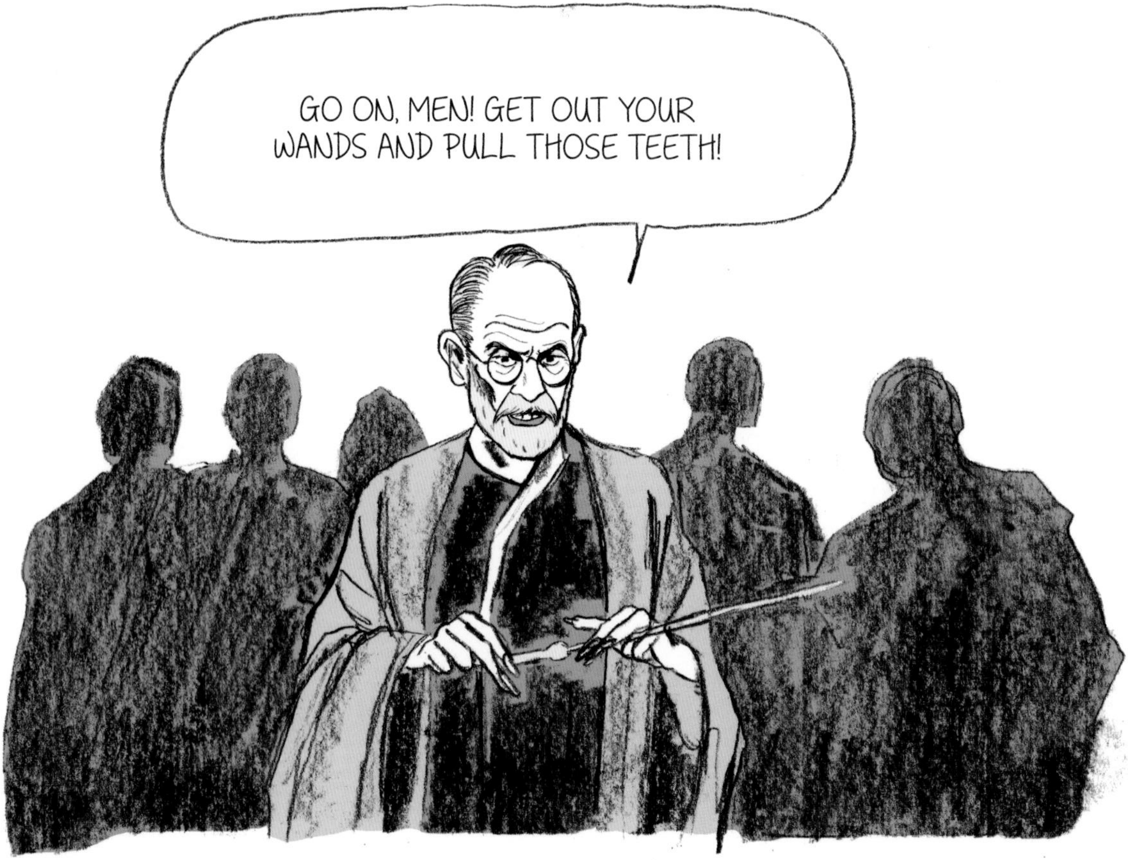
GO ON, MEN! GET OUT YOUR WANDS AND PULL THOSE TEETH!

The bodies and sexuality of women are still a topic controlled by men. We women have learned to subjugate ourselves, and that's hard to unlearn. I've slowly become cognizant of the desire to speak with my "down there" and to reflect on what went wrong all those years.

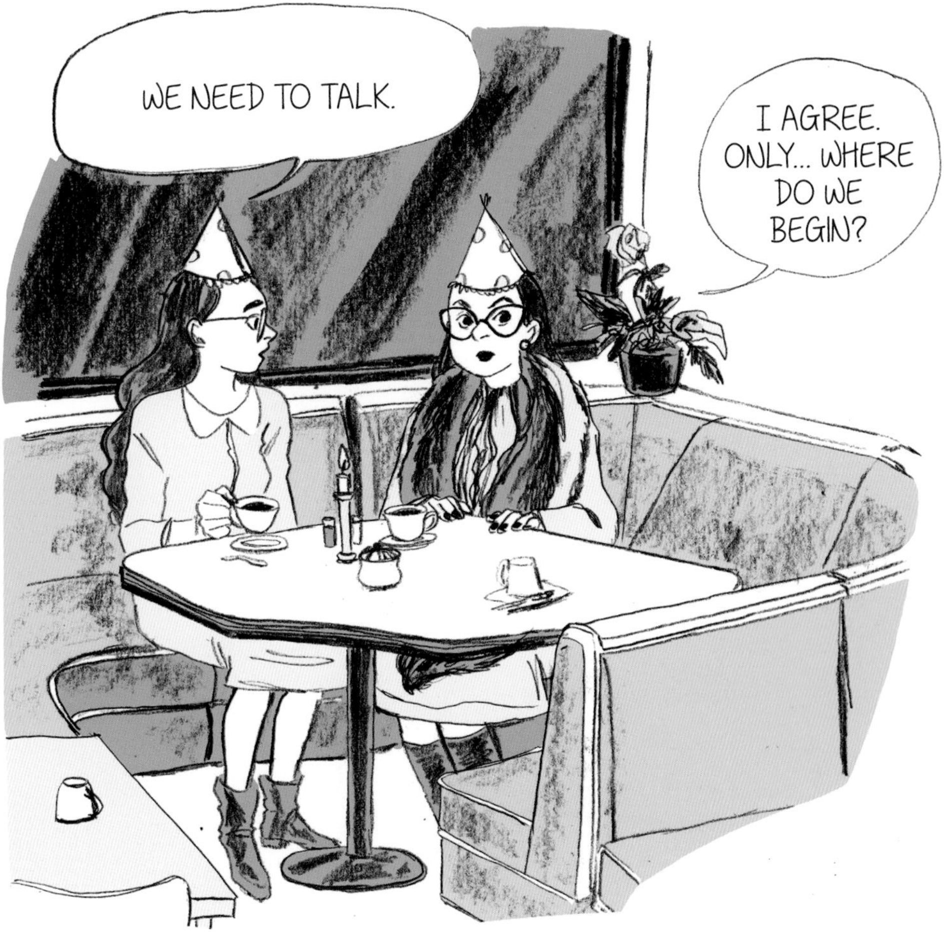
WE NEED TO TALK.
I AGREE. ONLY... WHERE DO WE BEGIN?

It didn't exactly help that I got my period at only ten years old. When it started, I was at school. My then-crush Christian was worried about me. But I had such bad stomach cramps, I didn't care at all.

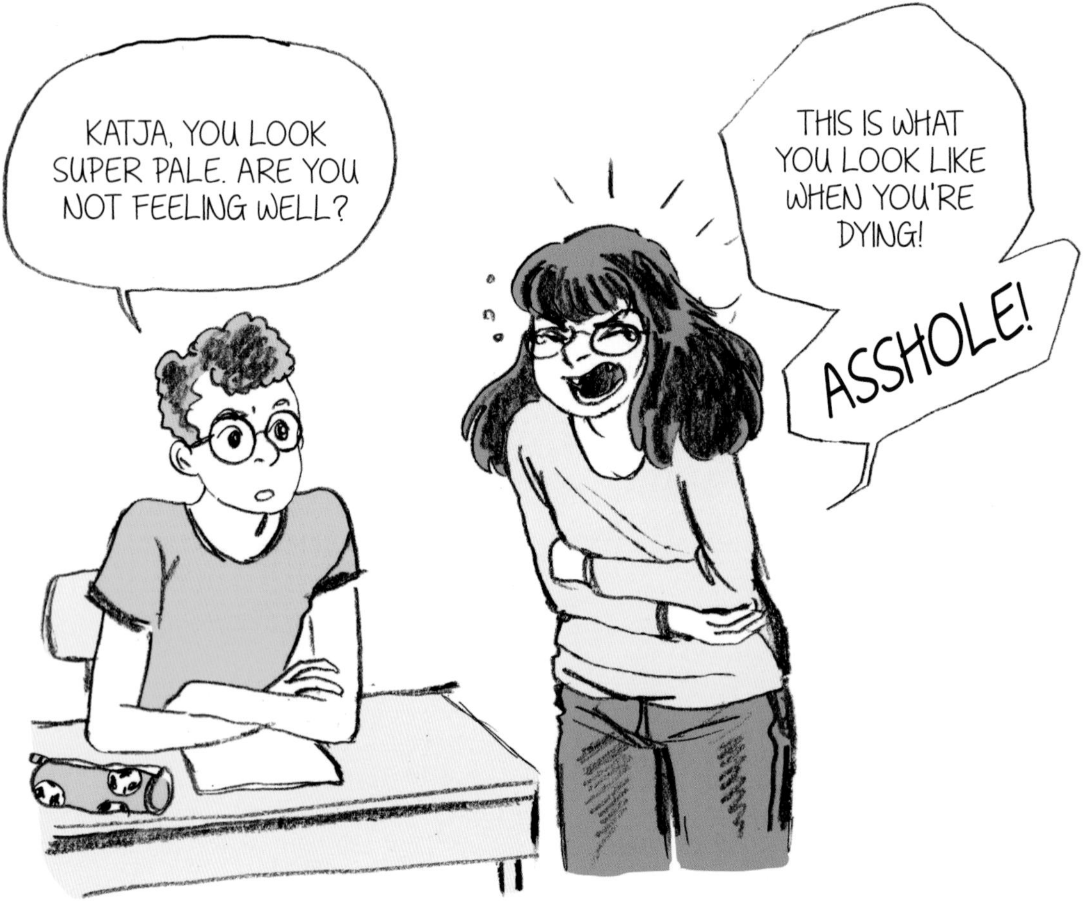
KATJA, YOU LOOK SUPER PALE. ARE YOU NOT FEELING WELL?
THIS IS WHAT YOU LOOK LIKE WHEN YOU'RE DYING!
ASSHOLE!

Since then, I felt a little bit dead every month. On the bathroom floor. (Becoming a woman isn't exactly what I'd call a hobby.)

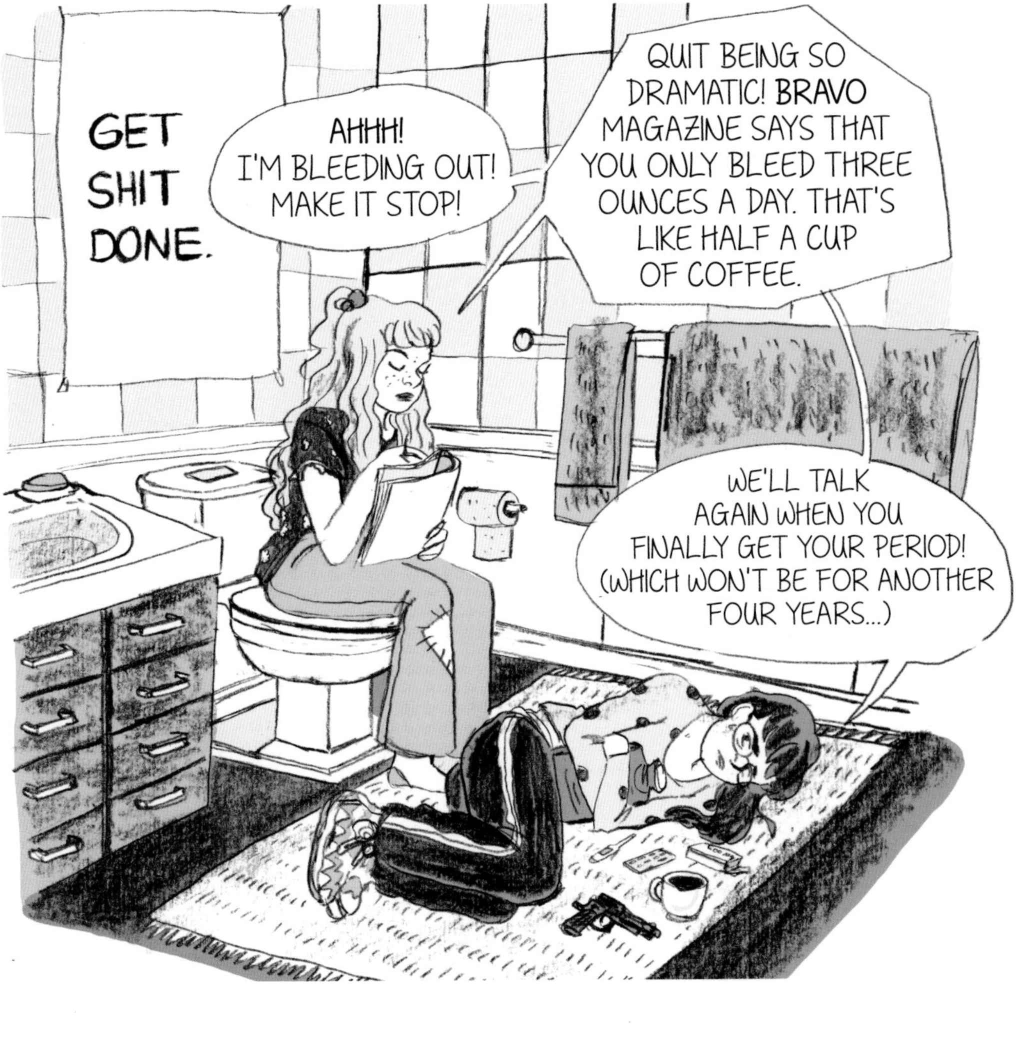
GET SHIT DONE.
AHHH! I'M BLEEDING OUT! MAKE IT STOP!
QUIT BEING SO DRAMATIC! BRAVO MAGAZINE SAYS THAT YOU ONLY BLEED THREE OUNCES A DAY. THAT'S LIKE HALF A CUP OF COFFEE.
WE'LL TALK AGAIN WHEN YOU FINALLY GET YOUR PERIOD! (WHICH WON'T BE FOR ANOTHER FOUR YEARS...)

I also thought that menstruation was disgusting and somehow unhygienic. At first, out of shame, I always bought pads with flowery scents. And those alone seem to announce--

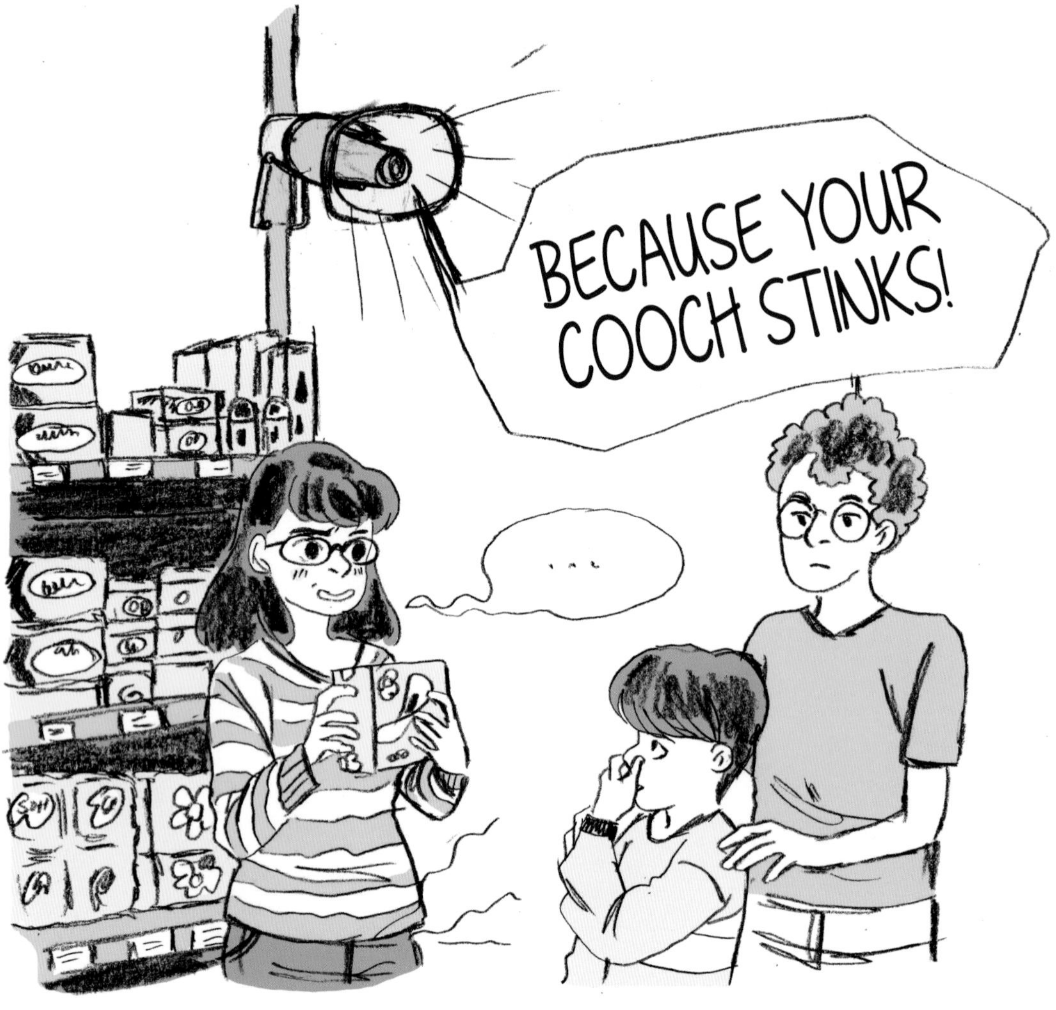
BECAUSE YOUR COOCH STINKS!
. . .

And because blood is totally unhygienic, and menstrual blood is the worst of all, it's always represented as blue liquid in advertisements. As if women were all aliens who bleed blue mouthwash.

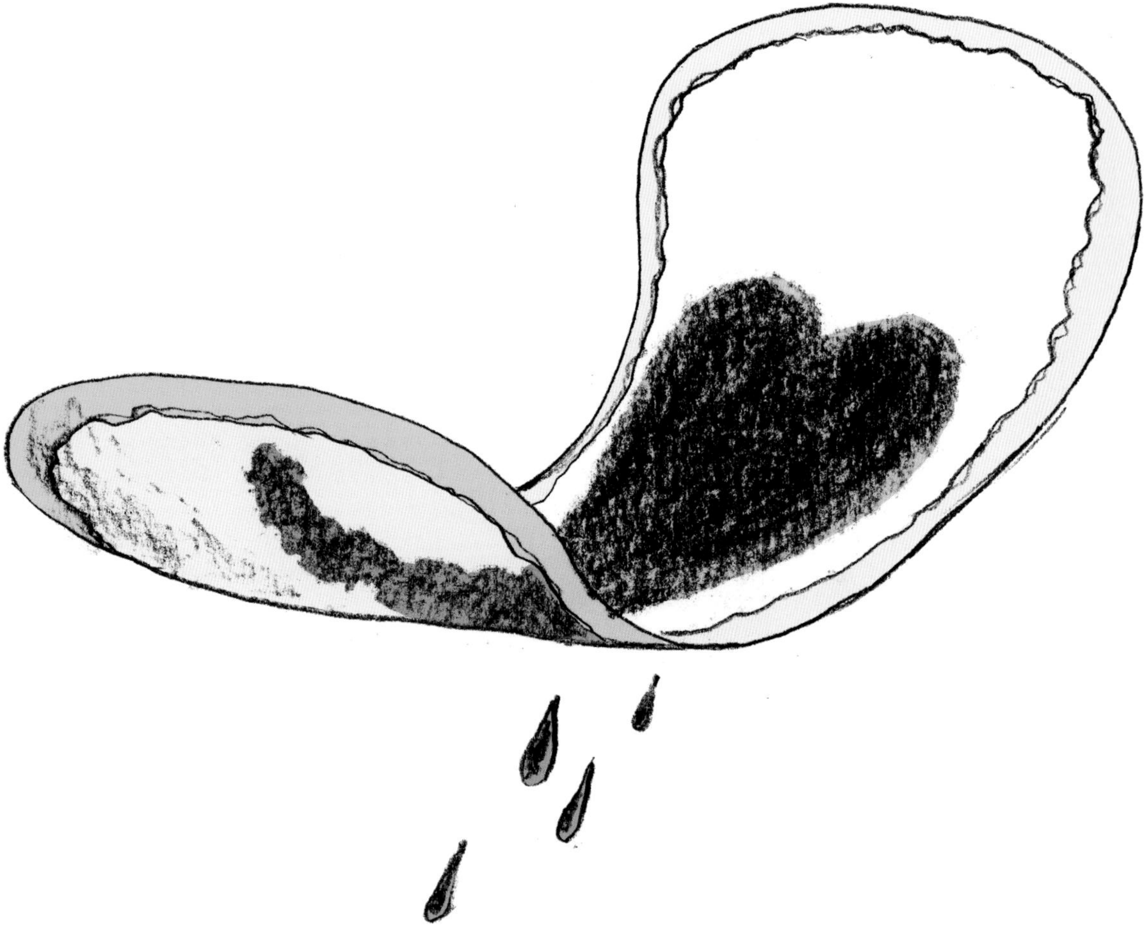

Moreover, I didn't know any comparable product that claimed that male sex parts were unhygienic.

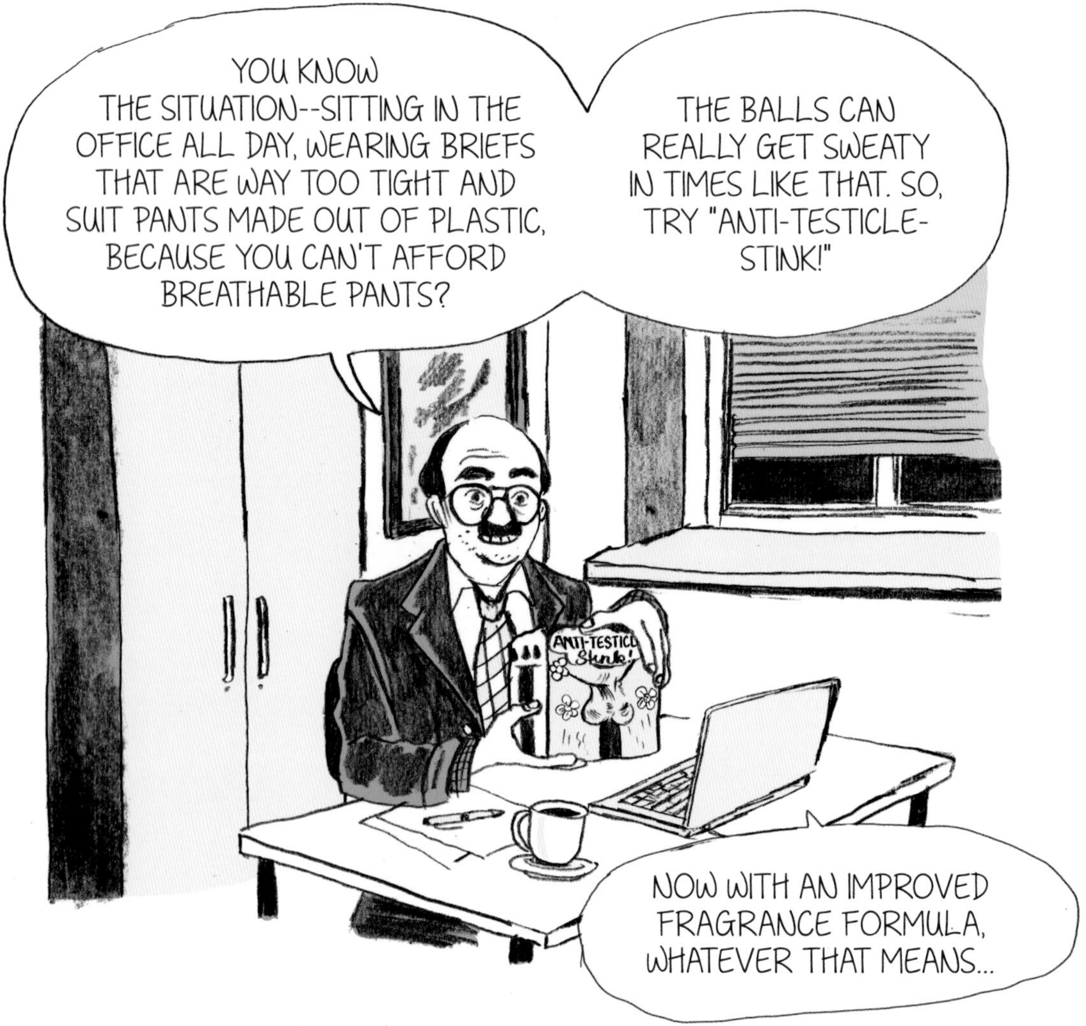
YOU KNOW THE SITUATION--SITTING IN THE OFFICE ALL DAY, WEARING BRIEFS THAT ARE WAY TOO TIGHT AND SUIT PANTS MADE OUT OF PLASTIC, BECAUSE YOU CAN'T AFFORD BREATHABLE PANTS?
THE BALLS CAN REALLY GET SWEATY IN TIMES LIKE THAT. SO, TRY "ANTI-TESTICLE-STINK!"
NOW WITH AN IMPROVED FRAGRANCE FORMULA, WHATEVER THAT MEANS...

And the constant public debate about pubic hair on vulvas gets us even further away from treating our bodies positively and learning how to enjoy them. Instead, bald vulvas are supposed to be more hygienic, although pubic hair a) protects against germs and b) is our own business.

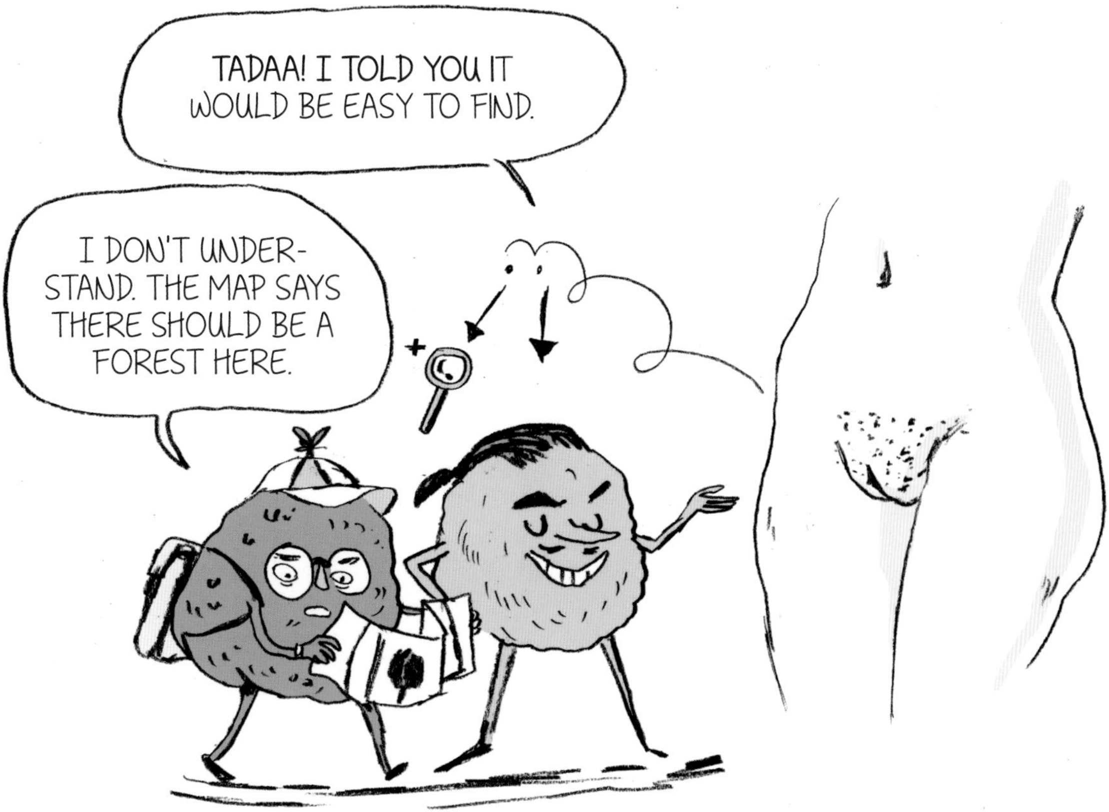

I DON'T UNDER-STAND. THE MAP SAYS THERE SHOULD BE A FOREST HERE.
TADAA! I TOLD YOU IT WOULD BE EASY TO FIND.

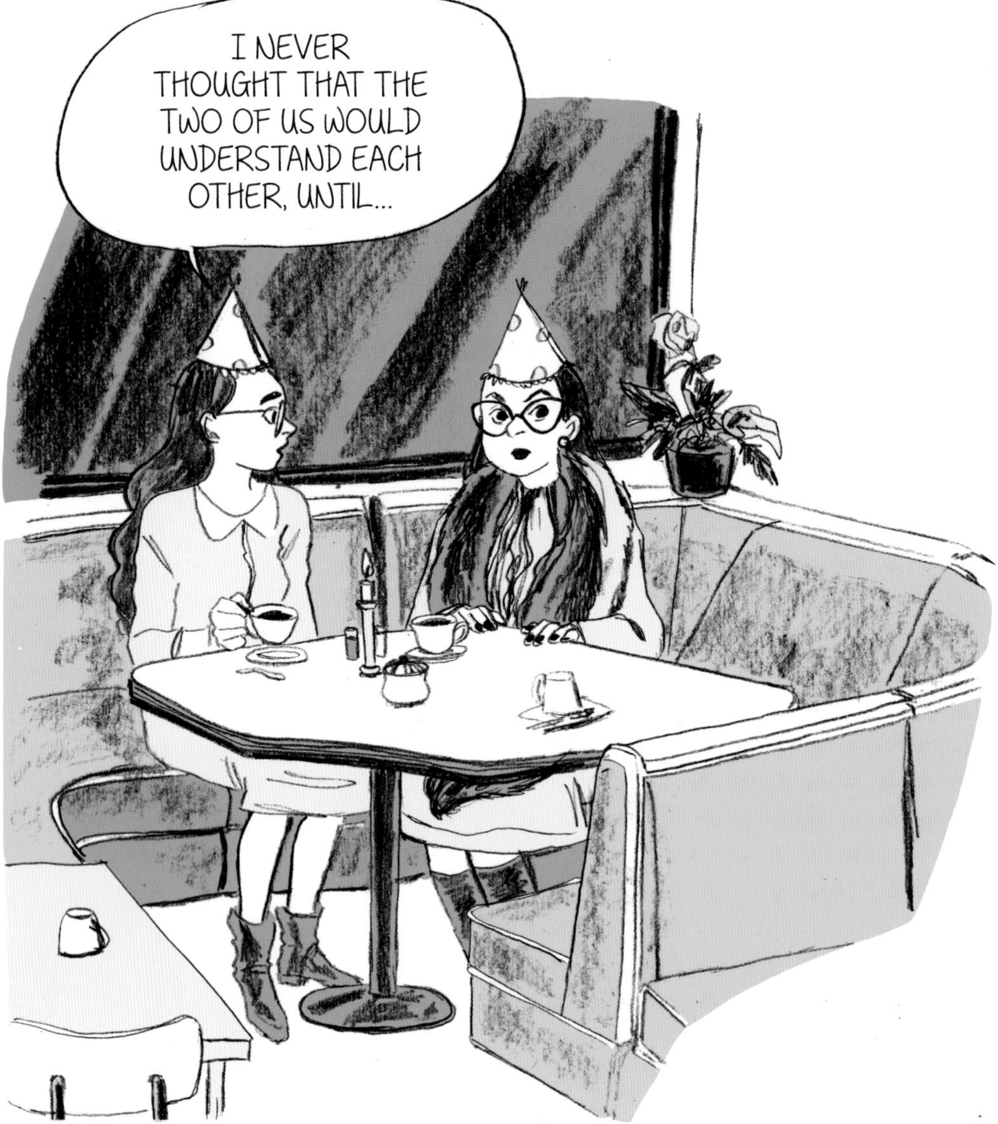
I NEVER THOUGHT THAT THE TWO OF US WOULD UNDERSTAND EACH OTHER, UNTIL...

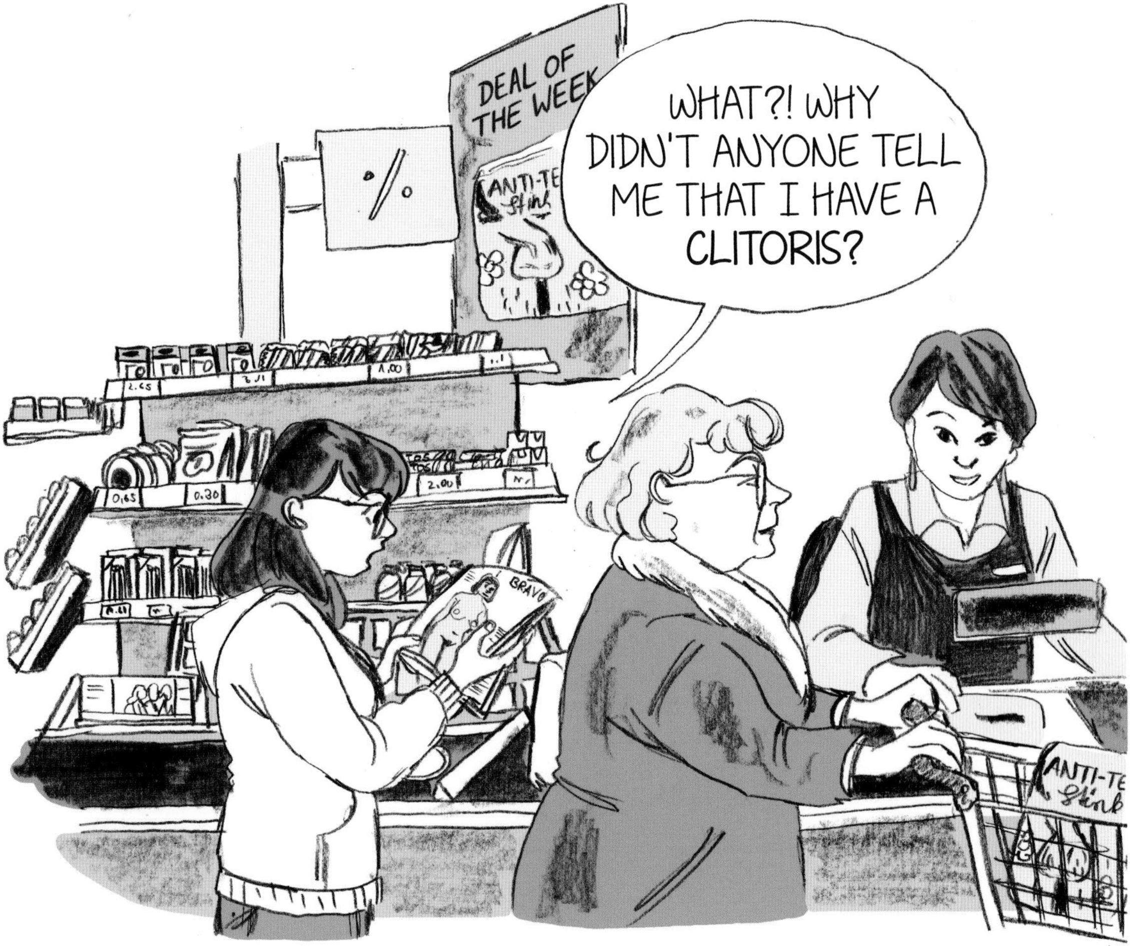
DEAL OF THE WEEK
%
WHAT?! WHY DIDN'T ANYONE TELL ME THAT I HAVE A CLITORIS?
BRAVO

Discovery of the Clitoris

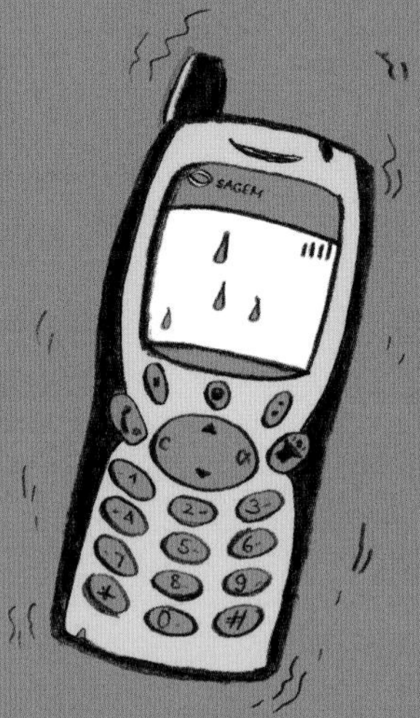
SAGEM

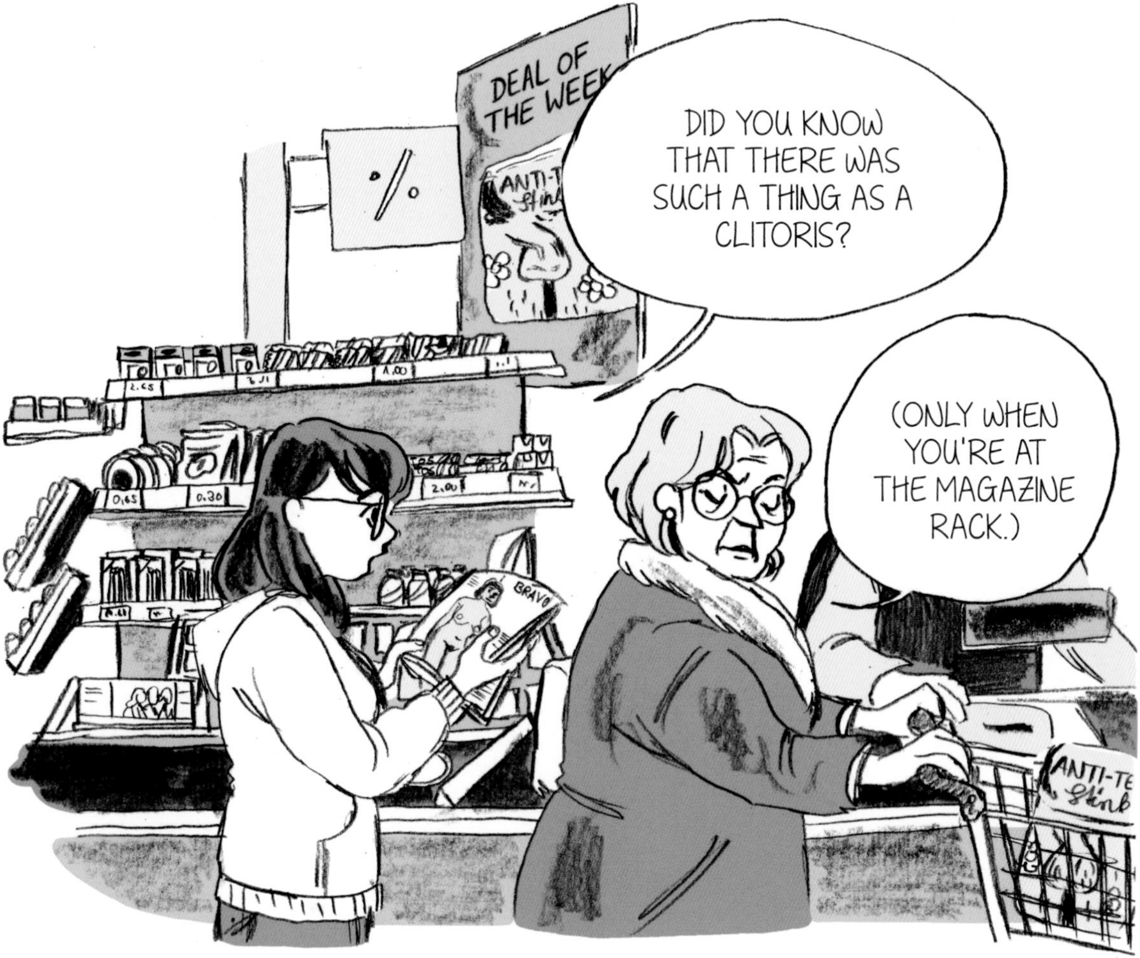
DEAL OF THE WEEK
DID YOU KNOW THAT THERE WAS SUCH A THING AS A CLITORIS?
BRAVO
(ONLY WHEN YOU'RE AT THE MAGAZINE RACK.)

So a vulva has something good after all! Wow! Naturally, I quickly went and tried out this "clitoris." I accidentally discovered that the vibration of my old cell phone worked amazingly to turn me on. (The vibration on phones today is nothing in comparison.)

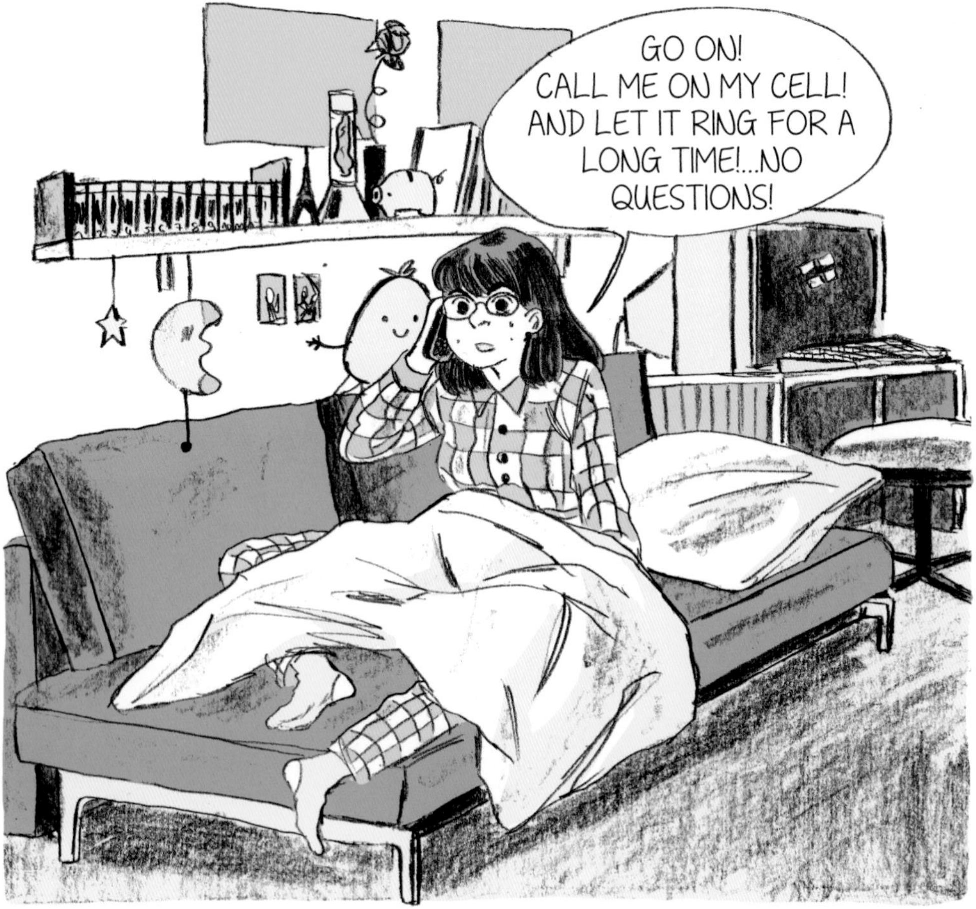
GO ON!
CALL ME ON MY CELL!
AND LET IT RING FOR A LONG TIME!...NO QUESTIONS!

But there was always this air of secrecy and indecency around masturbation. I was once even "caught" by my mother. Of course, she immediately shut the door. (Although a woman-to-woman conversation afterward wouldn't have been that complicated.)

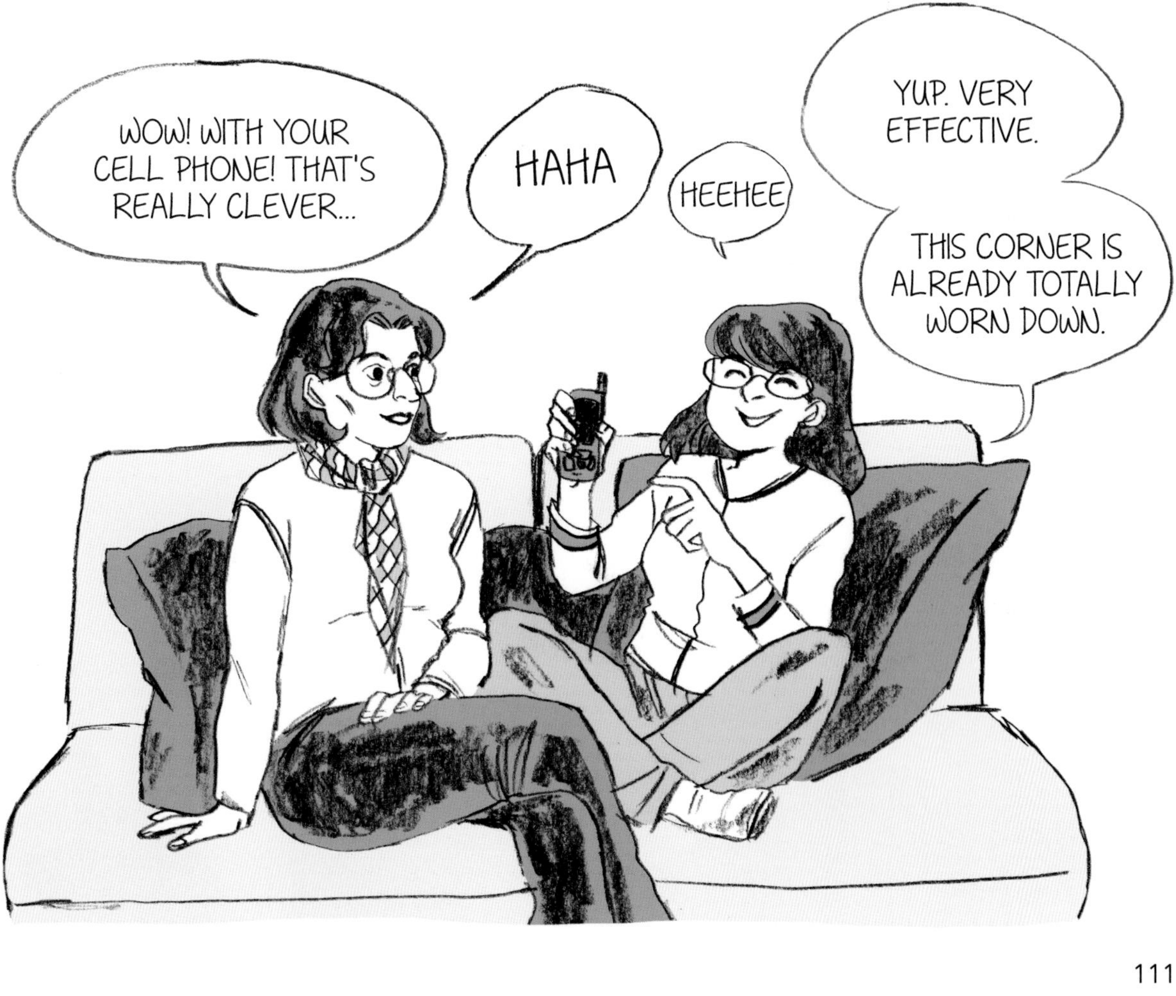
WOW! WITH YOUR CELL PHONE! THAT'S REALLY CLEVER...
HAHA
HEEHEE
YUP. VERY EFFECTIVE.
THIS CORNER IS ALREADY TOTALLY WORN DOWN.

Since no one talked about vulvas, orgasms, and desire, I didn't either. But I now knew how orgasms operated, so I didn't feel the need to do further research. I didn't look at my vulva until I was 20. Before, someone could have shown it to me and I wouldn't have recognized it...

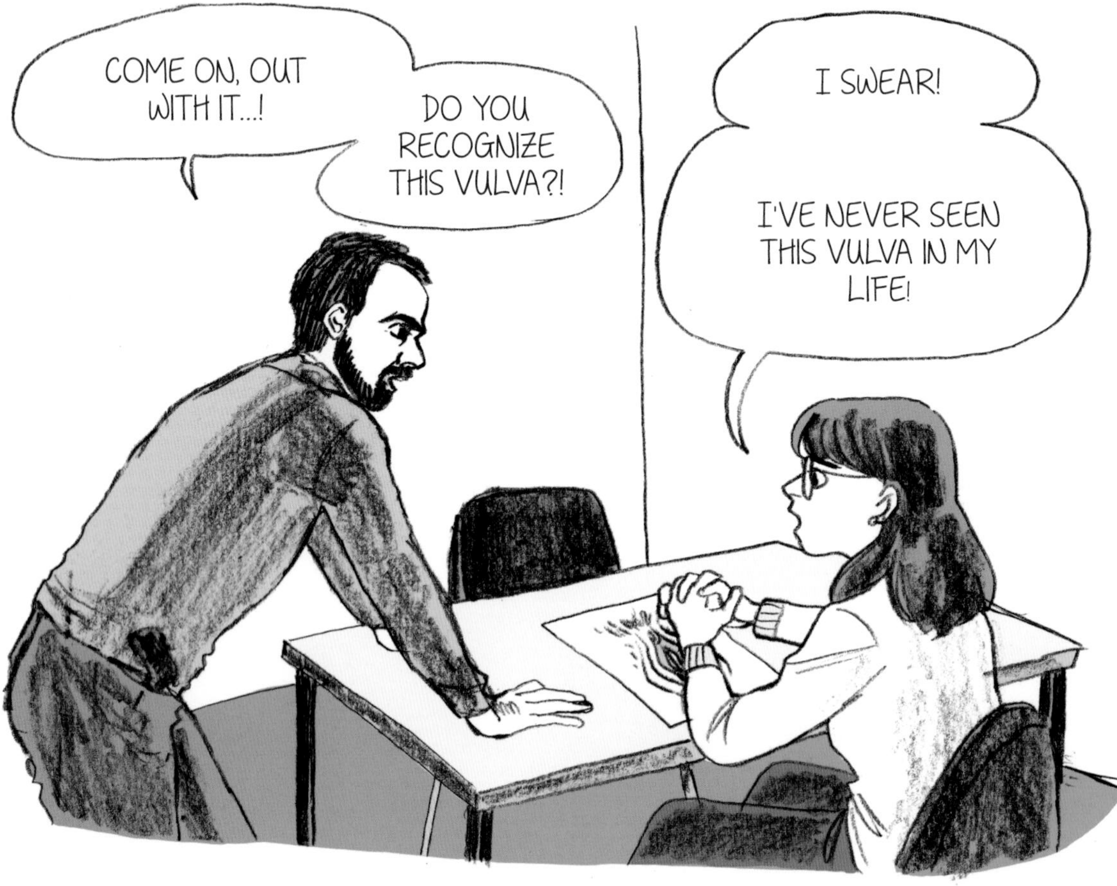
COME ON, OUT WITH IT...!
DO YOU RECOGNIZE THIS VULVA?!
I SWEAR!
I'VE NEVER SEEN THIS VULVA IN MY LIFE!

I had sex for the first time at 15. That was too young. I did it before understanding at all what it would mean to me.

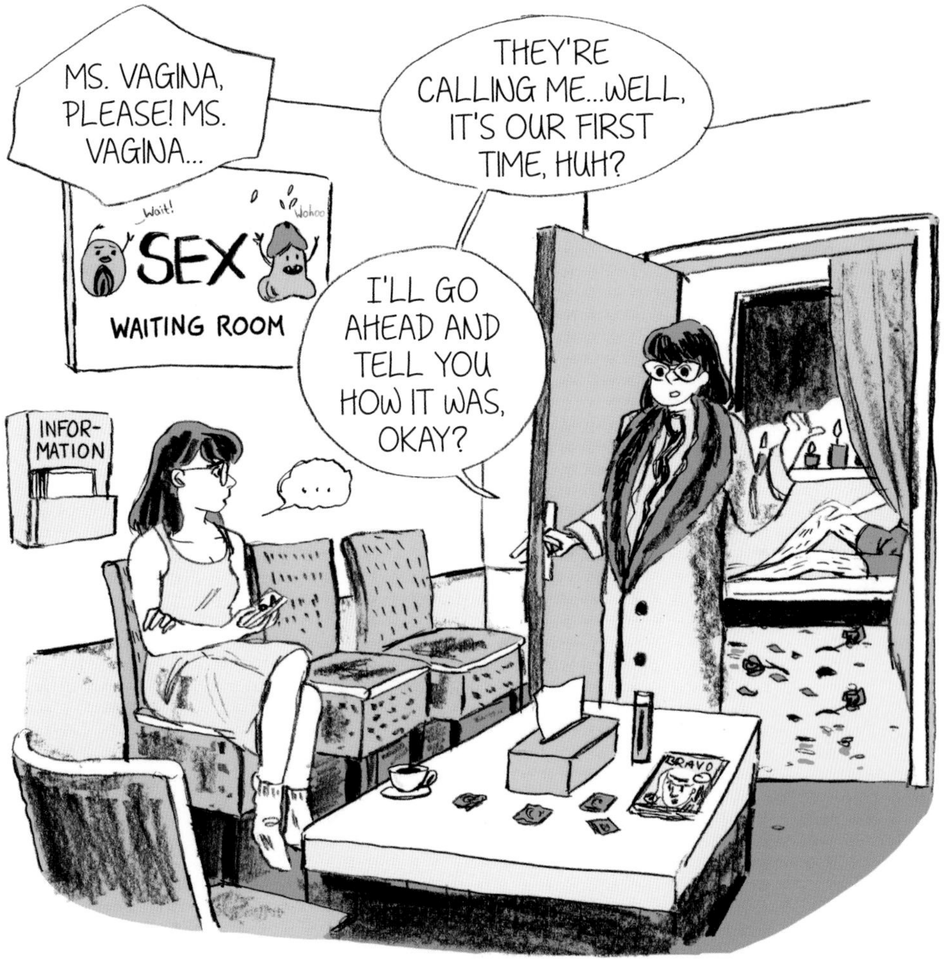

MS. VAGINA, PLEASE! MS. VAGINA...
THEY'RE CALLING ME...WELL, IT'S OUR FIRST TIME, HUH?
I'LL GO AHEAD AND TELL YOU HOW IT WAS, OKAY?
...
Wait!
SEX
Wohoo
WAITING ROOM
INFORMATION
BRAVO

I just wanted it behind me. It had nothing to do with desire. "Sex" often means just penetration. And that's not great for the woman the first time. For the man, penetration feels great--and somehow, it's accepted everywhere that the man's orgasm is the goal.

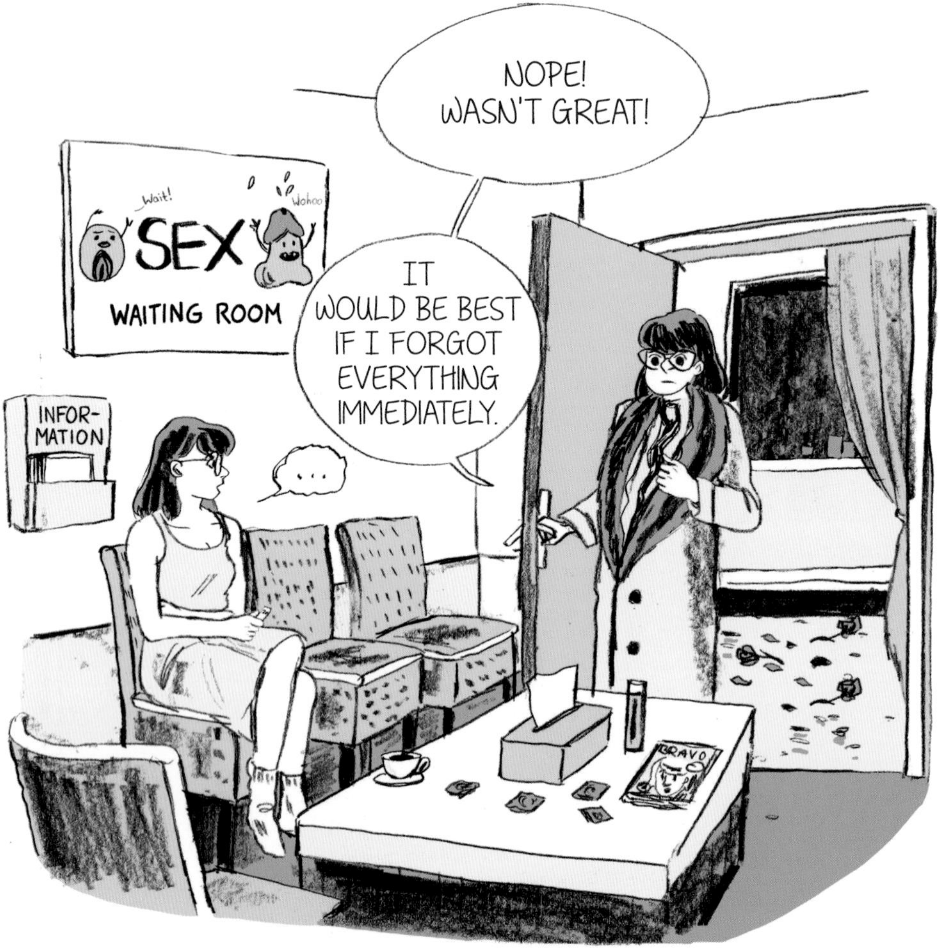
NOPE! WASN'T GREAT!
Wait!
Wohoo
SEX
WAITING ROOM
IT WOULD BE BEST IF I FORGOT EVERYTHING IMMEDIATELY.
INFOR-MATION
...
BRAVO

I have no memories at all of my first time. Neither of who it was with, nor how it happened. My first orgasm, in contrast, I still remember vividly. The truth lies somewhere between a romanticized picture of the first time and the first disillusioned post-coital cigarette. Only, I don't remember it. I have guesses, but the images have been erased.

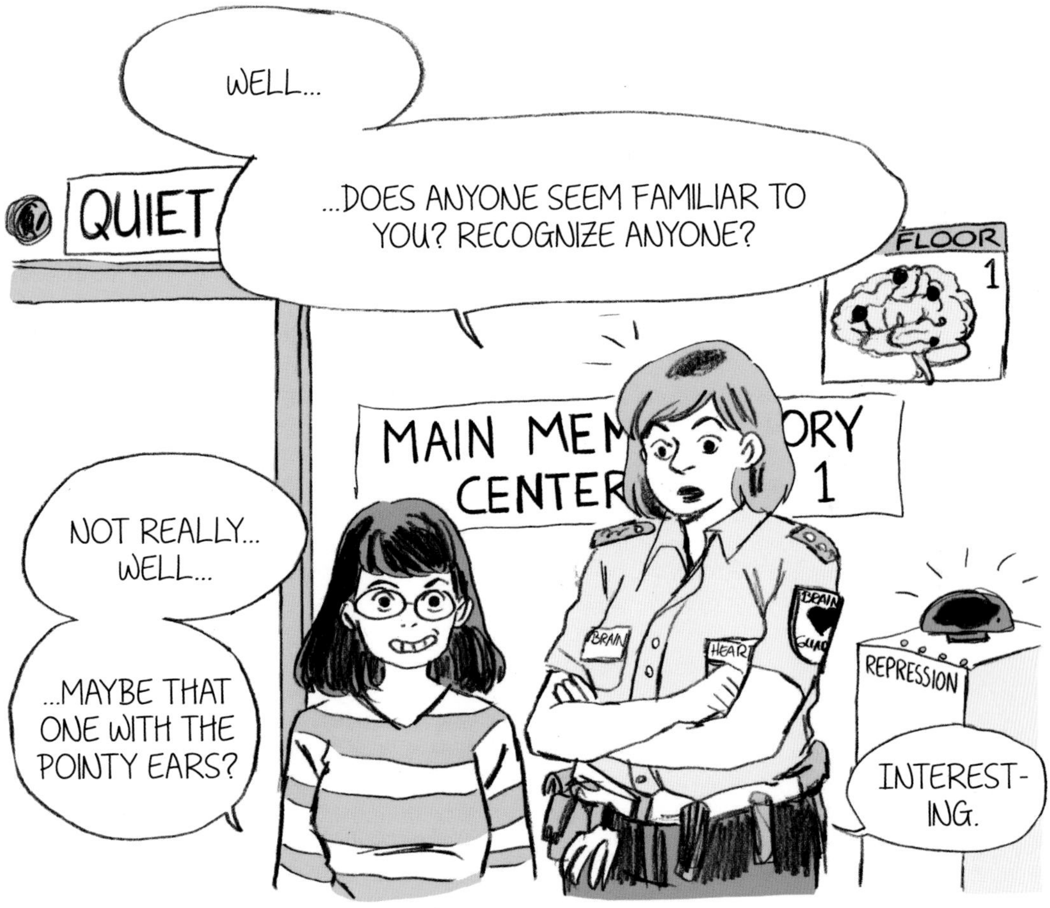
WELL...
...DOES ANYONE SEEM FAMILIAR TO YOU? RECOGNIZE ANYONE?
QUIET
FLOOR 1
MAIN MEM ORY CENTER 1
NOT REALLY... WELL...
...MAYBE THAT ONE WITH THE POINTY EARS?
BRAIN
HEART
REPRESSION
INTEREST-ING.

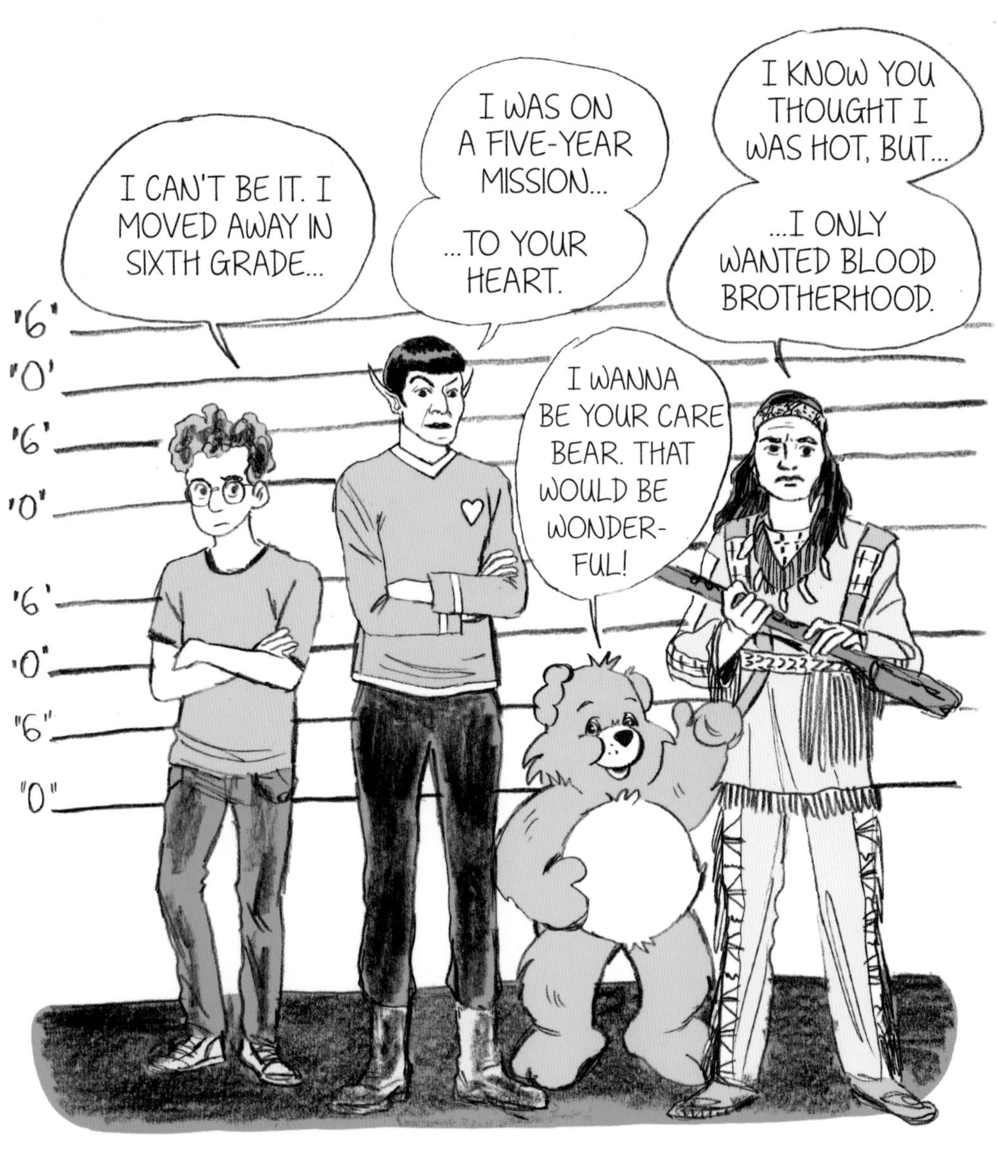

I CAN'T BE IT. I MOVED AWAY IN SIXTH GRADE...
I WAS ON A FIVE-YEAR MISSION...
...TO YOUR HEART.
I WANNA BE YOUR CARE BEAR. THAT WOULD BE WONDER-FUL!
I KNOW YOU THOUGHT I WAS HOT, BUT...
...I ONLY WANTED BLOOD BROTHERHOOD.
"6"
"0"
'6'
'0"
'6'
'0"
"6"
"0"

What remained, however, was the pain of my first time. A burning and ripping at the entrance of my vagina that lingered for a long time, and a feeling that a penis wasn't at all made to fit into a vagina. That the vagina was too narrow--a closed-off society.

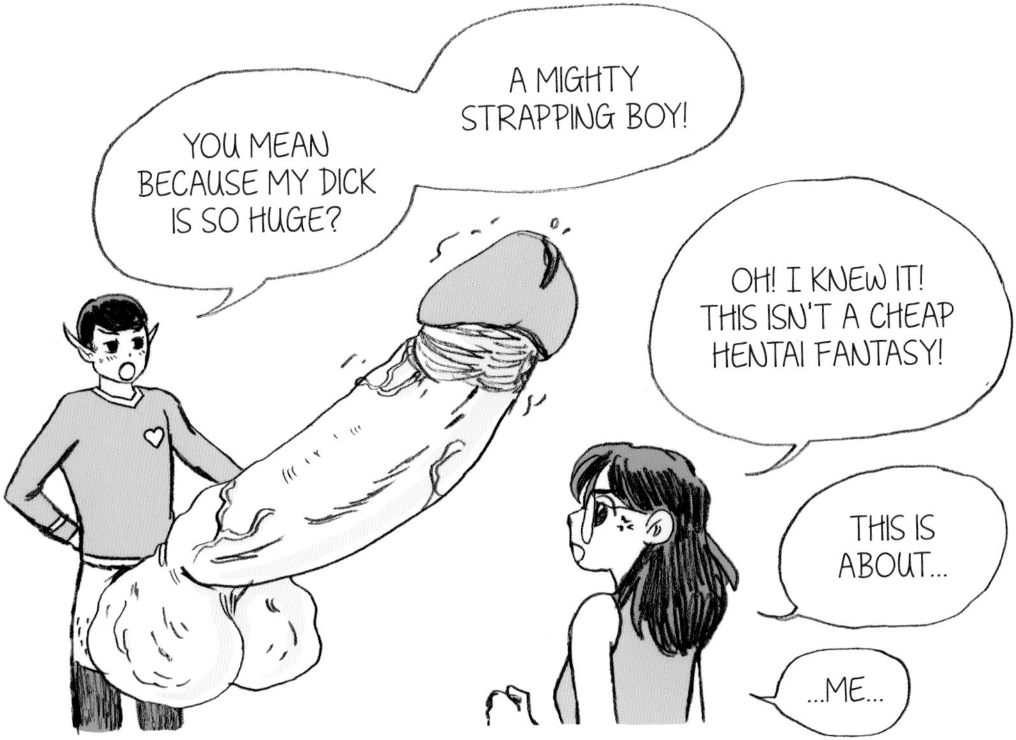
YOU MEAN BECAUSE MY DICK IS SO HUGE?
A MIGHTY STRAPPING BOY!
OH! I KNEW IT! THIS ISN'T A CHEAP HENTAI FANTASY!
THIS IS ABOUT...
...ME...

Then, at home, I came across the term "vaginismus"--a cramping of the vaginal muscles that makes the vagina feel closed. I was definitely cramped. And how! I wanted it to work. But under pressure, the cramping would only increase--as well as the wish to finally reward the man who had waited for so long to enter. I never thought of myself, it was always--

I'M TOTALLY BROKEN. MY VAGINA DOESN'T WORK.

It's absurd that I put up with pain instead of listening to myself and my body, which tried so desperately to tell me what I couldn't say back then: "No!" And--

I'M NOT READY YET. MAYBE WE COULD CUDDLE A BIT FIRST?

SOUNDS LOGICAL.

It's a shame that the word "sex," both when we say it and when we think it, is so often only associated with penetration. Language shapes reality. While sex can be so much more than the intrusion of a penis into a vagina, it often remains thought of as only penetration. For a man that can be very satisfying, but the arousal center of the woman, the clitoris, isn't stimulated by it. Ergo: Most women can't orgasm from vaginal intercourse.

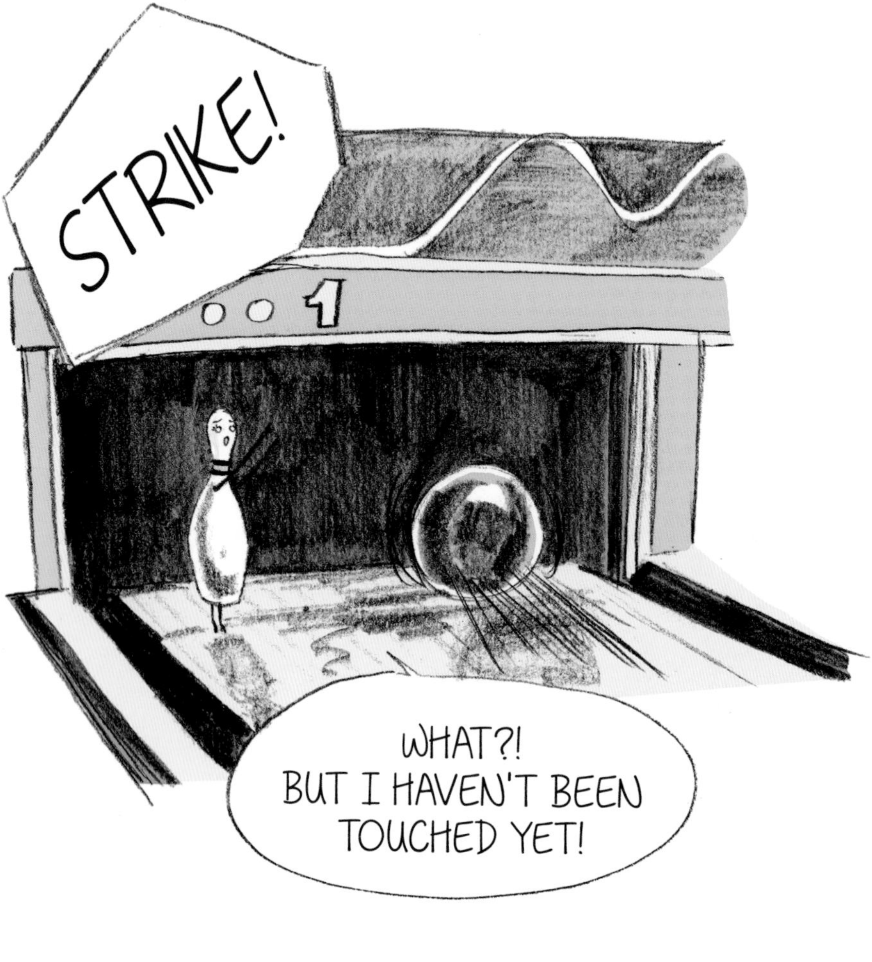
STRIKE!
1
WHAT?!
BUT I HAVEN'T BEEN
TOUCHED YET!

Most of the time, the clitoris is only stimulated during that short span of time that we call "foreplay." Often, though, my experience has been that foreplay is supposed to just lead into the actual act, where suddenly the pressure to worry about my partner's orgasm is back. Which is why I join in with the moaning to end sex more quickly. Wouldn't it be nice if the first time having sex didn't mean the first time with penetration, but instead the first jointly experienced orgasm?

THIS FOREPLAY WILL DEFINITELY HAVE AN ENCORE...HEEHEE

WHEN WILL YOU FINALLY ADMIT THAT YOU'RE ACTUALLY FROM THE PLANET VULVAN?!

FASCINATING...

The clitoris has 8,000 nerve endings. The penis glans, in comparison, has 4,000. So it's not more difficult for a woman to have an orgasm, it's clearly just harder to talk about it. You all must have noticed it--all these terms often sound medical. But it's **how** we talk that evokes desire! It's like a meal. The difference in enjoyment, whether we say:

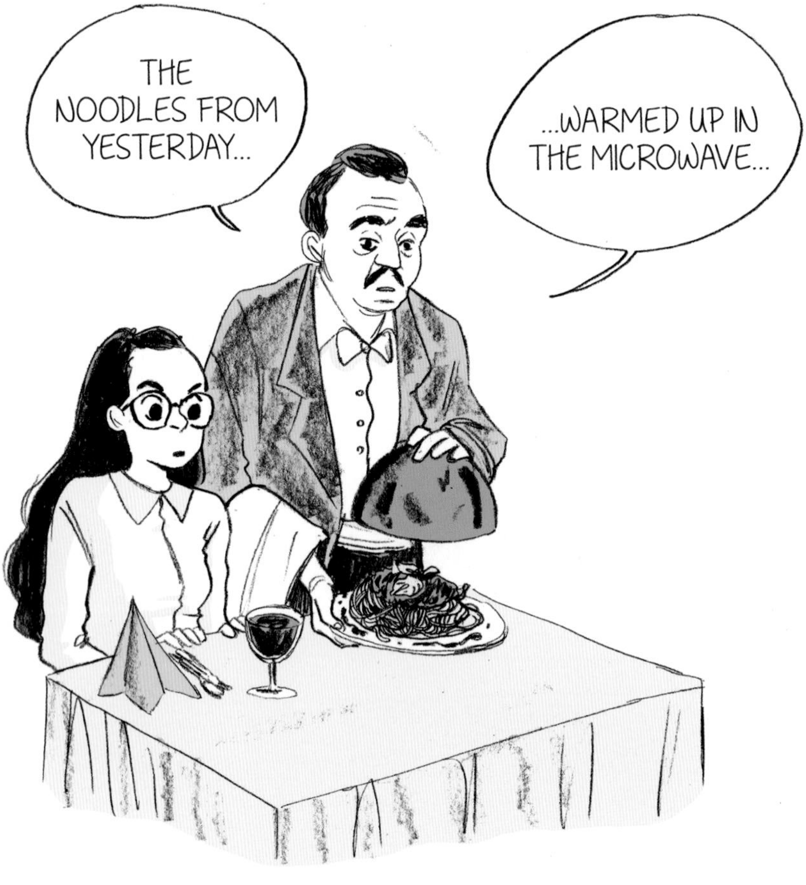
THE NOODLES FROM YESTERDAY...
...WARMED UP IN THE MICROWAVE...

Or whether we acknowledge that appetite comes before the food, and we say:

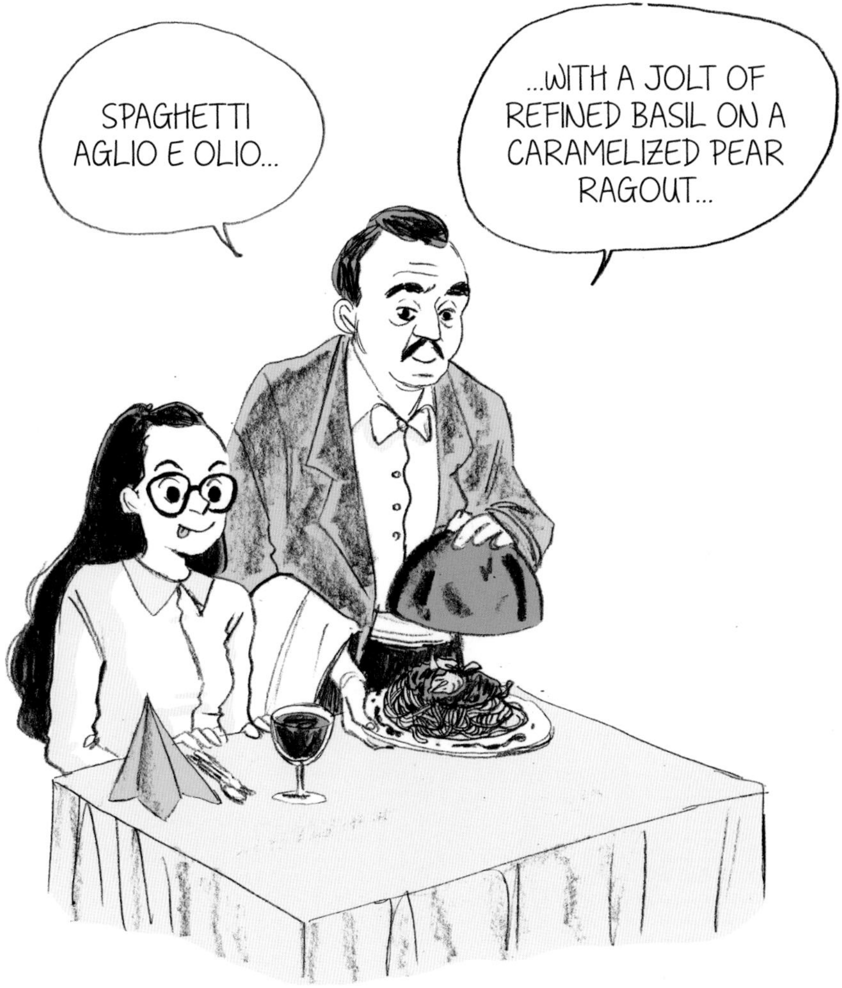
SPAGHETTI AGLIO E OLIO...
...WITH A JOLT OF REFINED BASIL ON A CARAMELIZED PEAR RAGOUT...

The vagina is the tubular part of the sex organ, and it goes from the vaginal entrance to the inside of the body. The vulva is the external, primary sex characteristic. Well--labia, pubic mound, clitoris. If we incorporated "vulva" into our day-to-day language, we'd also incorporate women's lust into our language, and with it, into our sex lives. And that seems fair to me.

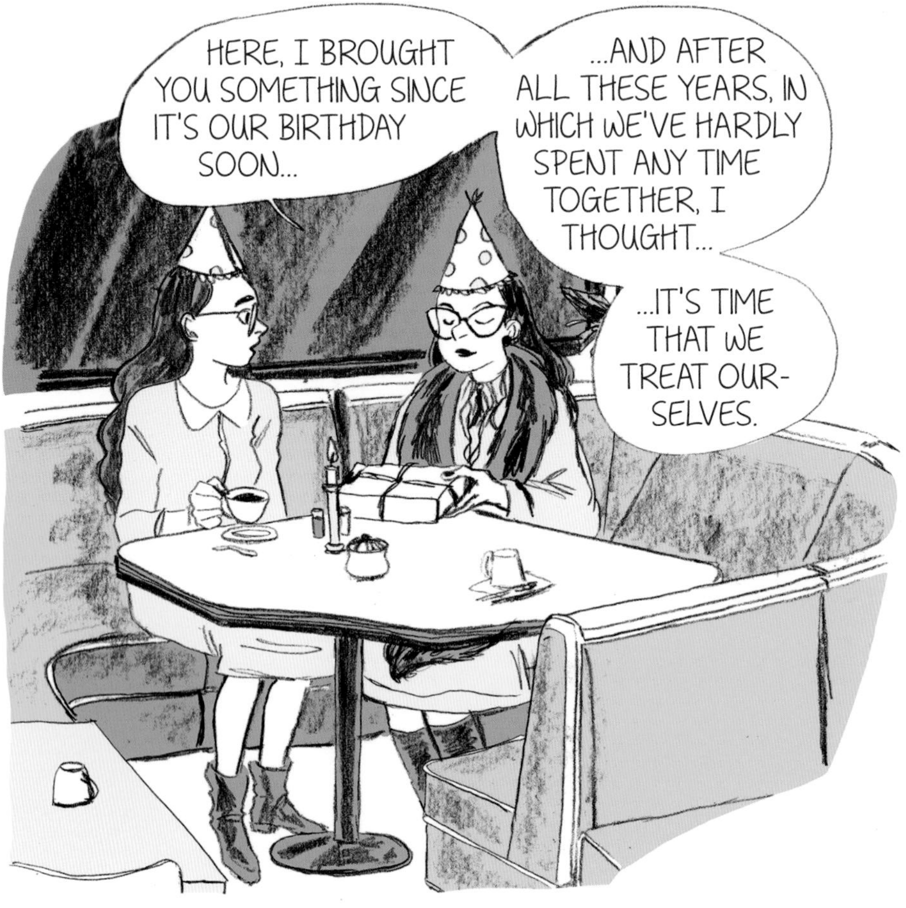
HERE, I BROUGHT YOU SOMETHING SINCE IT'S OUR BIRTHDAY SOON...
...AND AFTER ALL THESE YEARS, IN WHICH WE'VE HARDLY SPENT ANY TIME TOGETHER, I THOUGHT...
...IT'S TIME THAT WE TREAT OURSELVES.

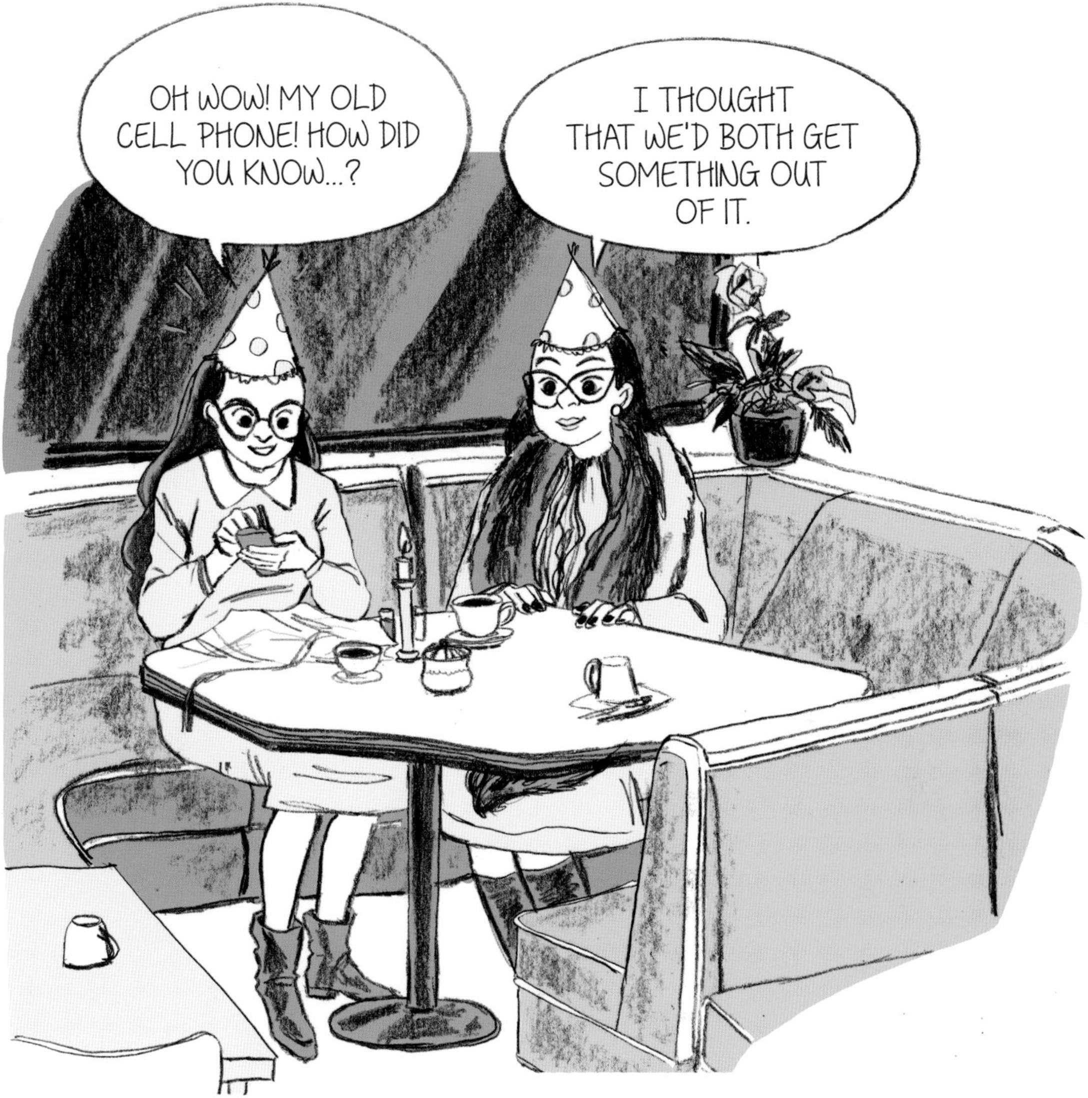
OH WOW! MY OLD CELL PHONE! HOW DID YOU KNOW...?
I THOUGHT THAT WE'D BOTH GET SOMETHING OUT OF IT.

It's like so many words that sound strange when you first hear them. The more often you say them, the more naturally they fall from your lips. Okay, now let's all say "vulva" loud and clear.

I'll help! On three! 1, 2, 3...

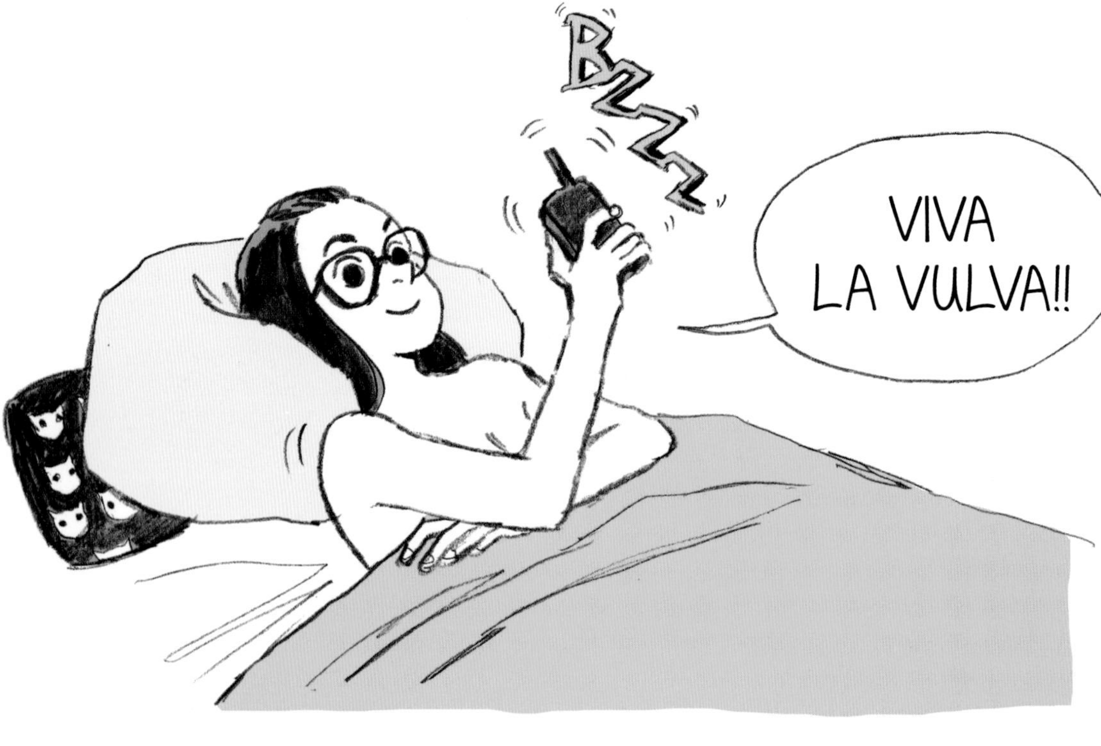
BZZZ
VIVA LA VULVA!!

The Toy Trap

When I was very young, I had to stay alone in a hospital for several days. It was an old, creepy building, and at night the branches of a willow whipped against the window panes. When my parents came to visit me, they brought me my very first Barbie doll, and I forgot about my fear. Even today, toys are a healing, comforting thing for me.

Friends who know me well know that I love toys. Other people who come to visit find me strange sometimes, because I store toys in a glass showcase. Before, I used to hide my passion for collecting, and I would hang a blanket over the case. This only made me look more strange.

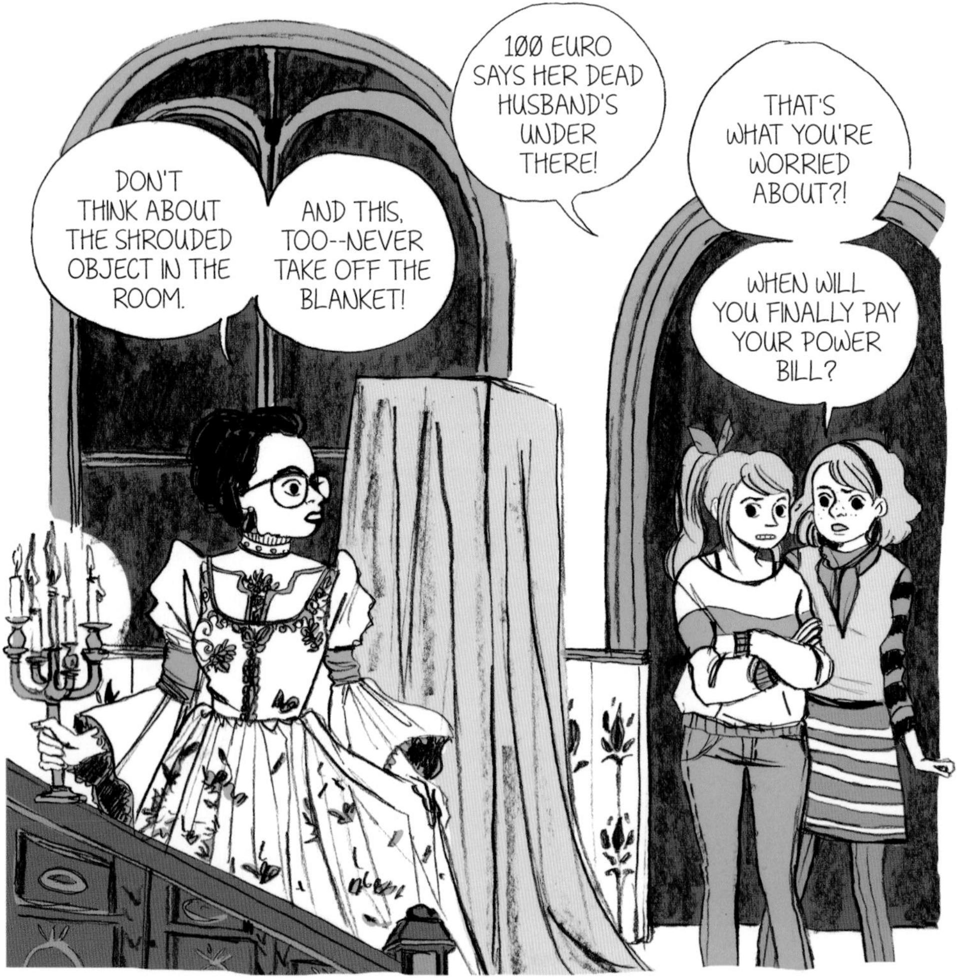
DON'T THINK ABOUT THE SHROUDED OBJECT IN THE ROOM.
AND THIS, TOO--NEVER TAKE OFF THE BLANKET!
100 EURO SAYS HER DEAD HUSBAND'S UNDER THERE!
THAT'S WHAT YOU'RE WORRIED ABOUT?!
WHEN WILL YOU FINALLY PAY YOUR POWER BILL?

Nowadays I make no secret of my passion for collecting. Just the opposite!

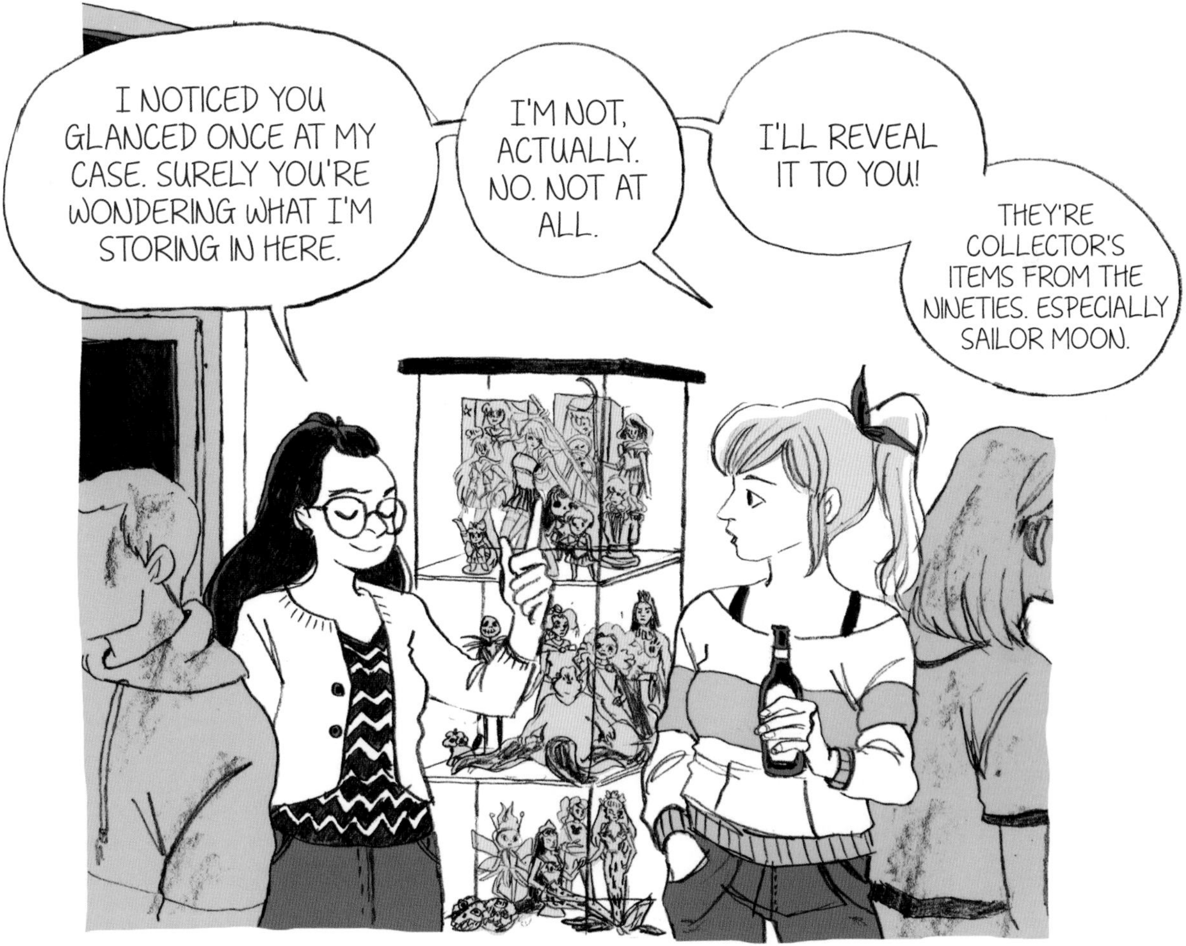
I NOTICED YOU GLANCED ONCE AT MY CASE. SURELY YOU'RE WONDERING WHAT I'M STORING IN HERE.
I'M NOT, ACTUALLY. NO. NOT AT ALL.
I'LL REVEAL IT TO YOU!
THEY'RE COLLECTOR'S ITEMS FROM THE NINETIES. ESPECIALLY SAILOR MOON.

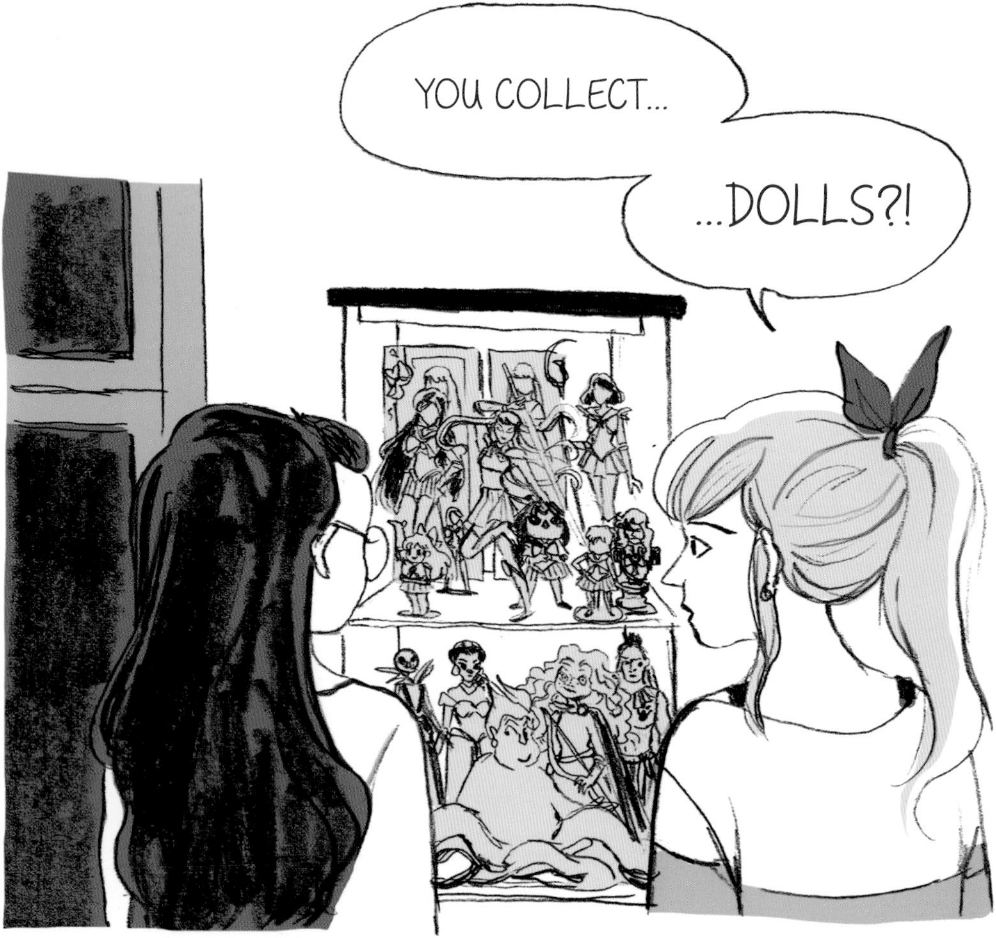
YOU COLLECT...
...DOLLS?!

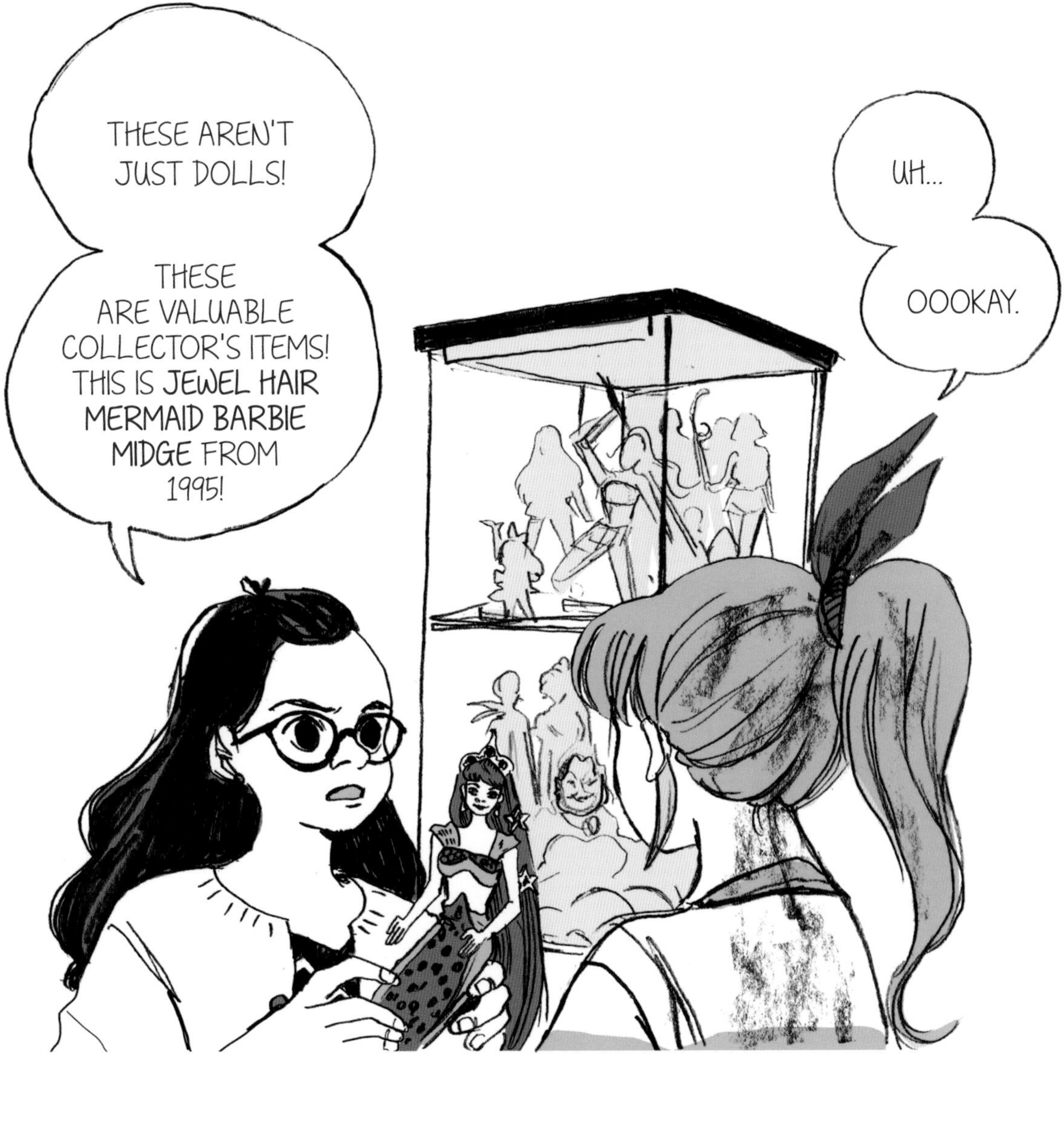
THESE AREN'T JUST DOLLS!
THESE ARE VALUABLE COLLECTOR'S ITEMS! THIS IS JEWEL HAIR MERMAID BARBIE MIDGE FROM 1995!
UH...
OOOKAY.

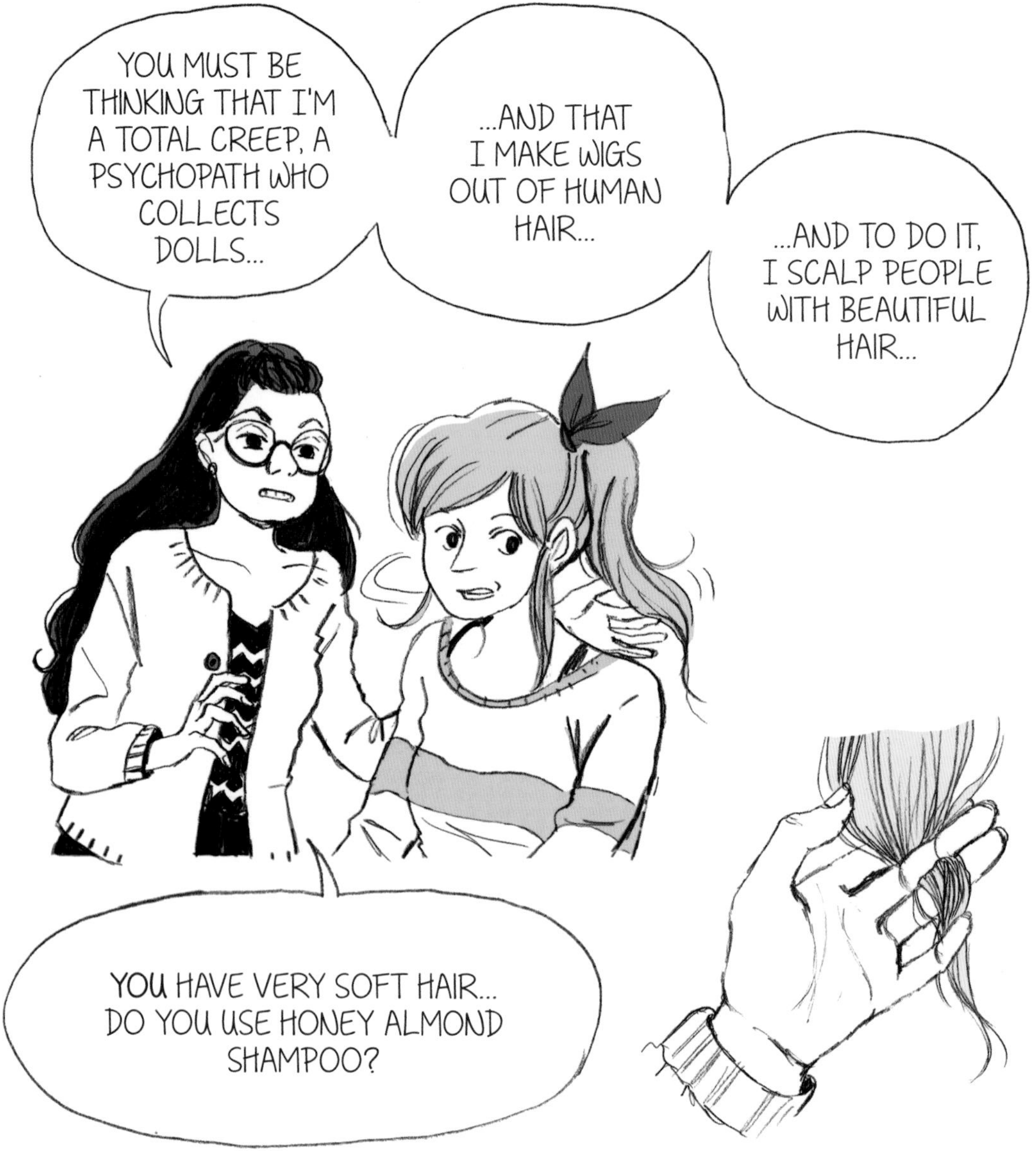
YOU MUST BE THINKING THAT I'M A TOTAL CREEP, A PSYCHOPATH WHO COLLECTS DOLLS...
...AND THAT I MAKE WIGS OUT OF HUMAN HAIR...
...AND TO DO IT, I SCALP PEOPLE WITH BEAUTIFUL HAIR...
YOU HAVE VERY SOFT HAIR... DO YOU USE HONEY ALMOND SHAMPOO?

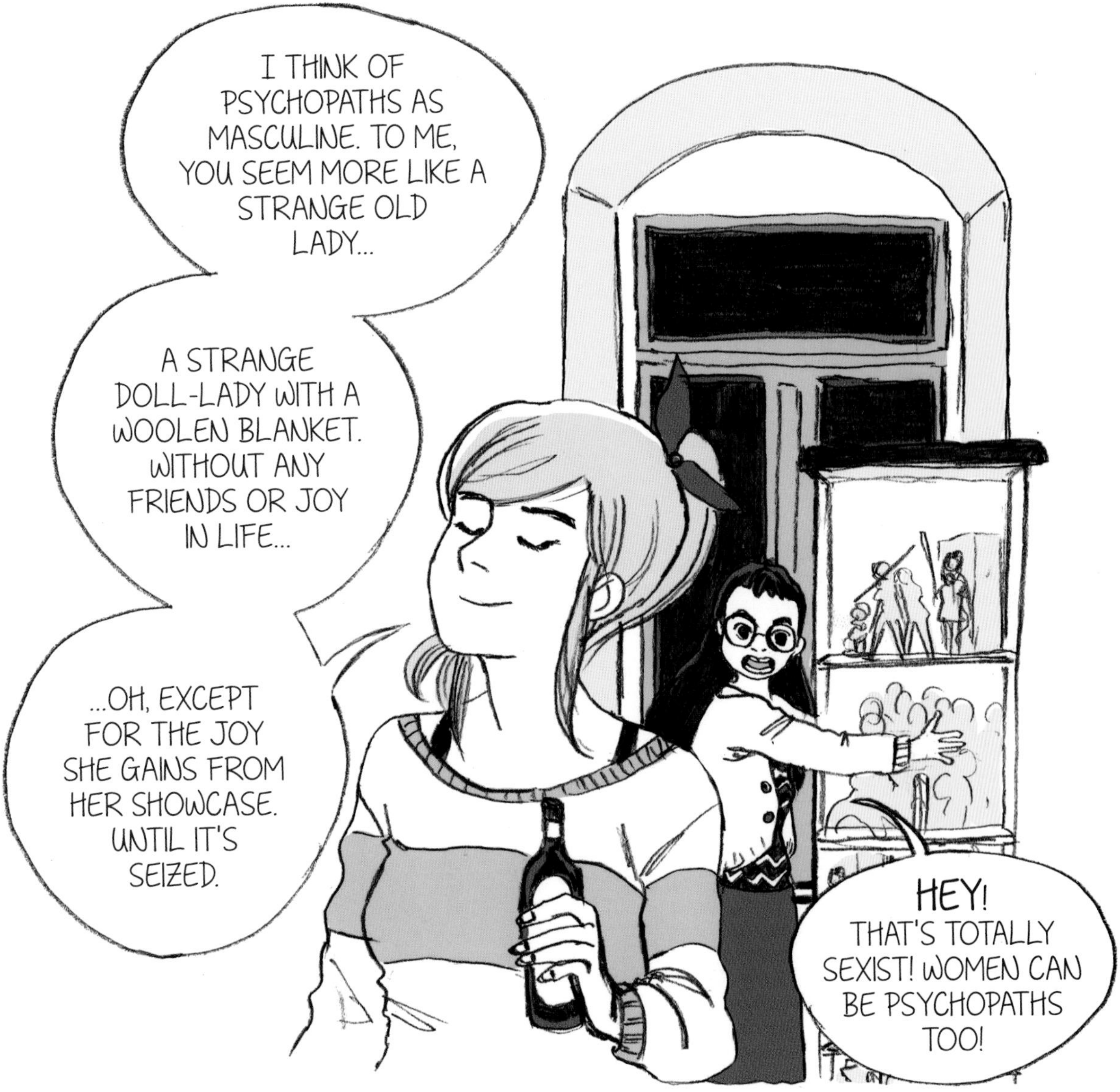
I THINK OF PSYCHOPATHS AS MASCULINE. TO ME, YOU SEEM MORE LIKE A STRANGE OLD LADY...
A STRANGE DOLL-LADY WITH A WOOLEN BLANKET. WITHOUT ANY FRIENDS OR JOY IN LIFE...
...OH, EXCEPT FOR THE JOY SHE GAINS FROM HER SHOWCASE. UNTIL IT'S SEIZED.
HEY! THAT'S TOTALLY SEXIST! WOMEN CAN BE PSYCHOPATHS TOO!

As a child, I had thousands of Barbies! I could play out truly epic tales with them. From the outside, my games must have looked innocent. After all, dolls are "only" something for girls.

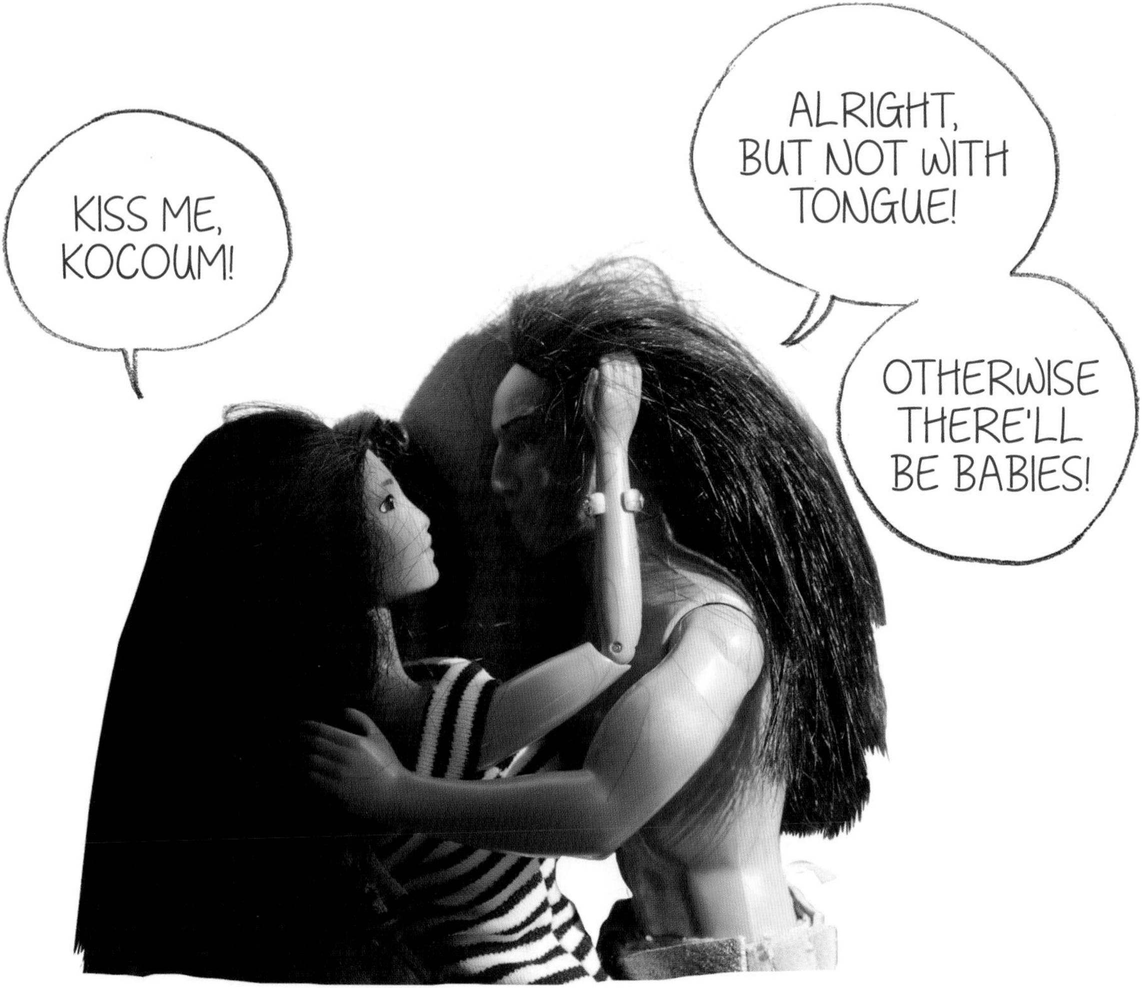
KISS ME, KOCOUM!
ALRIGHT, BUT NOT WITH TONGUE!
OTHERWISE THERE'LL BE BABIES!

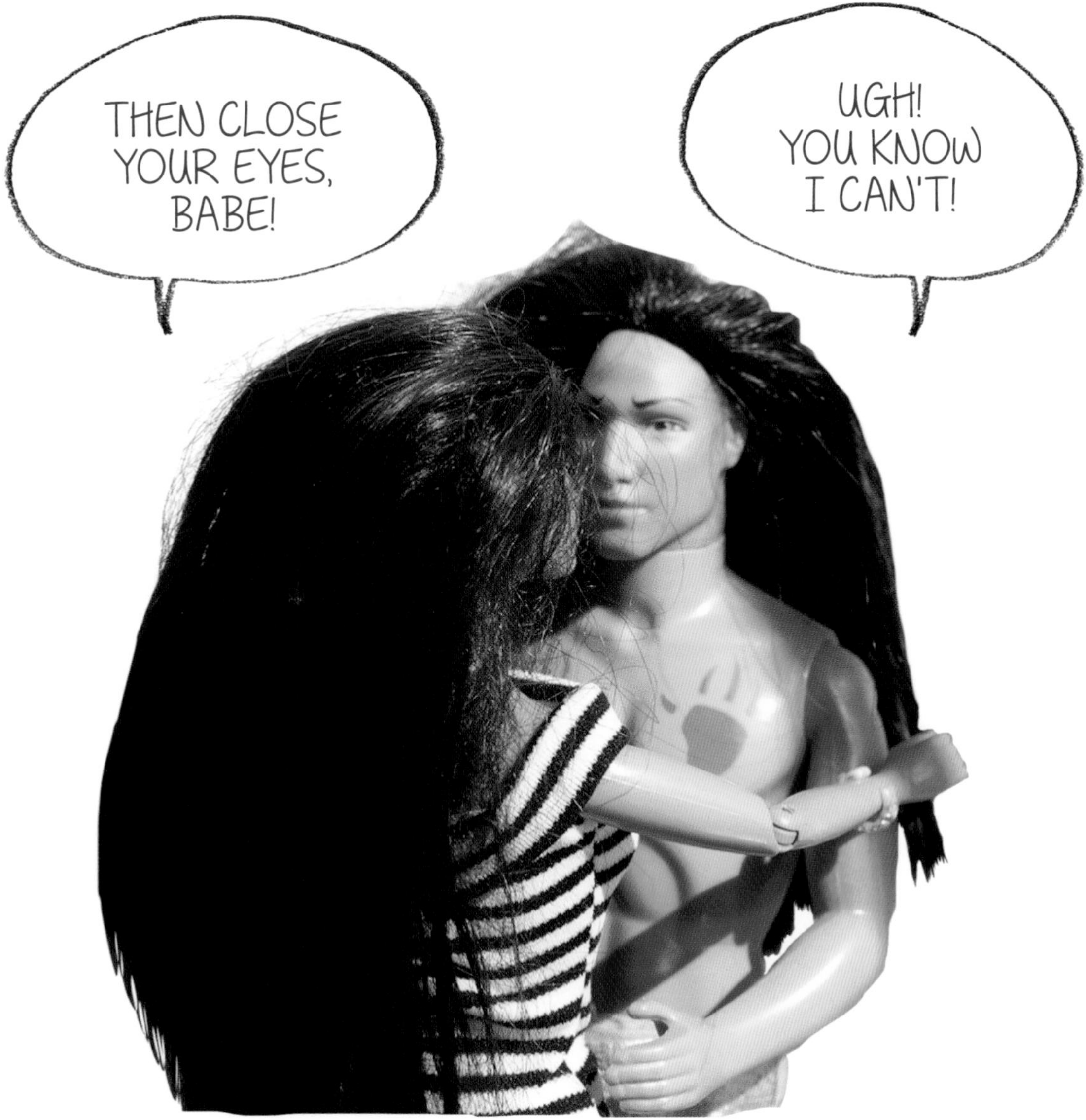
THEN CLOSE YOUR EYES, BABE!
UGH! YOU KNOW I CAN'T!

Looking closer, my games were actually a lot more intense...

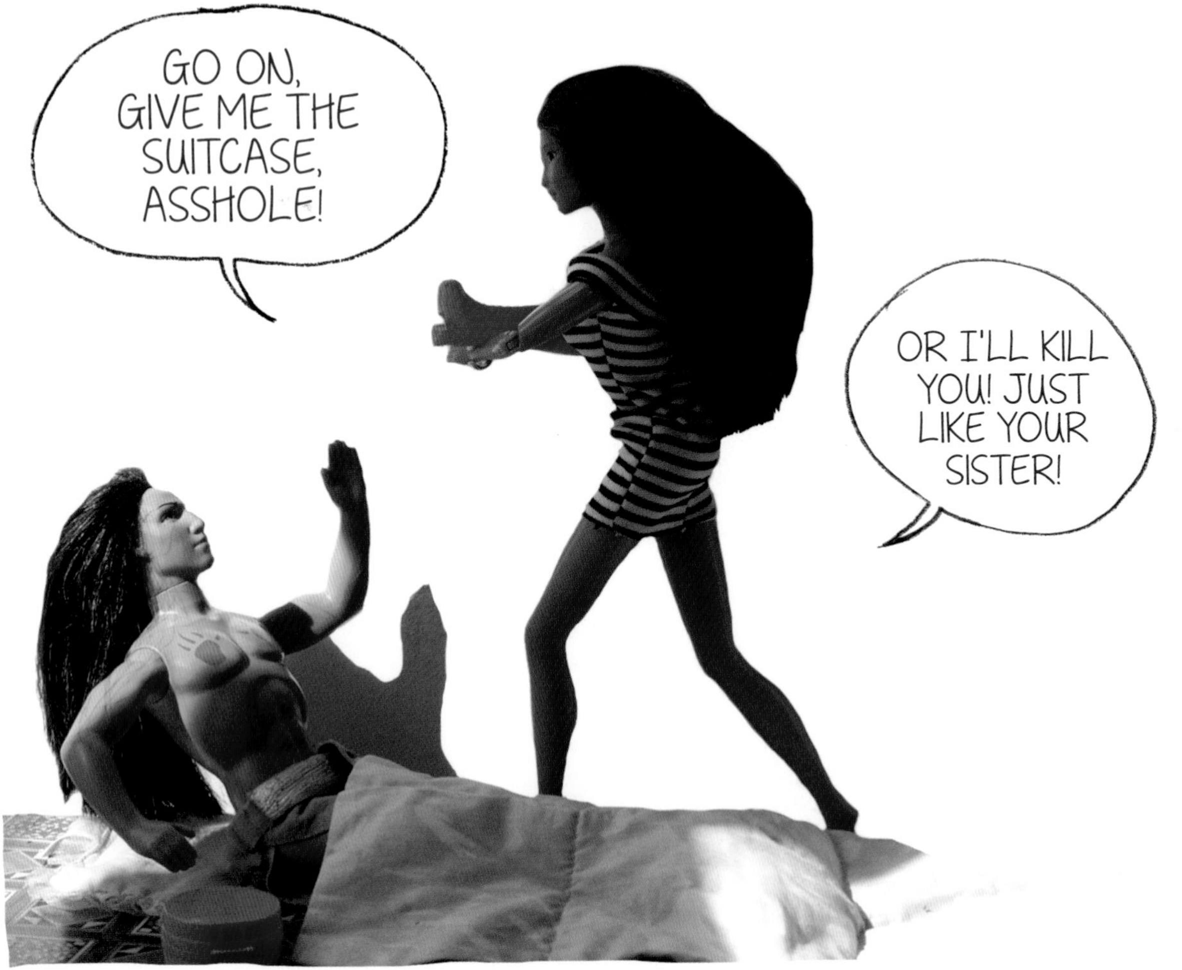

GO ON, GIVE ME THE SUITCASE, ASSHOLE!
OR I'LL KILL YOU! JUST LIKE YOUR SISTER!

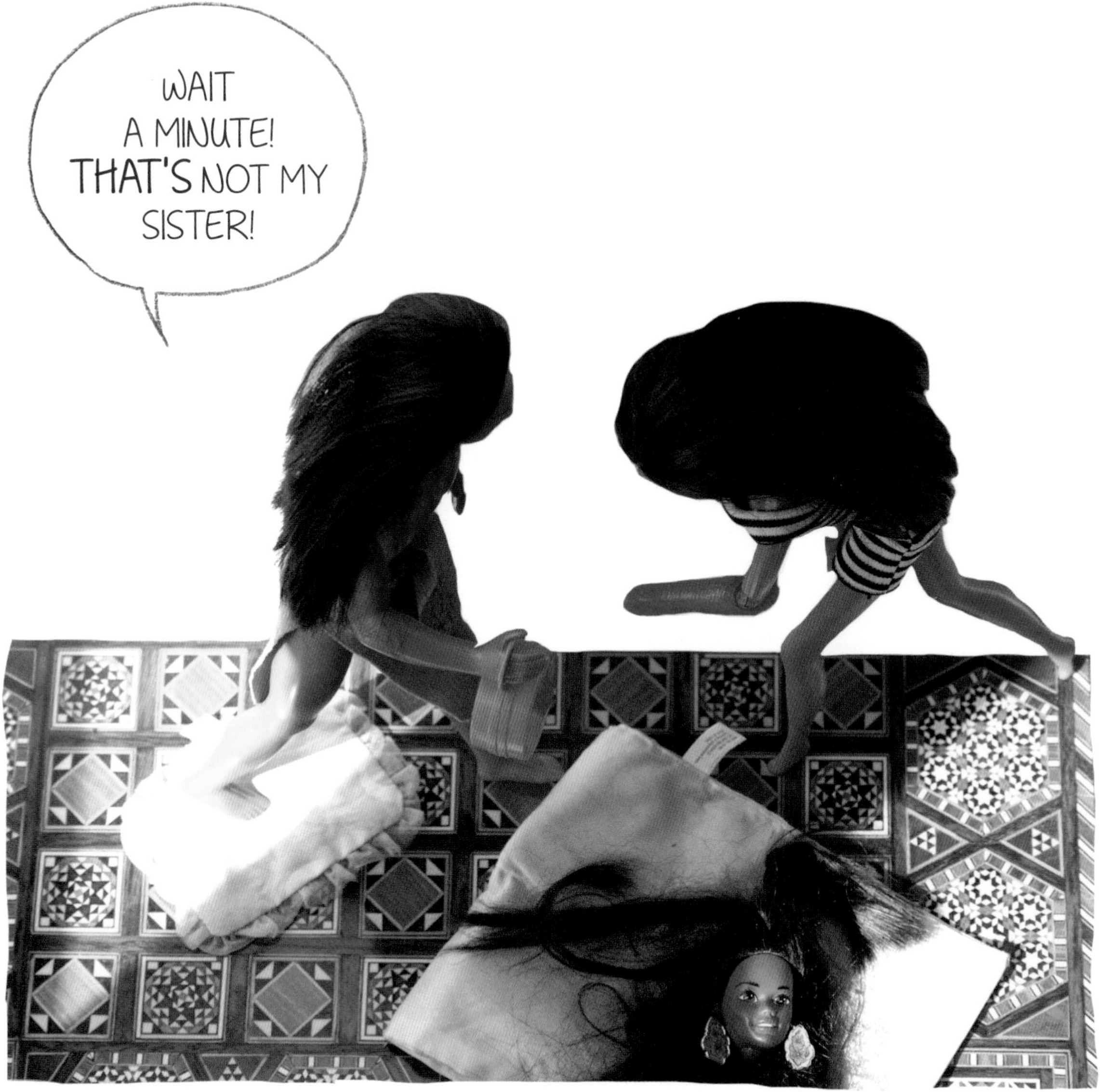
WAIT A MINUTE! THAT'S NOT MY SISTER!

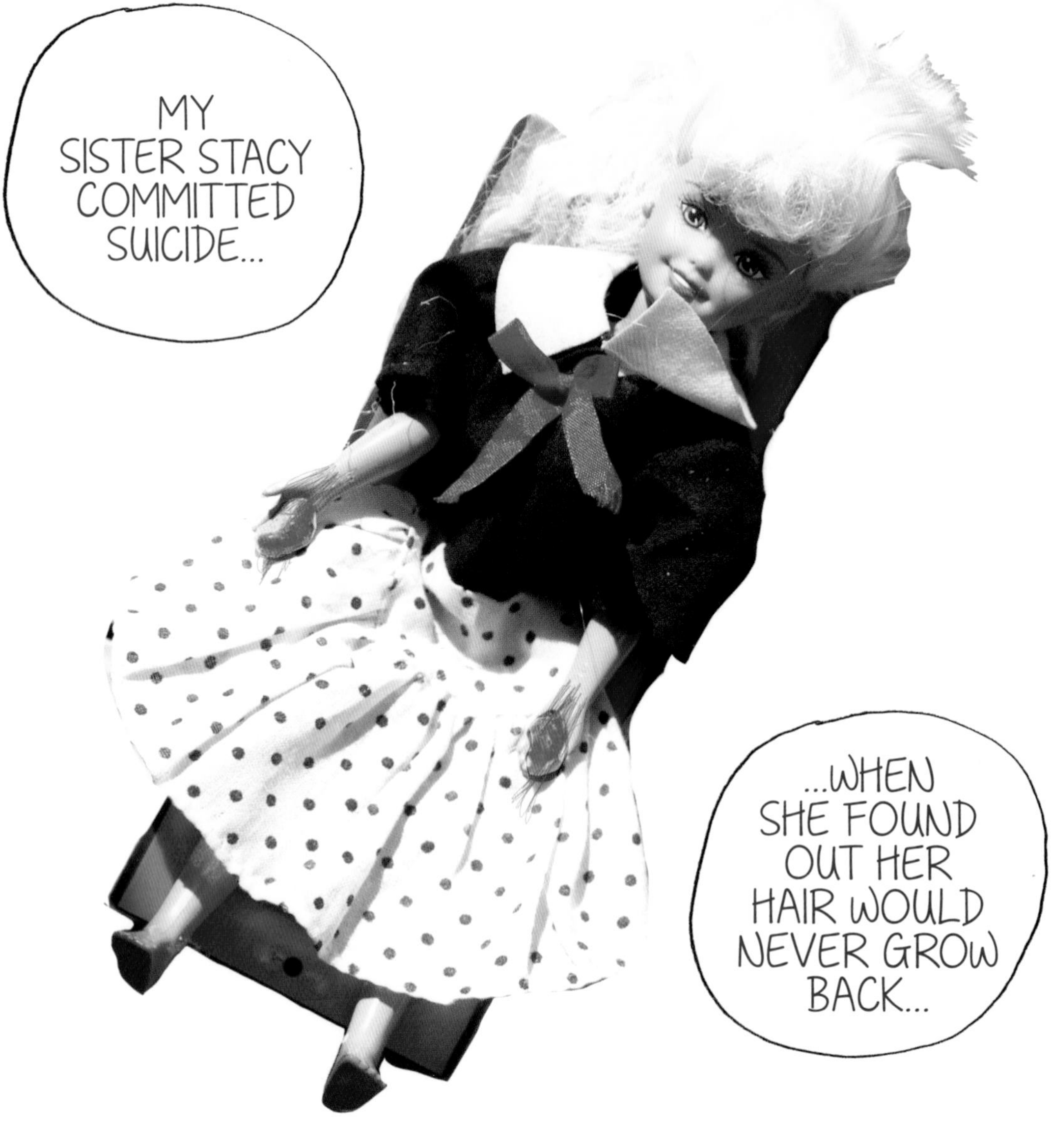
MY SISTER STACY COMMITTED SUICIDE...
...WHEN SHE FOUND OUT HER HAIR WOULD NEVER GROW BACK...

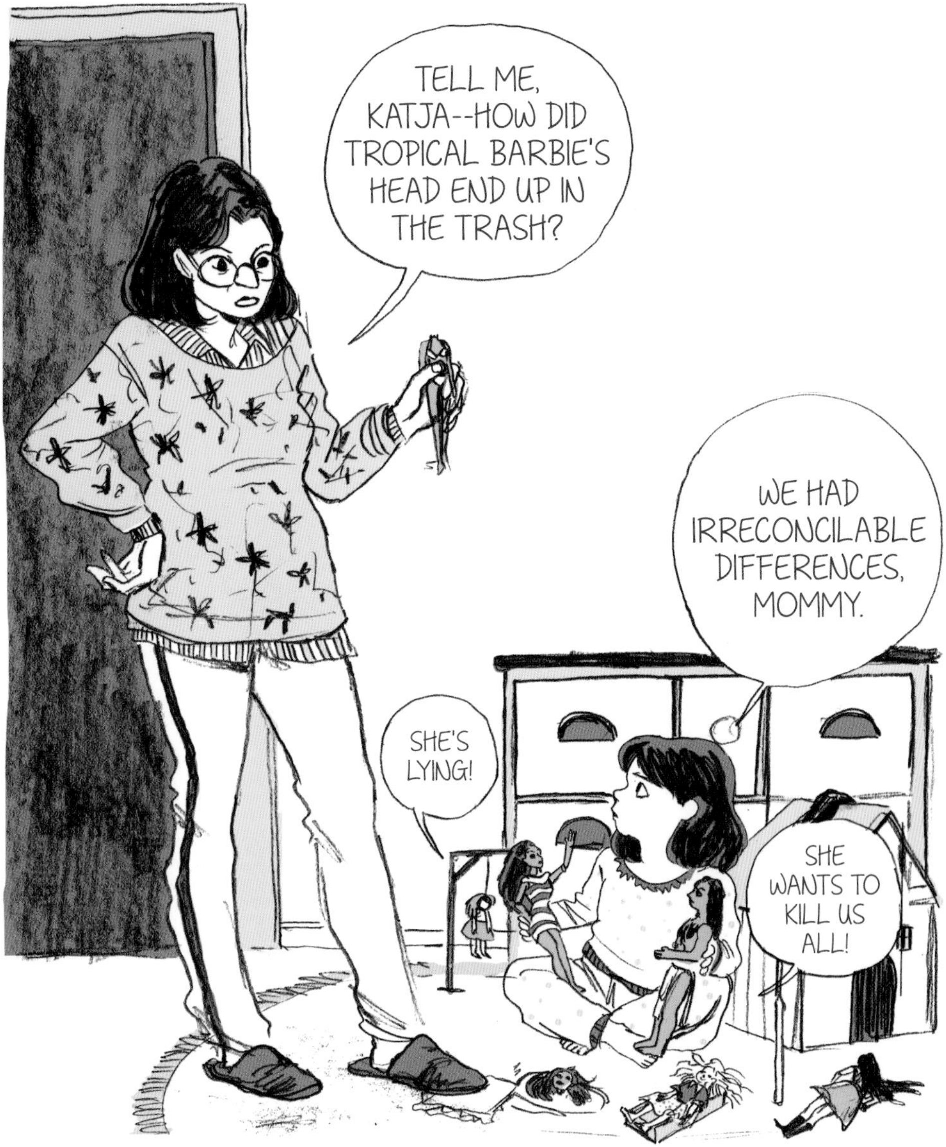
TELL ME, KATJA--HOW DID TROPICAL BARBIE'S HEAD END UP IN THE TRASH?
WE HAD IRRECONCILABLE DIFFERENCES, MOMMY.
SHE'S LYING!
SHE WANTS TO KILL US ALL!

You can also play great war battles in Legos. My brother had this cool knight's castle with a drawbridge, a dragon, and a wizard.

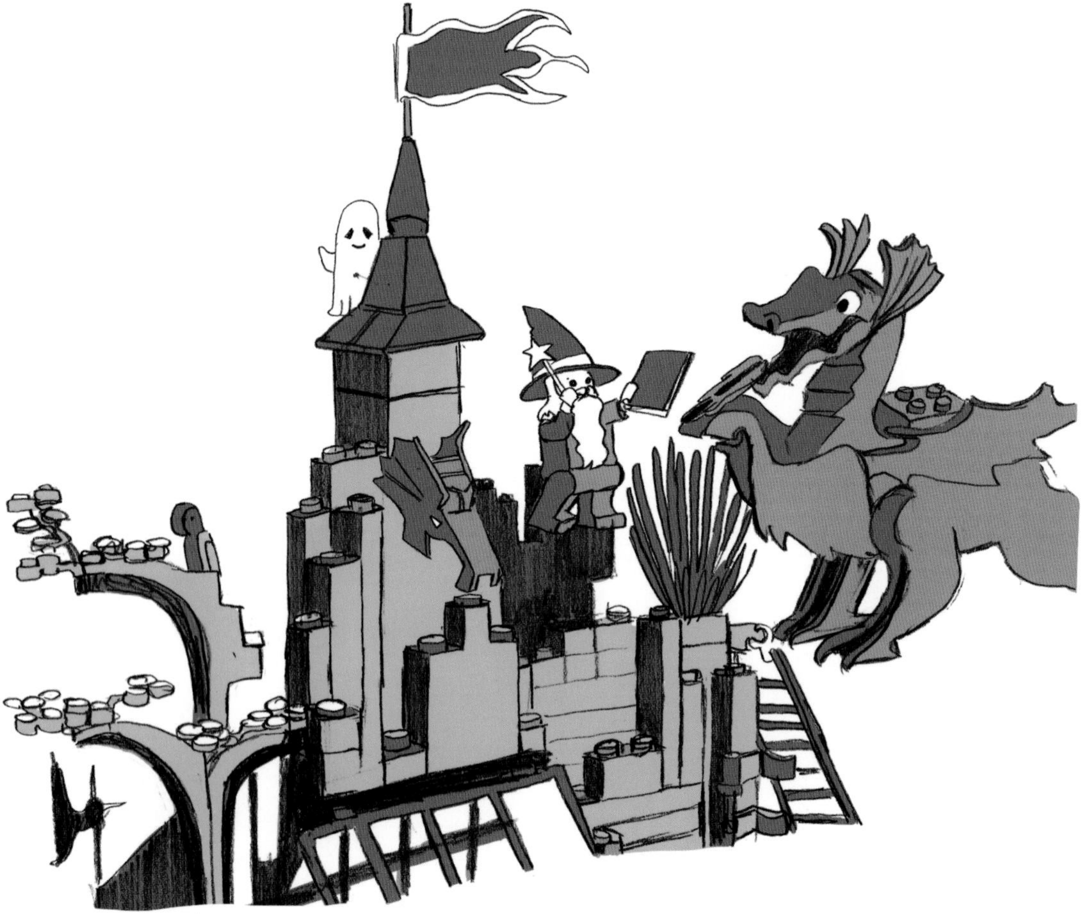

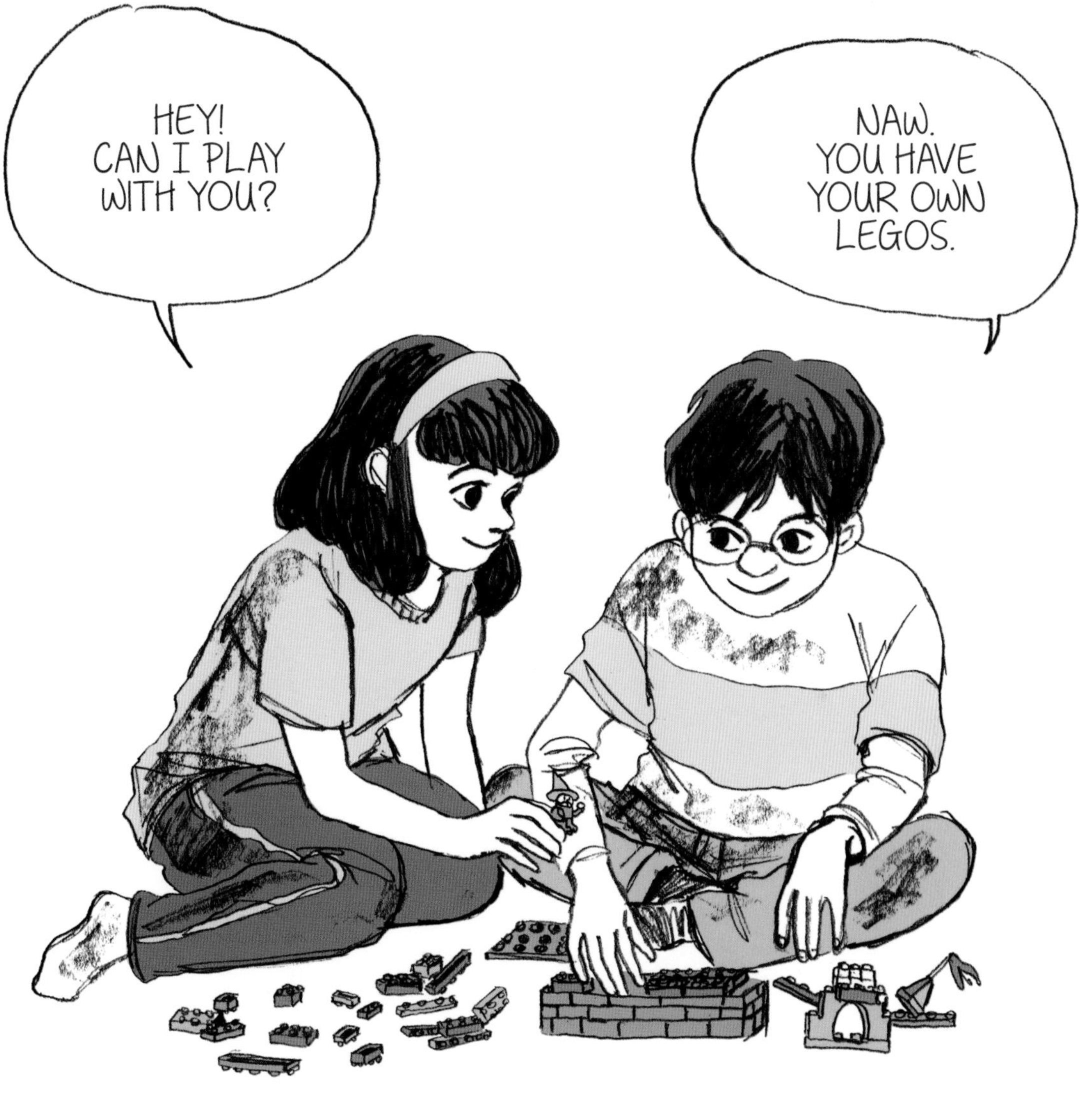
HEY!
CAN I PLAY
WITH YOU?
NAW.
YOU HAVE
YOUR OWN
LEGOS.

I had exactly **one** Lego set. It was intended for girls and it was quite pink. Instead of a dragon and a drawbridge, there was a beach bar and a girl surfer. (And this weird dude in a boat.)

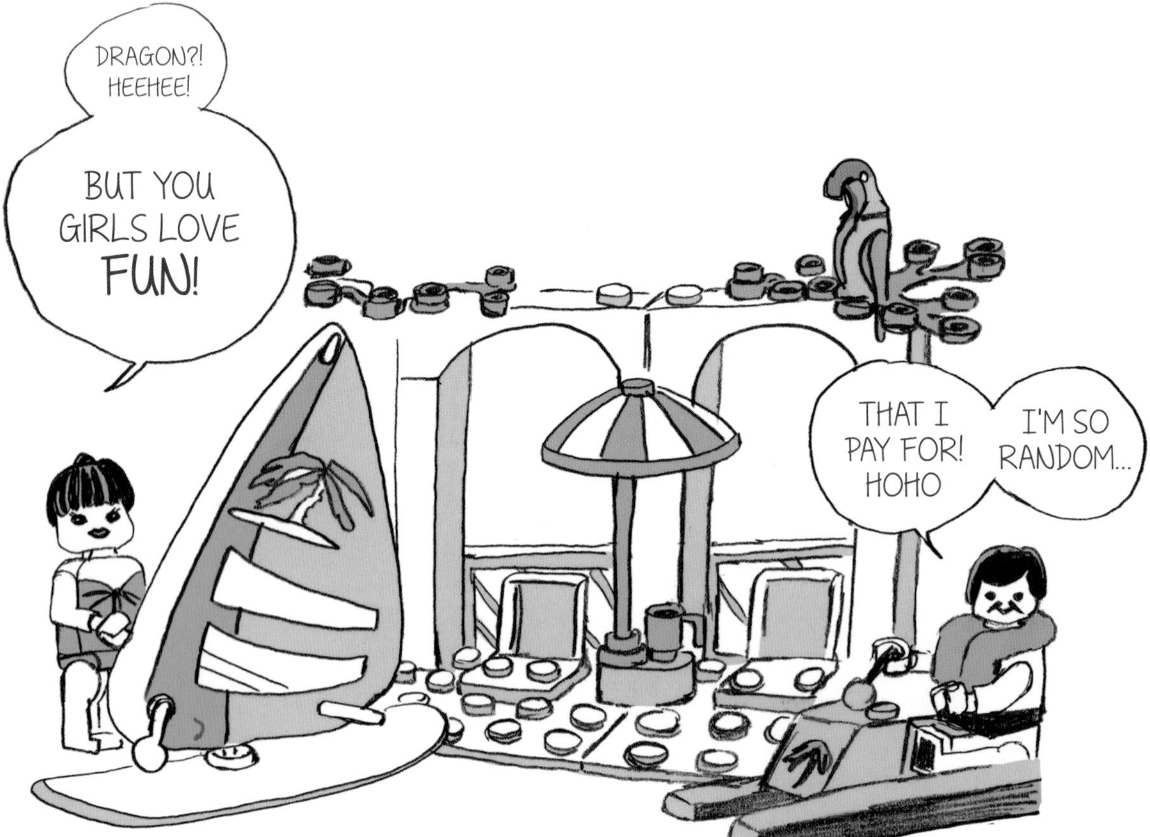

DRAGON?! HEEHEE!
BUT YOU GIRLS LOVE **FUN**!
THAT I PAY FOR! HOHO
I'M SO RANDOM...

Since I, of course, already understood the complexity of the toy industry and their gender marketing techniques, according to whose power structures I was supposed to be fed "girl toys," I tried reasonably to clarify the matter with my brother...

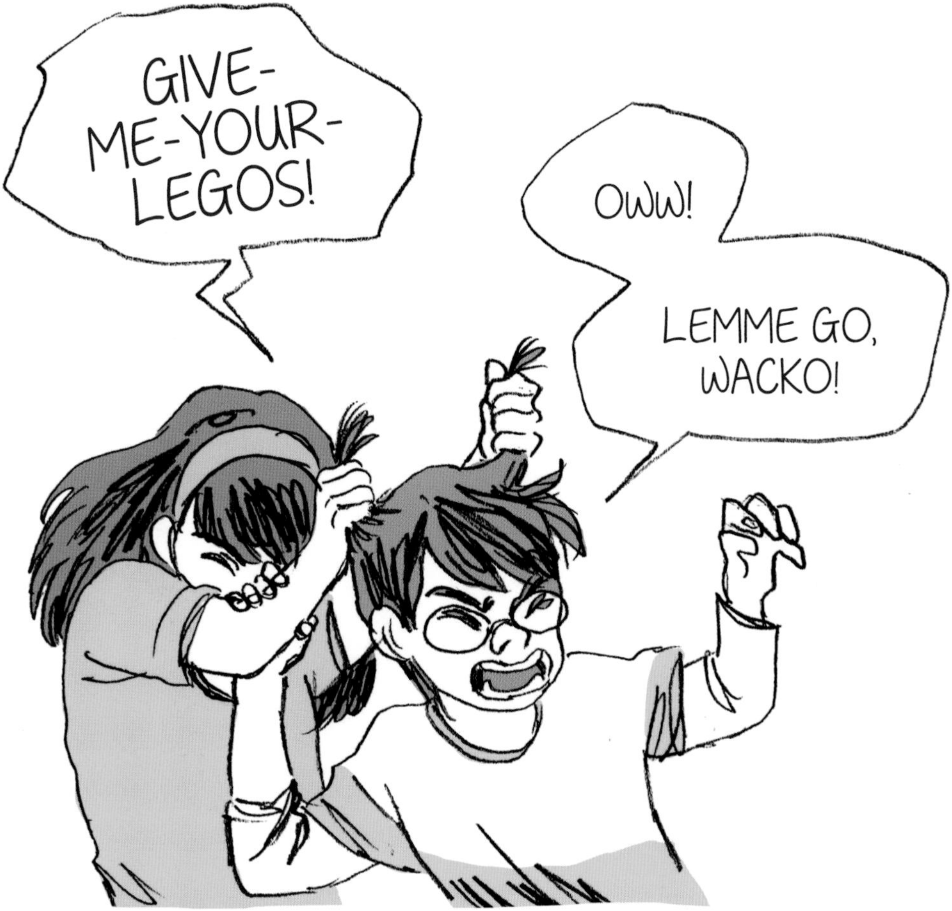

GIVE-ME-YOUR-LEGOS!
OWW!
LEMME GO, WACKO!

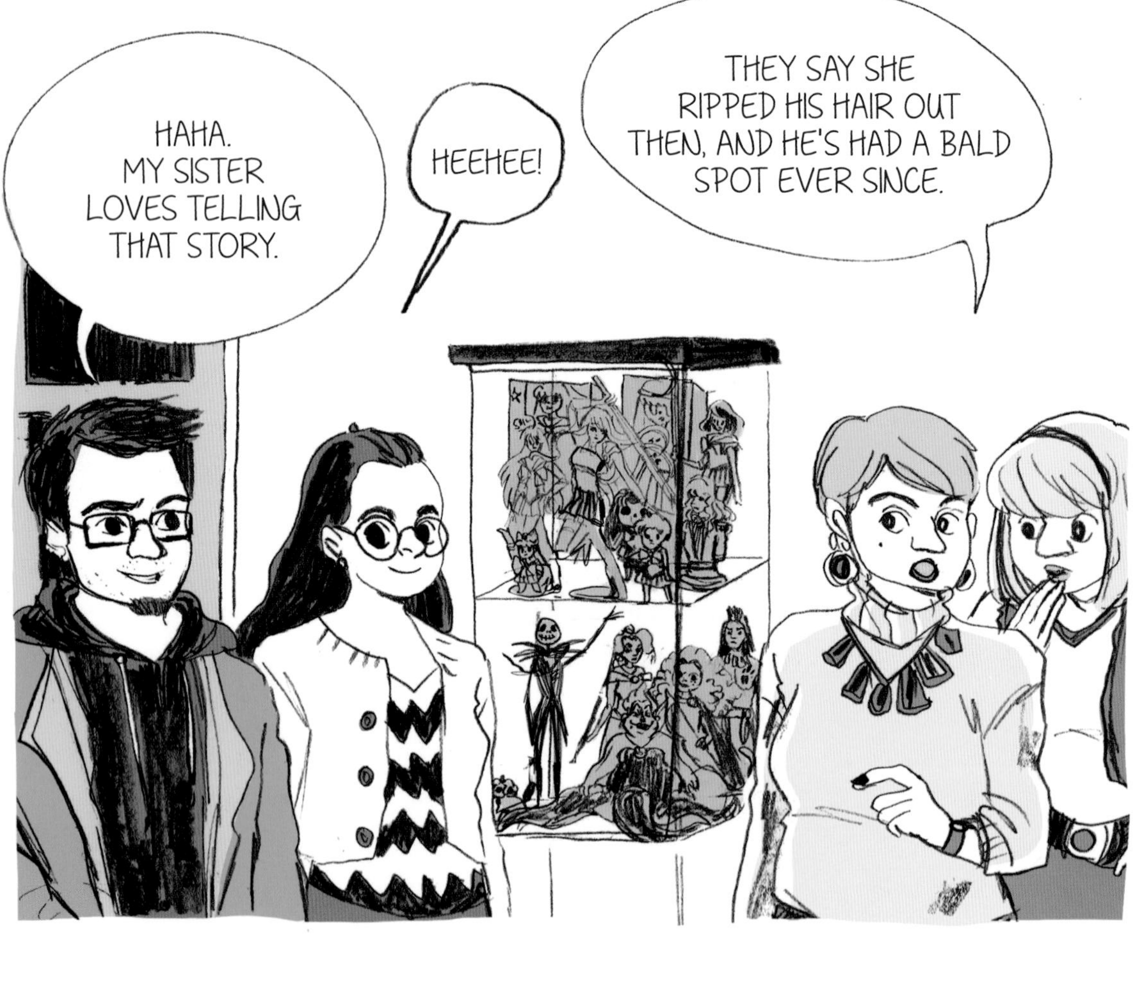
HAHA. MY SISTER LOVES TELLING THAT STORY.
HEEHEE!
THEY SAY SHE RIPPED HIS HAIR OUT THEN, AND HE'S HAD A BALD SPOT EVER SINCE.

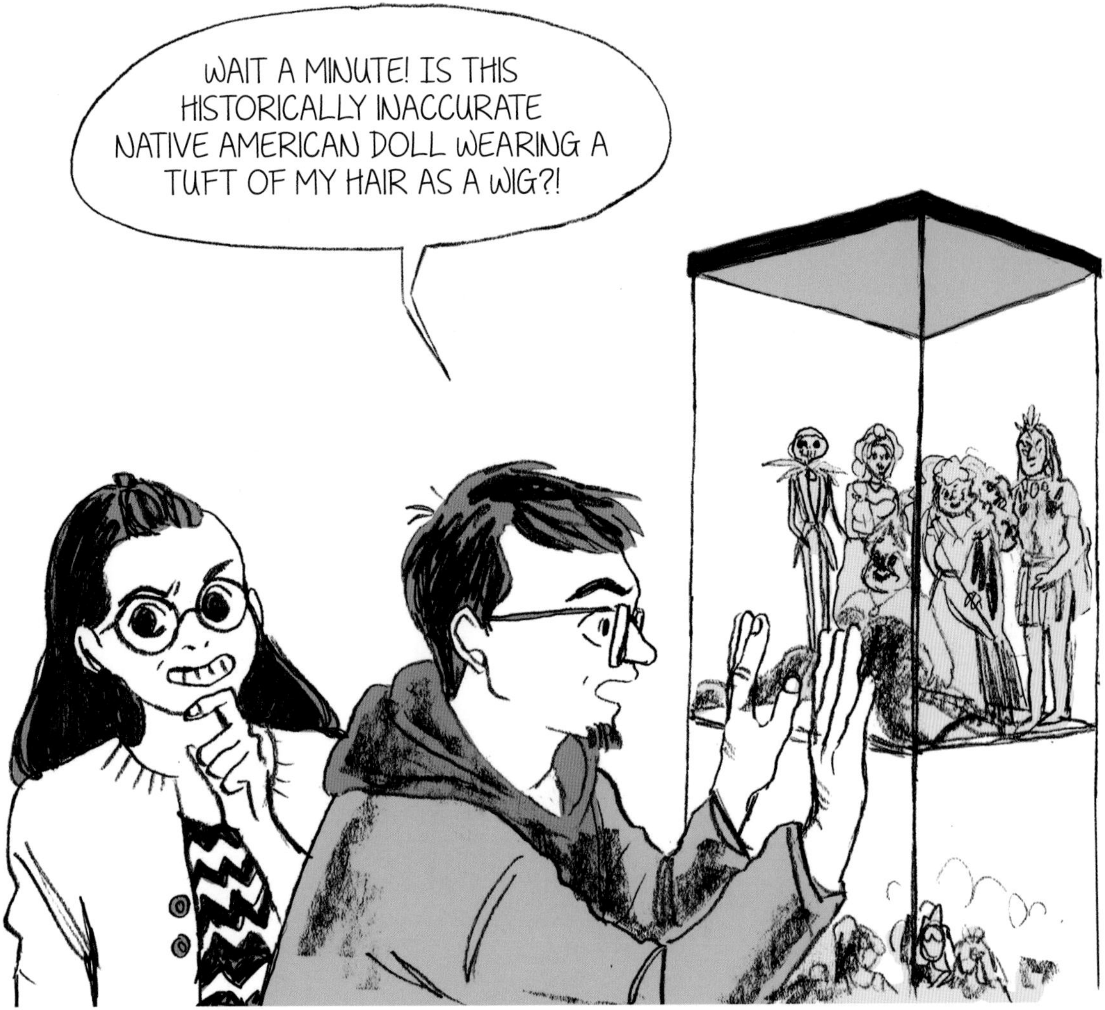
WAIT A MINUTE! IS THIS HISTORICALLY INACCURATE NATIVE AMERICAN DOLL WEARING A TUFT OF MY HAIR AS A WIG?!

I still love going into a toy store today. But I have the impression that the separation between "girls'" and "boys'" toys has grown even more rigid.

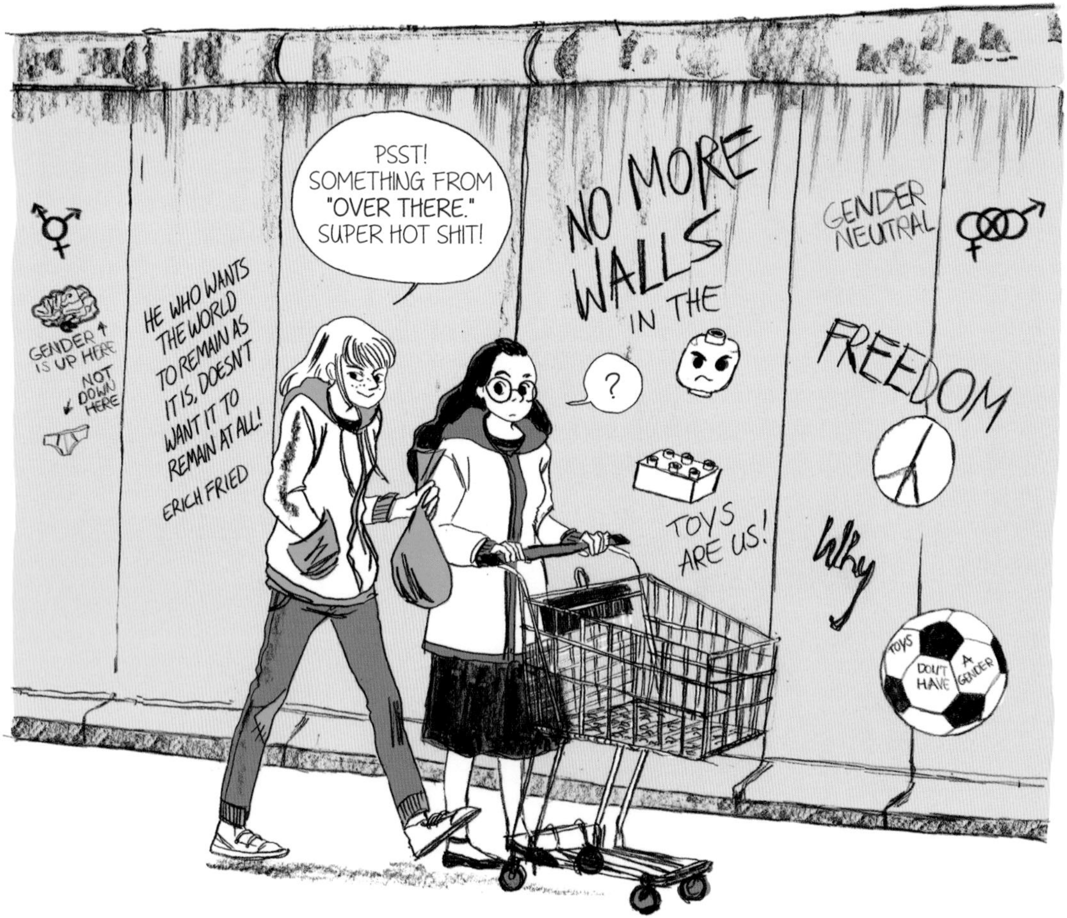
PSST! SOMETHING FROM "OVER THERE." SUPER HOT SHIT!
?
NO MORE WALLS IN THE
FREEDOM
GENDER NEUTRAL
GENDER IS UP HERE
NOT DOWN HERE
HE WHO WANTS THE WORLD TO REMAIN AS IT IS, DOESN'T WANT IT TO REMAIN AT ALL!
ERICH FRIED
TOYS ARE US!
Why
TOYS DON'T HAVE A GENDER

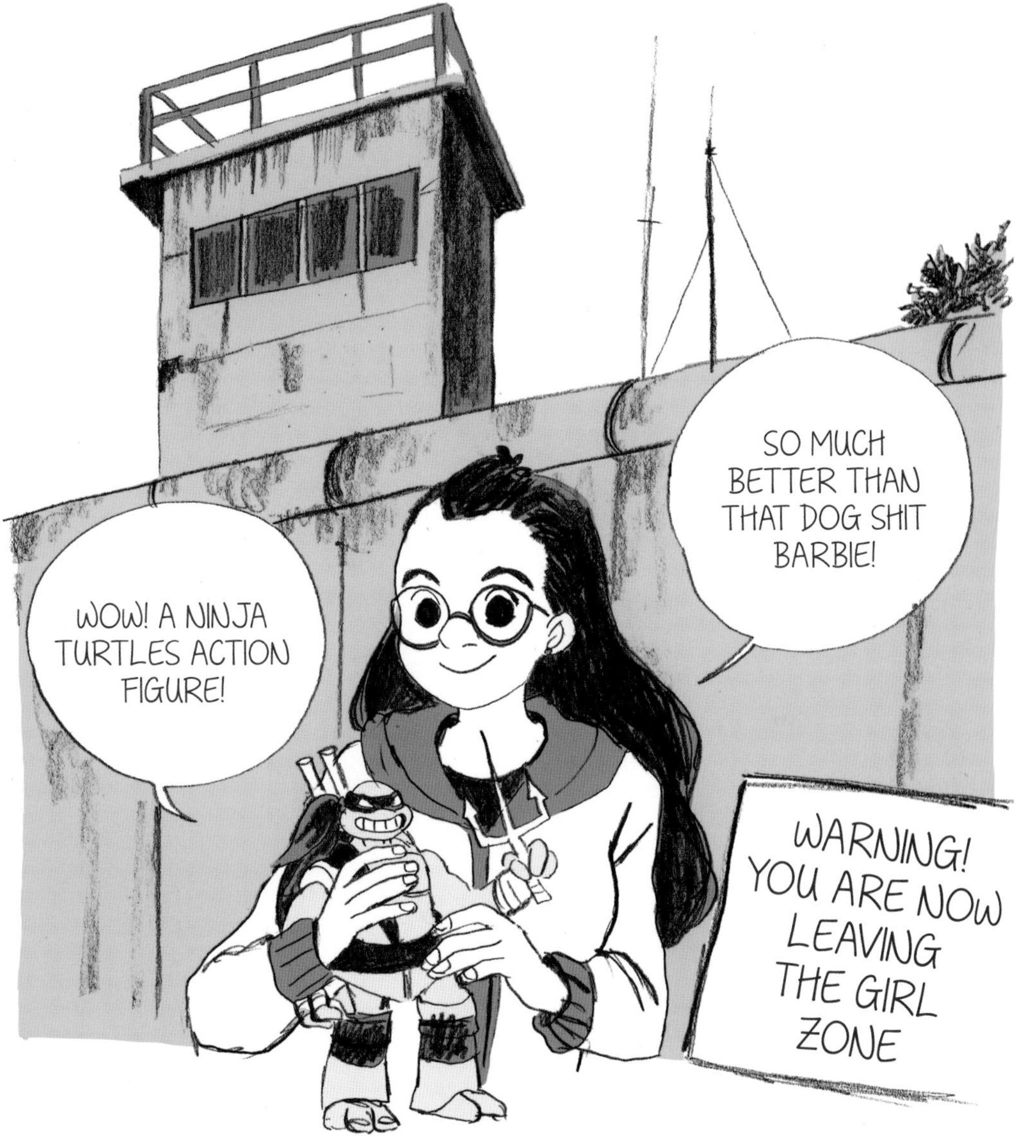
WOW! A NINJA TURTLES ACTION FIGURE!
SO MUCH BETTER THAN THAT DOG SHIT BARBIE!
WARNING! YOU ARE NOW LEAVING THE GIRL ZONE

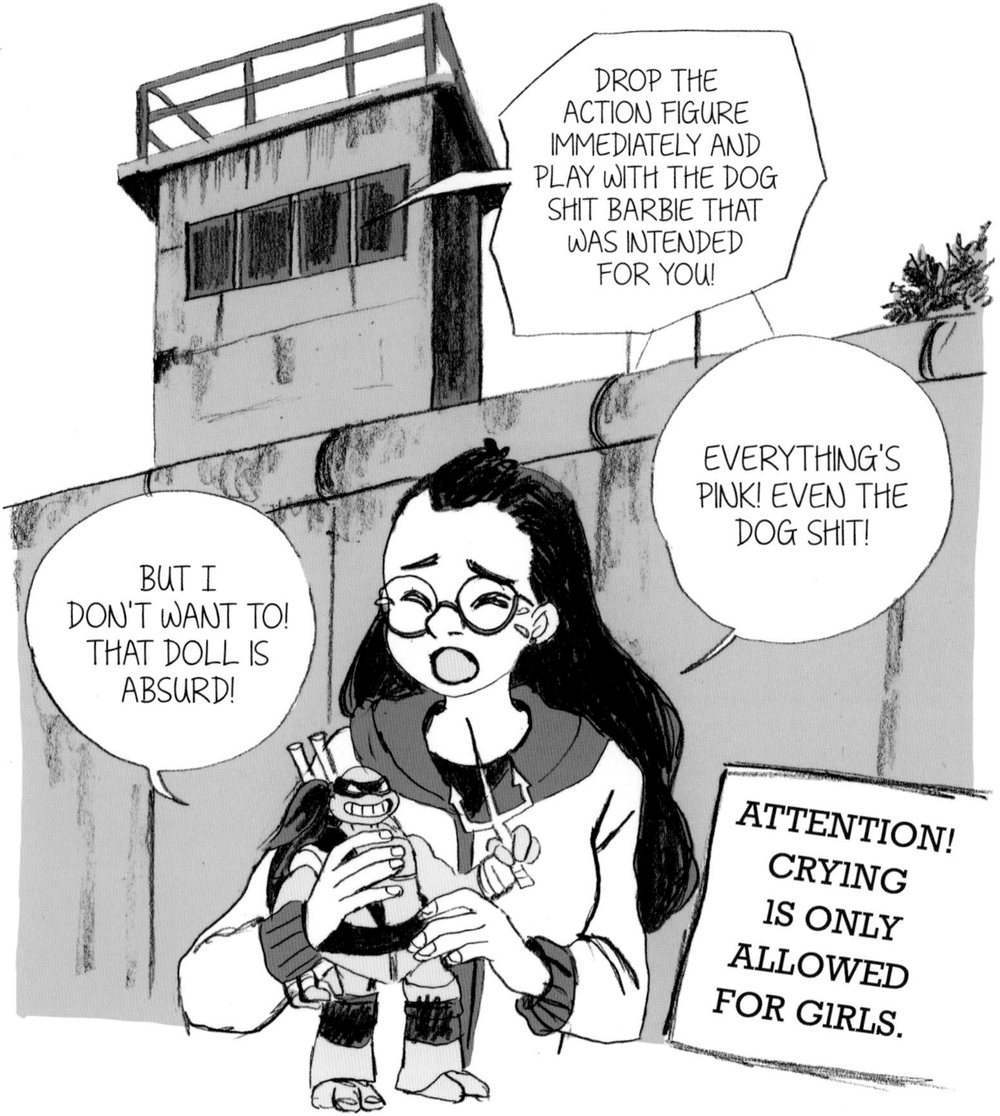
DROP THE ACTION FIGURE IMMEDIATELY AND PLAY WITH THE DOG SHIT BARBIE THAT WAS INTENDED FOR YOU!
EVERYTHING'S PINK! EVEN THE DOG SHIT!
BUT I DON'T WANT TO! THAT DOLL IS ABSURD!
ATTENTION! CRYING IS ONLY ALLOWED FOR GIRLS.

I visited my niece and nephew for Easter recently and I wanted to give them a gift. It was hard to find something that wasn't designated by gender but would still be something they'd both like. In order to keep my "cool aunt" reputation, I ended up following the system and buying my nephew Pokémon cards. I thought that on this topic, at least, I could really shine as an aunt.

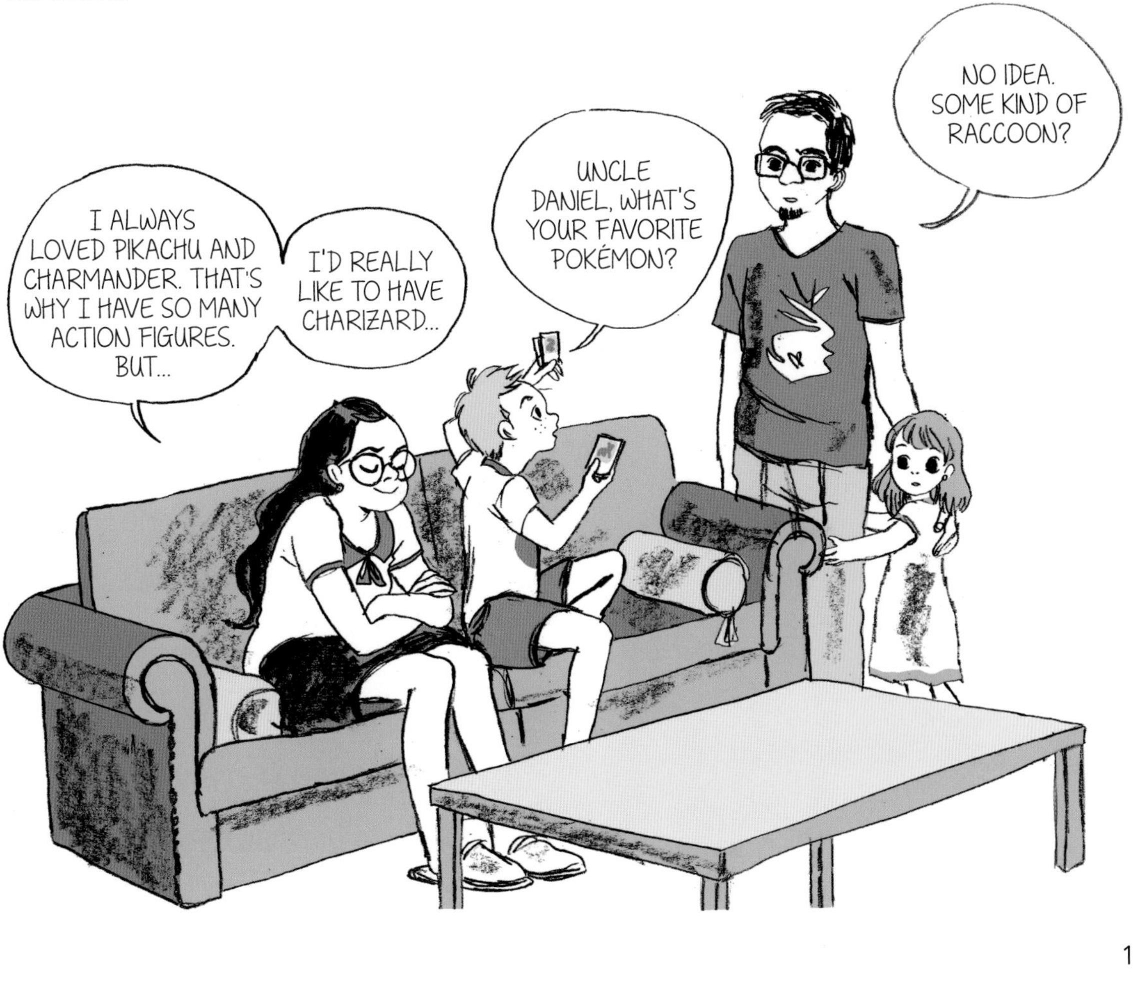
I ALWAYS LOVED PIKACHU AND CHARMANDER. THAT'S WHY I HAVE SO MANY ACTION FIGURES. BUT...
I'D REALLY LIKE TO HAVE CHARIZARD...
UNCLE DANIEL, WHAT'S YOUR FAVORITE POKÉMON?
NO IDEA. SOME KIND OF RACCOON?

That's when I came to the painful realization--my nephew thinks my brother's cooler than me because he's a man, and it's automatically assumed that he therefore knows Pokémon better than I do.

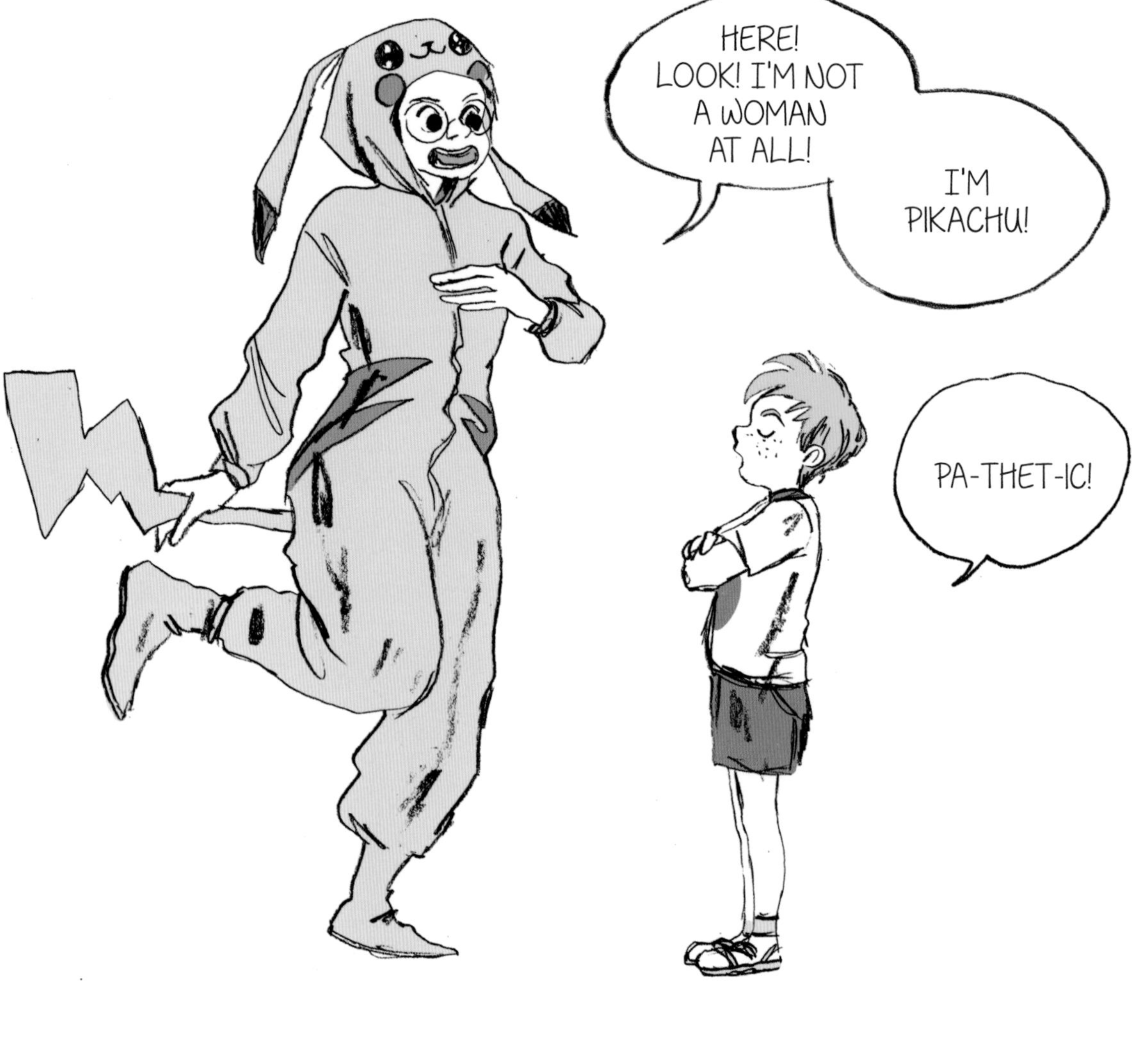
HERE! LOOK! I'M NOT A WOMAN AT ALL!
I'M PIKACHU!
PA-THET-IC!

That same day, I "caught" my nephew in his room with a Barbie in hand.
It was so embarrassing for him that he shut the door in my face.

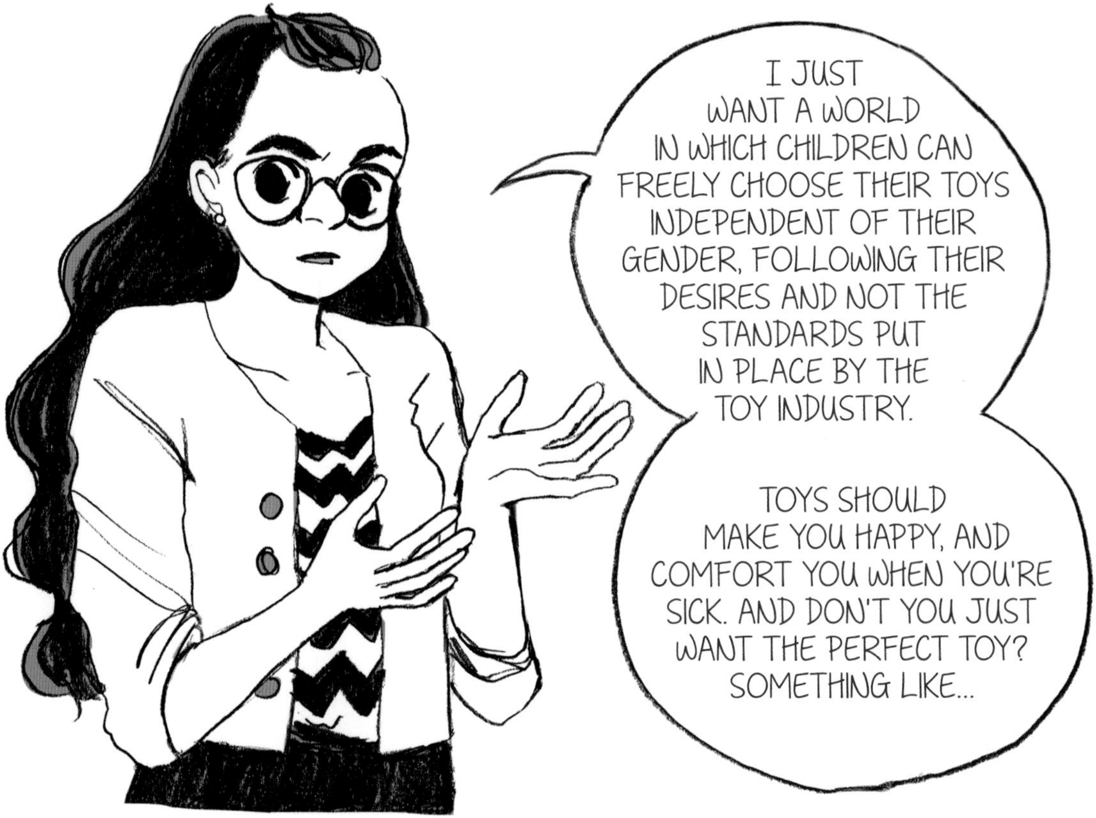
I JUST WANT A WORLD IN WHICH CHILDREN CAN FREELY CHOOSE THEIR TOYS INDEPENDENT OF THEIR GENDER, FOLLOWING THEIR DESIRES AND NOT THE STANDARDS PUT IN PLACE BY THE TOY INDUSTRY.
TOYS SHOULD MAKE YOU HAPPY, AND COMFORT YOU WHEN YOU'RE SICK. AND DON'T YOU JUST WANT THE PERFECT TOY? SOMETHING LIKE...

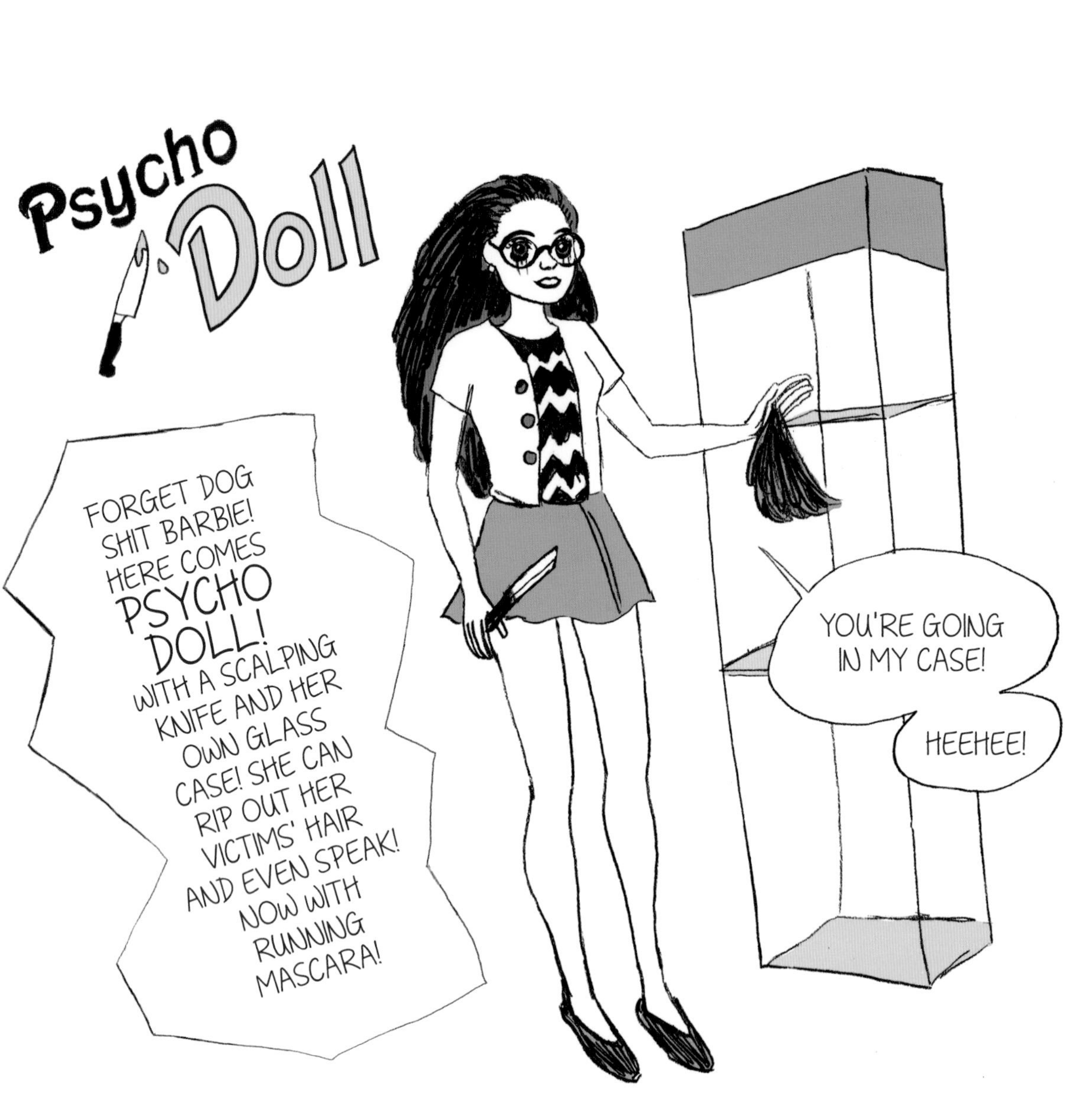
Psycho Doll
FORGET DOG SHIT BARBIE! HERE COMES PSYCHO DOLL! WITH A SCALPING KNIFE AND HER OWN GLASS CASE! SHE CAN RIP OUT HER VICTIMS' HAIR AND EVEN SPEAK! NOW WITH RUNNING MASCARA!
YOU'RE GOING IN MY CASE!
HEEHEE!

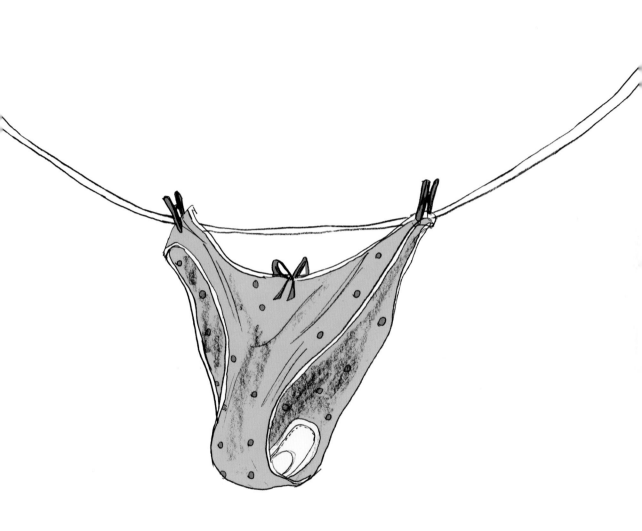

A slightly idealized depiction of a reader ;-)

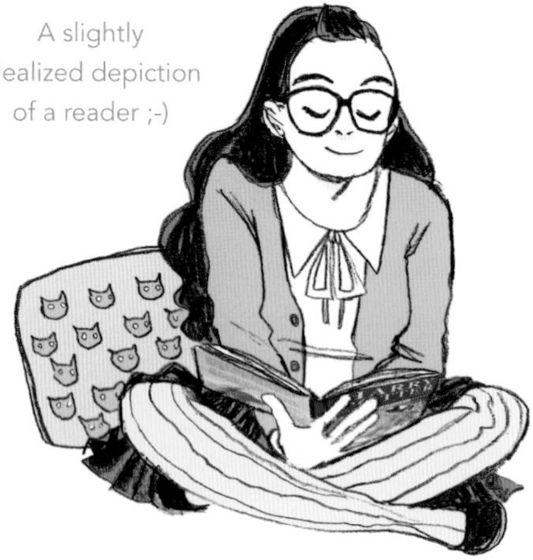

In *Girlsplaining*, many pop culture references show up. Here is a short, incomplete selection—in no particular order—of books, TV series, and films that have guided my work and comics, or that currently inspire me and provoke thought.

Katja's Suggested Readings

Novels/Stories

- Naomi Alderman, *The Power*
- Siri Hustvedt, *The Summer Without Men*
- Margaret Atwood, *The Handmaid's Tale*
- Lucia Berlin, *A Manual for Cleaning Women*
- Yael Inokai, *Mahlstrom*
- Joan Lindsay, *Picnic at Hanging Rock*

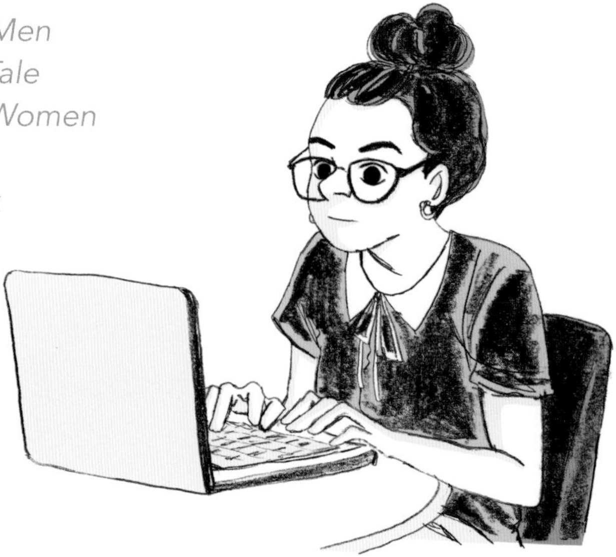

Essays/Columns

- Margarete Stokowski, "Untemrum frei"
- Rebecca Solnit, "Men Explain Things to Me"

Comics

- Olivia Vieweg, *Endzeit*
- Asia Wiegand, *Sterne sehen*
- Vera Brosgol, *Be Prepared*
- Dominik Wendland, *Tüti*
- Mariko Tamaki & Jillian Tamaki, *This One Summer*

Katja's Watch Recommendations, with Binge-Watching Guarantee

TV Series/Shows

- *Hannah Gadsby: Nanette*
- *Sailor Moon*
- *Steven Universe*
- *Orange is the New Black*
- *Glow*
- *Godless*
- *Alias Grace*
- *Mad Men*
- *Sharp Objects*
- *Big Little Lies*
- *Buffy*

Films

- *The Florida Project*
- *Call Me by Your Name*
- *Lady Bird*
- *American Honey*
- *Thelma*
- *Lady Macbeth*
- *The Beguiled*
- *Yoni Erdmann*
- *Three Billboards Outside Ebbing, Missouri*
- *Swimming Pool*

7/10/18 Berlin

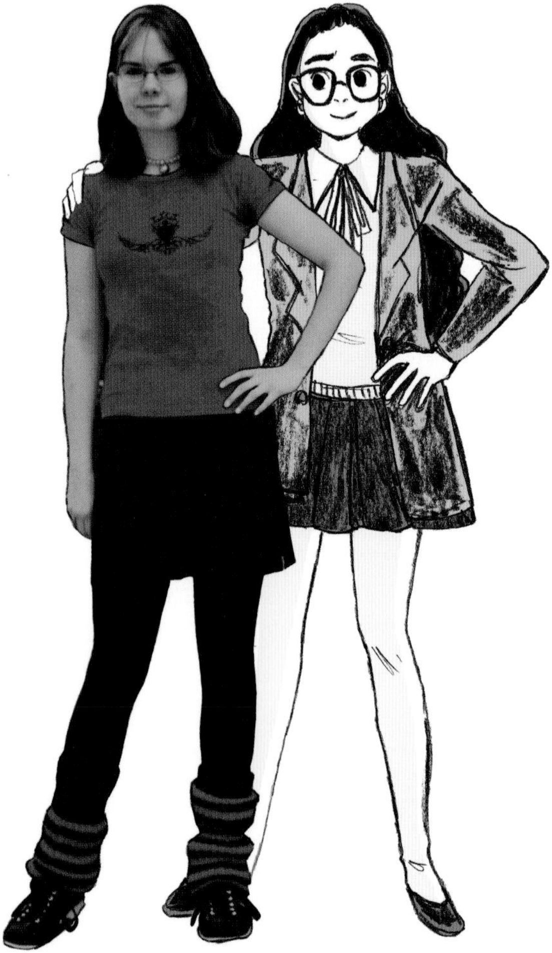

Dear 15-year-old me!

You know how we often lay on our bed crying because someone asserted that our butt was ugly, and we believed them? How, in the middle of summer vacation, we put hair removal cream on our inflamed legs and couldn't swim for two weeks afterward? How we were always running after some brainless guy, because we couldn't value and love ourselves? I'M SORRY FOR ALL OF IT! You were a cool girl—you followed your heart back then, made comics despite all obstacles, wrote stories, did theater, and sang in choir! Hats off!!! I think we handled everything fabulously. (Just take a look at our bio —>)

I'm going to take care of us, and celebrate that with self-love.

About the Creator

© Adrian vom Baur

Katja Klengel, born in Jena, Germany in 1988, studied art at the Dresden Academy of Fine Arts. She quickly gave up classic painting in favor of the comics medium, which had fascinated her since childhood. With time, she developed a unique drawing style in which she blended the influence of the *Sailor Moon* comics by Naoko Takeuchi with the aesthetic of American graphic novels.

During her studies, Katja Klengel published the comics series *"Als ich so alt war"* ("When I was this old") in the *Frankfurter Allgemeine Zeitung*. She simultaneously began an autobiographical comics diary on her blog Blattonisch, which she continues to keep today. In 2014, she moved to Berlin and pursued a second degree in screenwriting at the German Film and Television Academy. For her fantasy series project *Vesta* she won the prestigious 2018 Förderpreis from the Mitteldeutsche Medienförderung.

Since then, Katja has been working on *Vesta* and other TV series concepts, and keeps busy as co-organizer of the comics reading series "Reading Panels."

Special Thanks

Thank you to everyone who provided such generous support for *Girlsplaining*!

Lisa Ludwig of Broadly Germany and Sarah Burrini, without whom these columns wouldn't have existed.

Thank you to the whole team at Reprodukt, without whom the book wouldn't exist: Dirk, Barbara, who were always on hand with help and guidance, for your diligence and good eye; Michael for [the German edition] lettering (my Achilles heel); Klara for the scanning, the lovely book-making, and calm-keeping. Felix, Mona, and Filip for the whole organization all around.

Thanks to Adrian for everything, but particularly for making life easier, for coloring, and for retouching.

And I also thank my incredible friends: especially Jan, my roommates, and Yael.

—**Katja**

DISCOVER
GROUNDBREAKING TITLES

FRANK "BIG BLACK" SMITH
BIG BLACK
STAND AT ATTICA
JARED REINMUTH
AMÉZIANE
Four days in 1971 changed the course of American history.

LEV GROSSMAN
LILAH STURGES PIUS BAK
THE MAGICIANS
NEW CLASS

ROXANE GAY
TRACY LYNNE OLIVER
THE SACRIFICE OF DARKNESS
REBECCA KIRBY
JAMES FENNER

KURT VONNEGUT
with RYAN NORTH & ALBERT MONTEYS
SLAUGHTER
or the children's crusade
HOUSE-FIVE
a graphic novel adaptation

SABAA TAHIR
A THIEF AMONG THE TREES

EMEI BURELL
WE SERVED THE PEOPLE
MY MOTHER'S STORIES

ARCHAIA

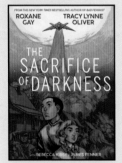

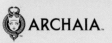

AVAILABLE AT YOUR LOCAL COMICS SHOP AND BOOKSTORE

To find a comics shop in your area, visit www.comicshoplocator.com

WWW.**BOOM-STUDIOS**.COM

Big Black: Stand at Attica
Frank "Big Black" Smith, Jared Reinmuth, Améziane
ISBN: 978-1-68415-479-1 | $19.99 US

The Magicians: New Class
Lev Grossman, Lilah Sturges, Pius Bak
ISBN: 978-1-68415-565-1 | $19.99 US

The Sacrifice of Darkness
Roxane Gay, Tracy Lynne Oliver, Rebecca Kirby
ISBN: 978-1-68415-624-5 | $24.99 US

Slaughterhouse-Five
Kurt Vonnegut, Ryan North, Albert Monteys
ISBN: 978-1-68415-625-2 | $24.99 US

A Thief Among the Trees: An Ember in the Ashes Graphic Novel
Sabaa Tahir, Nicole Andelfinger, Sonia Liao
ISBN: 978-1-68415-524-8 | $19.99 US

We Served the People: My Mother's Stories
Emei Burell
ISBN: 978-1-68415-504-0 | $24.99 US

Bear
Ben Queen, Joe Todd-Stanton
ISBN: 978-1-68415-531-6 | $24.99 US

Girl on Film
Cecil Castellucci, Vicky Leta, Melissa Duffy, V. Gagnon, Jon Berg
ISBN: 978-1-68415-453-1 | $19.99 US

Happiness Will Follow
Mike Hawthorne
ISBN: 978-1-68415-545-3 | $24.99 US

The Man Who Came Down the Attic Stairs
Celine Loup
ISBN: 978-1-68415-352-7 | $14.99 US

Waves
Ingrid Chabbert, Carole Maurel
ISBN: 978-1-68415-346-6 | $14.99 US

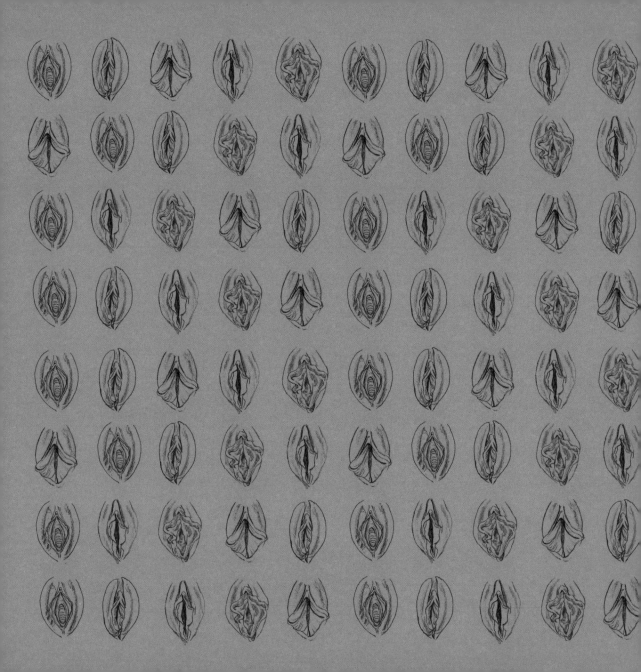